The Works of
Alice Dunbar-Nelson

THE SCHOMBURG LIBRARY OF
NINETEENTH-CENTURY BLACK WOMEN WRITERS

General Editor, Henry Louis Gates, Jr.

Titles are listed chronologically; collections that include works published over a span of years are listed according to the publication date of their initial work.

Phillis Wheatley, *The Collected Works of Phillis Wheatley*

Six Women's Slave Narratives: M. Prince; Old Elizabeth; M. J. Jackson; L. A. Delaney; K. Drumgoold; A. L. Burton

Spiritual Narratives: M. W. Stewart; J. Lee; J. A. J. Foote; V. W. Broughton

Ann Plato, *Essays*

Collected Black Women's Narratives: N. Prince; L. Picquet; B. Veney; S. K. Taylor

Frances E. W. Harper, *Complete Poems of Frances E. W. Harper*

Charlotte Forten Grimké, *The Journals of Charlotte Forten Grimké*

Mary Seacole, *Wonderful Adventures of Mrs. Seacole in Many Lands*

Harriet Jacobs, *Incidents in the Life of a Slave Girl*

Collected Black Women's Poetry, Volumes 1–4: M. E. Tucker; A. I. Menken; M. W. Fordham; P. J. Thompson; C. A. Thompson; H. C. Ray; L. A. J. Moorer; J. D. Heard; E. Bibb; M. P. Johnson; Mrs. H. Linden

Elizabeth Keckley, *Behind the Scenes. Or, Thirty Years a Slave, and Four Years in the White House*

C. W. Larison, M.D., *Silvia Dubois, A Biografy of the Slav Who Whipt Her Mistres and Gand Her Fredom*

Mrs. A. E. Johnson, *Clarence and Corinne; or, God's Way*

Octavia V. Rogers Albert, *The House of Bondage: or Charlotte Brooks and Other Slaves*

Emma Dunham Kelley, *Megda*

Anna Julia Cooper, *A Voice From the South*

Frances E. W. Harper, *Iola Leroy, or Shadows Uplifted*

Amanda Smith, *An Autobiography: The Story of the Lord's Dealings with Mrs. Amanda Smith the Colored Evangelist*

Mrs. A. E. Johnson, *The Hazeley Family*

Mrs. N. F. Mossell, *The Work of the Afro-American Woman*

Alice Dunbar-Nelson, *The Works of Alice Dunbar-Nelson*, Volumes 1–3

Emma D. Kelley-Hawkins, *Four Girls at Cottage City*

Pauline E. Hopkins, *Contending Forces: A Romance Illustrative of Negro Life North and South*

Pauline Hopkins, *The Magazine Novels of Pauline Hopkins*

Hallie Q. Brown, *Homespun Heroines and Other Women of Distinction*

The Works

of

Alice Dunbar-Nelson

Volume 2

Edited by
GLORIA T. HULL

❧ ❧ ❧

❧ ❧ ❧

New York   Oxford
OXFORD UNIVERSITY PRESS
1988

Oxford University Press

Oxford New York Toronto
Delhi Bombay Calcutta Madras Karachi
Petaling Jaya Singapore Hong Kong Tokyo
Nairobi Dar es Salaam Cape Town
Melbourne Auckland

and associated companies in
Beirut Berlin Ibadan Nicosia

Copyright © 1988 by Oxford University Press, Inc.

Published by Oxford University Press, Inc.,
200 Madison Avenue, New York, New York 10016

Oxford is a registered trademark of Oxford University Press

Library of Congress Cataloging-in-Publication Data

Dunbar-Nelson, Alice Moore, 1875–1935.
The works of Alice Dunbar-Nelson.
(The Schomburg library on nineteenth-century black women writers)
Bibliography: v. 2. p.
1. Afro-Americans—Literary collections. I. Hull,
Gloria T. II. Title. III. Series.
PS3507.U6228 1988   818'.5209   87-14118
ISBN 0-19-505251-X (v. 2)
ISBN 0-19-505267-6 (set)

ISBN 0-19-505251-X Cloth

2 4 6 8 10 9 7 5 3 1

Printed in the United States of America
on acid-free paper

The
Schomburg Library
of
Nineteenth-Century
Black Women Writers
is
Dedicated
in Memory
of
PAULINE AUGUSTA COLEMAN GATES

1916–1987

PUBLISHER'S NOTE

Whenever possible, the volumes in this set were reproduced directly from original materials. When availability, physical condition of original texts, or other circumstances prohibited this, volumes or portions of volumes were reset.

FOREWORD
In Her Own Write

Henry Louis Gates, Jr.

One muffled strain in the Silent South, a jarring chord and a
vague and uncomprehended cadenza has been and still is the
Negro. And of that muffled chord, the one mute and voiceless note has been the sadly expectant Black Woman, ...

The "other side" has not been represented by one who "lives
there." And not many can more sensibly realize and more
accurately tell the weight and the fret of the "long dull pain"
than the open-eyed but hitherto voiceless Black Woman of
America.

. . . as our Caucasian barristers are not to blame if they
cannot *quite* put themselves in the dark man's place, neither
should the dark man be wholly expected fully and adequately
to reproduce the exact Voice of the Black Woman.

—ANNA JULIA COOPER, *A Voice From the South* (1892)

The birth of the Afro-American literary tradition occurred
in 1773, when Phillis Wheatley published a book of poetry.
Despite the fact that her book garnered for her a remarkable
amount of attention, Wheatley's journey to the printer had
been a most arduous one. Sometime in 1772, a young African girl walked demurely into a room in Boston to undergo
an oral examination, the results of which would determine
the direction of her life and work. Perhaps she was shocked
upon entering the appointed room. For there, perhaps gath-

ered in a semicircle, sat eighteen of Boston's most notable citizens. Among them were John Erving, a prominent Boston merchant; the Reverend Charles Chauncy, pastor of the Tenth Congregational Church; and John Hancock, who would later gain fame for his signature on the Declaration of Independence. At the center of this group was His Excellency, Thomas Hutchinson, governor of Massachusetts, with Andrew Oliver, his lieutenant governor, close by his side.

Why had this august group been assembled? Why had it seen fit to summon this young African girl, scarcely eighteen years old, before it? This group of "the most respectable Characters in *Boston*," as it would later define itself, had assembled to question closely the African adolescent on the slender sheaf of poems that she claimed to have "written by herself." We can only speculate on the nature of the questions posed to the fledgling poet. Perhaps they asked her to identify and explain—for all to hear—exactly who were the Greek and Latin gods and poets alluded to so frequently in her work. Perhaps they asked her to conjugate a verb in Latin or even to translate randomly selected passages from the Latin, which she and her master, John Wheatley, claimed that she "had made some Progress in." Or perhaps they asked her to recite from memory key passages from the texts of John Milton and Alexander Pope, the two poets by whom the African claimed to be most directly influenced. We do not know.

We do know, however, that the African poet's responses were more than sufficient to prompt the eighteen august gentlemen to compose, sign, and publish a two-paragraph "Attestation," an open letter "To the Publick" that prefaces Phillis Wheatley's book and that reads in part:

> We whose Names are under-written, do assure the World, that the Poems specified in the following Page, were (as we

verily believe) written by Phillis, a young Negro Girl, who was but a few Years since, brought an uncultivated Barbarian from *Africa,* and has ever since been, and now is, under the Disadvantage of serving as a Slave in a Family in this Town. She has been examined by some of the best Judges, and is thought qualified to write them.

So important was this document in securing a publisher for Wheatley's poems that it forms the signal element in the prefatory matter preceding her *Poems on Various Subjects, Religious and Moral,* published in London in 1773.

Without the published "Attestation," Wheatley's publisher claimed, few would believe that an African could possibly have written poetry all by herself. As the eighteen put the matter clearly in their letter, "Numbers would be ready to suspect they were not really the Writings of Phillis." Wheatley and her master, John Wheatley, had attempted to publish a similar volume in 1772 in Boston, but Boston publishers had been incredulous. One year later, "Attestation" in hand, Phillis Wheatley and her master's son, Nathaniel Wheatley, sailed for England, where they completed arrangements for the publication of a volume of her poems with the aid of the Countess of Huntington and the Earl of Dartmouth.

This curious anecdote, surely one of the oddest oral examinations on record, is only a tiny part of a larger, and even more curious, episode in the Enlightenment. Since the beginning of the sixteenth century, Europeans had wondered aloud whether or not the African "species of men," as they were most commonly called, *could* ever create formal literature, could ever master "the arts and sciences." If they could, the argument ran, then the African variety of humanity was fundamentally related to the European variety. If not, then it seemed clear that the African was destined by nature

to be a slave. This was the burden shouldered by Phillis
Wheatley when she successfully defended herself and the authorship of her book against counterclaims and doubts.

Indeed, with her successful defense, Wheatley launched
two traditions at once—the black American literary tradition
and the black woman's literary tradition. If it is extraordinary
that not just one but both of these traditions were founded
simultaneously by a black woman—certainly an event unique
in the history of literature—it is also ironic that this important fact of common, coterminous literary origins seems to
have escaped most scholars.

That the progenitor of the black literary tradition was a
woman means, in the most strictly literal sense, that all sub-
sequent black writers have evolved in a matrilinear line of
descent, and that each, consciously or unconsciously, has extended and revised a canon whose foundation was the poetry
of a black woman. Early black writers seem to have been
keenly aware of Wheatley's founding role, even if most of
her white reviewers were more concerned with the implica-
tions of her race than her gender. Jupiter Hammon, for example, whose 1760 broadside "An Evening Thought. Salvation by Christ, With Penitential Cries" was the first
individual poem published by a black American, acknowledged Wheatley's influence by selecting her as the subject of
his second broadside, "An Address to Miss Phillis Wheatly
[*sic*], Ethiopian Poetess, in Boston," which was published at
Hartford in 1778. And George Moses Horton, the second
Afro-American to publish a book of poetry in English (1829),
brought out in 1838 an edition of his *Poems By A Slave*
bound together with Wheatley's work. Indeed, for fifty-six
years, between 1773 and 1829, when Horton published *The
Hope of Liberty*, Wheatley was the *only* black person to have
published a book of imaginative literature in English. So

central was this black woman's role in the shaping of the Afro-American literary tradition that, as one historian has maintained, the history of the reception of Phillis Wheatley's poetry *is* the history of Afro-American literary criticism. Well into the nineteenth century, Wheatley and the black literary tradition were the same entity.

But Wheatley is not the only black woman writer who stands as a pioneering figure in Afro-American literature. Just as Wheatley gave birth to the genre of black poetry, Ann Plato was the first Afro-American to publish a book of essays (1841) and Harriet E. Wilson was the first black person to publish a novel in the United States (1859).

Despite this pioneering role of black women in the tradition, however, many of their contributions before this century have been all but lost or unrecognized. As Hortense Spillers observed as recently as 1983,

> With the exception of a handful of autobiographical narratives from the nineteenth century, the black woman's realities are virtually suppressed until the period of the Harlem Renaissance and later. Essentially the black woman as artist, as intellectual spokesperson for her own cultural apprenticeship, has not existed before, for anyone. At the source of [their] own symbol-making task, [the community of black women writers] confronts, therefore, a tradition of work that is quite recent, its continuities, broken and sporadic.

Until now, it has been extraordinarily difficult to establish the formal connections between early black women's writing and that of the present, precisely because our knowledge of their work has been broken and sporadic. Phillis Wheatley, for example, while certainly the most reprinted and discussed poet in the tradition, is also one of the least understood. Ann Plato's seminal work, *Essays* (which includes biographies and poems), has not been reprinted since it was published a cen-

tury and a half ago. And Harriet Wilson's *Our Nig,* her
compelling novel of a black woman's expanding consciousness in a racist Northern antebellum environment, never received even *one* review or comment at a time when virtually
all works written by black people were heralded by abolitionists as salient arguments against the existence of human slavery. Many of the books reprinted in this set experienced a
similar fate, the most dreadful fate for an author: that of
being ignored then relegated to the obscurity of the rare book
section of a university library. We can only wonder how
many other texts in the black woman's tradition have been
lost to this generation of readers or remain unclassified or
uncatalogued and, hence, unread.

This was not always so, however. Black women writers
dominated the final decade of the nineteenth century, perhaps
spurred to publish by an 1886 essay entitled "The Coming
American Novelist," which was published in *Lippincott's
Monthly Magazine* and written by "A Lady From Philadelphia." This pseudonymous essay argued that the "Great
American Novel" would be written by a black person. Her
argument is so curious that it deserves to be repeated:

> When we come to formulate our demands of the Coming
> American Novelist, we will agree that he must be native-
> born. His ancestors may come from where they will, but we
> must give him a birthplace and have the raising of him. Still,
> the longer his family has been here the better he will represent
> us. Suppose he should have no country but ours, no traditions
> but those he has learned here, no longings apart from us, no
> future except in our future—the orphan of the world, he
> finds with us his home. And with all this, suppose he refuses
> to be fused into that grand conglomerate we call the "Amer-
> ican type." With us, he is not of us. He is original, he has
> humor, he is tender, he is passive and fiery, he has been

taught what we call justice, and he has his own opinion about
it. He has suffered everything a poet, a dramatist, a novelist
need suffer before he comes to have his lips anointed. And
with it all he is in one sense a spectator, a little out of the
race. How would these conditions go towards forming an
original development? In a word, suppose the coming novelist
is of African origin? When one comes to consider the subject,
there is no improbability in it. One thing is certain,—our
great novel will not be written by the typical American.

An atypical American, indeed. Not only would the great
American novel be written by an African-American, it would
be written by an African-American *woman:*

> Yet farther: I have used the generic masculine pronoun
> because it is convenient; but Fate keeps revenge in store. It
> was a woman who, taking the wrongs of the African as her
> theme, wrote the novel that awakened the world to their
> reality, and why should not the coming novelist be a woman
> as well as an African? She—the woman of that race—has
> some claims on Fate which are not yet paid up.

It is these claims on fate that we seek to pay by publishing
The Schomburg Library of Nineteenth-Century Black Women
Writers.

This theme would be repeated by several black women
authors, most notably by Anna Julia Cooper, a prototypical
black feminist whose 1892 *A Voice From the South* can be
considered to be one of the original texts of the black feminist movement. It was Cooper who first analyzed the fal-
lacy of referring to "the Black man" when speaking of black
people and who argued that just as white men cannot speak
through the consciousness of black men, neither can black
men "fully and adequately . . . reproduce the exact Voice of
the Black Woman." Gender and race, she argues, cannot be

conflated, except in the instance of a black woman's voice, and it is this voice which must be uttered and to which we must listen. As Cooper puts the matter so compellingly:

> It is not the intelligent woman vs. the ignorant woman; nor the white woman vs. the black, the brown, and the red,—it is not even the cause of woman vs. man. Nay, 'tis woman's strongest vindication for speaking that *the world needs to hear her voice*. It would be subversive of every human interest that the cry of one-half the human family be stifled. Woman in stepping from the pedestal of statue-like inactivity in the domestic shrine, and daring to think and move and speak,— to undertake to help shape, mold, and direct the thought of her age, is merely completing the circle of the world's vision. Hers is every interest that has lacked an interpreter and a defender. Her cause is linked with that of every agony that has been dumb—every wrong that needs a voice.
>
> It is no fault of man's that he has not been able to see truth from her standpoint. It does credit both to his head and heart that no greater mistakes have been committed or even wrongs perpetrated while she sat making tatting and snipping paper flowers. Man's own innate chivalry and the mutual interdependence of their interests have insured his treating her cause, in the main at least, as his own. And he is pardonably surprised and even a little chagrined, perhaps, to find his legislation not considered "perfectly lovely" in every respect. But in any case his work is only impoverished by her remaining dumb. The world has had to limp along with the wobbling gait and one-sided hesitancy of a man with one eye. Suddenly the bandage is removed from the other eye and the whole body is filled with light. It sees a circle where before it saw a segment. The darkened eye restored, every member rejoices with it.

The myopic sight of the darkened eye can only be restored when the full range of the black woman's voice, with its own special timbres and shadings, remains mute no longer.

Similarly, Victoria Earle Matthews, an author of short stories and essays, and a cofounder in 1896 of the National Association of Colored Women, wrote in her stunning essay, "The Value of Race Literature" (1895), that "when the literature of our race is developed, it will of necessity be different in all essential points of greatness, true heroism and real Christianity from what we may at the present time, for convenience, call American literature." Matthews argued that this great tradition of Afro-American literature would be the textual outlet "for the unnaturally suppressed inner lives which our people have been compelled to lead." Once these "unnaturally suppressed inner lives" of black people are unveiled, no "grander diffusion of mental light" will shine more brightly, she concludes, than that of the articulate Afro-American woman:

> And now comes the question, What part shall we women play in the Race Literature of the future? . . . within the compass of one small journal ["Woman's Era"] we have struck out a new line of departure—a journal, a record of Race interests gathered from all parts of the United States, carefully selected, moistened, winnowed and garnered by the ablest intellects of educated colored women, shrinking at no lofty theme, shirking no serious duty, aiming at every possible excellence, and determined to do their part in the future uplifting of the race.
>
> If twenty women, by their concentrated efforts in one literary movement, can meet with such success as has engendered, planned out, and so successfully consummated this convention, what much more glorious results, what wider spread success, what grander diffusion of mental light will not come forth at the bidding of the enlarged hosts of women writers, already called into being by the stimulus of your efforts?
>
> And here let me speak one word for my journalistic sisters

who have already entered the broad arena of journalism. Before the "Woman's Era" had come into existence, no one except themselves can appreciate the bitter experience and sore disappointments under which they have at all times been compelled to pursue their chosen vocations.

If their brothers of the press have had their difficulties to contend with, I am here as a sister journalist to state, from the fullness of knowledge, that their task has been an easy one compared with that of the colored woman in journalism.

Woman's part in Race Literature, as in Race building, is the most important part and has been so in all ages. . . . All through the most remote epochs she has done her share in literature. . . .

One of the most important aspects of this set is the republication of the salient texts from 1890 to 1910, which literary historians could well call "The Black Woman's Era." In addition to Mary Helen Washington's definitive edition of Cooper's *A Voice From the South,* we have reprinted two novels by Amelia Johnson, Frances Harper's *Iola Leroy,* two novels by Emma Dunham Kelley, Alice Dunbar-Nelson's two impressive collections of short stories, and Pauline Hopkins's three serialized novels as well as her monumental novel, *Contending Forces*—all published between 1890 and 1910. Indeed, black women published more works of fiction in these two decades than black men had published in the previous half century. Nevertheless, this great achievement has been ignored.

Moreover, the writings of nineteenth-century Afro-American women in general have remained buried in obscurity, accessible only in research libraries or in overpriced and poorly edited reprints. Many of these books have never been reprinted at all; in some instances only one or two copies are extant. In these works of fiction, poetry, autobiography, biography, essays, and journalism resides the mind of the nineteenth-century Afro-American woman. Until these works are made readily available to teachers and their students, a significant segment of the black tradition will remain silent.

Oxford University Press, in collaboration with the Schomburg Center for Research in Black Culture, is publishing thirty volumes of these compelling works, each of which contains an introduction by an expert in the field. The set includes such rare texts as Johnson's *The Hazeley Family* and *Clarence and Corinne*, Plato's *Essays*, the most complete edition of Phillis Wheatley's poems and letters, Emma Dunham Kelley's pioneering novel *Megda*, several previously unpublished stories and a novel by Alice Dunbar-Nelson, and the first collected volumes of Pauline Hopkins's three serialized novels and Frances Harper's poetry. We also present four volumes of poetry by such women as Mary Eliza Tucker Lambert, Adah Menken, Josephine Heard, and Maggie Johnson. Numerous slave and spiritual narratives, a newly discovered novel—*Four Girls at Cottage City*—by Emma Dunham Kelley (-Hawkins), and the first American edition of *Wonderful Adventures of Mrs. Seacole in Many Lands* are also among the texts included.

In addition to resurrecting the works of black women authors, it is our hope that this set will facilitate the resurrection of the Afro-American woman's literary tradition itself by unearthing its nineteenth-century roots. In the works of Nella Larsen and Jessie Fauset, Zora Neale Hurston and Ann Petry, Lorraine Hansberry and Gwendolyn Brooks, Paule Marshall and Toni Cade Bambara, Audre Lorde and Rita Dove, Toni Morrison and Alice Walker, Gloria Naylor and Jamaica Kincaid, these roots have branched luxuriantly. The eighteenth- and nineteenth-century authors whose works are presented in this set founded and nurtured the black women's literary tradition, which must be revived, explicated, analyzed, and debated before we can understand more completely the formal shaping of this tradition within a tradition, a coded literary universe through which, regrettably, we are only just beginning to navigate our way. As Anna Cooper said nearly one hundred years ago, we have been blinded by the loss of sight in one eye and have therefore been unable to detect the full *shape* of the Afro-American literary tradition.

Literary works configure into a tradition not because of some mystical collective unconscious determined by the biology of race or gender, but because writers read other writers and *ground* their representations of experience in models of language provided largely by other writers to whom they feel akin. It is through this mode of literary revision, amply evident in the *texts* themselves—in formal echoes, recast metaphors, even in parody—that a "tradition" emerges and defines itself.

This is formal bonding, and it is only through formal bonding that we can know a literary tradition. The collective publication of these works by black women now, for the first time, makes it possible for scholars and critics, male and female, black and white, to *demonstrate* that black women writers read, and revised, other black women writers. To demonstrate this set of formal literary relations is to demonstrate that sexuality, race, and gender are both the condition and the basis of *tradition*—but tradition as found in discrete acts of language use.

A word is in order about the history of this set. For the past decade, I have taught a course, first at Yale and then at Cornell, entitled "Black Women and Their Fictions," a course that I inherited from Toni Morrison, who developed it in the mid-1970s for Yale's Program in Afro-American Studies. Although the course was inspired by the remarkable accomplishments of black women novelists since 1970, I gradually extended its beginning date to the late nineteenth century, studying Frances Harper's *Iola Leroy* and Anna Julia Cooper's *A Voice From the South*, both published in 1892. With the discovery of Harriet E. Wilson's seminal novel, *Our Nig* (1859), and Jean Yellin's authentication of Harriet Jacobs's brilliant slave narrative, *Incidents in the Life of a Slave Girl* (1861), a survey course spanning over a century and a quarter emerged.

But the discovery of *Our Nig*, as well as the interest in nineteenth-century black women's writing that this discovery generated, convinced me that even the most curious and diligent scholars knew very little of the extensive history of the creative writings of Afro-American women before 1900. Indeed, most scholars of Afro-American literature had never even read most of the books published by black women, simply because these books—of poetry, novels, short stories, essays, and autobiography—were mostly accessible only in rare book sections of university libraries. For reasons unclear to me even today, few of these marvelous renderings of the Afro-American woman's consciousness were reprinted in the late 1960s and early 1970s, when so many other texts of the Afro-American literary tradition were resurrected from the dark and silent graveyard of the out-of-print and were reissued in facsimile editions aimed at the hungry readership for canonical texts in the nascent field of black studies.

So, with the help of several superb research assistants — including David Curtis, Nicola Shilliam, Wendy Jones, Sam Otter, Janadas Devan, Suvir Kaul, Cynthia Bond, Elizabeth Alexander, and Adele Alexander—and with the expert advice of scholars such as William Robinson, William Andrews, Mary Helen Washington, Maryemma Graham, Jean Yellin, Houston A. Baker, Jr., Richard Yarborough, Hazel Carby, Joan R. Sherman, Frances Foster, and William French, dozens of bibliographies were used to compile a list of books written or narrated by black women mostly before 1910. Without the assistance provided through this shared experience of scholarship, the scholar's true legacy, this project could not have been conceived. As the list grew, I was struck by how very many of these titles that I, for example, had never even heard of, let alone read, such as Ann Plato's *Essays,* Louisa Picquet's slave narrative, or Amelia Johnson's two novels, *Clarence and Corinne* and *The Hazeley Family.* Through our research with the Black Periodical Fiction and Poetry Project (funded by NEH and the Ford Foundation), I also realized that several novels by black women, including three works of fiction by Pauline Hopkins, had been serialized in black periodicals, but had never been collected and published as books. Nor had the several books of poetry published by black women, such as the prolific Frances E. W. Harper, been collected and edited. When I discovered still another "lost" novel by an Afro-American woman (*Four Girls at Cottage City,* published in 1898 by Emma Dunham Kelley-Hawkins), I decided to attempt to edit a collection of reprints of these works and to publish them as a "library" of black women's writings, in part so that I could read them myself.

Convincing university and trade publishers to undertake this project proved to be a difficult task. Despite the commercial success of *Our Nig* and of the several reprint series of women's works (such as Virago, the Beacon Black Women Writers Series, and Rutgers' American Women Writers Series), several presses rejected the project as "too large," "too limited," or as "commercially unviable." Only two publishers recognized the viability and the import of the project and, of these, Oxford's commitment to publish the titles simultaneously as a set made the press's offer irresistible.

While attempting to locate original copies of these exceedingly rare books, I discovered that most of the texts were housed at the Schomburg Center for Research in Black Culture, a branch of The New York Public Library, under the direction of Howard Dodson. Dodson's infectious enthusiasm for the project and his generous collaboration, as well as that of his stellar staff (especially Diana Lachatanere, Sharon Howard, Ellis Haizip, Richard Newman, and Betty Gubert), led to a joint publishing initiative that produced this set as part of the Schomburg's major fund-raising campaign. Without Dodson's foresight and generosity of spirit, the set would not have materialized. Without William P. Sisler's masterful editorship at Oxford and his staff's careful attention to detail, the set would have remained just another grand idea that tends to languish in a scholar's file cabinet.

I would also like to thank Dr. Michael Winston and Dr. Thomas C. Battle, Vice-President of Academic Affairs and the Director of the Moorland-Spingarn Research Center (respectively) at Howard University, for their unending encouragement, support, and collaboration in this project, and Esme E. Bhan at Howard for her meticulous research and bibliographical skills. In addition, I would like to acknowledge the aid of the staff at the libraries of Duke University, Cornell University (especially Tom Weissinger and Donald Eddy), the Boston Public Library, the Western Reserve Historical Society, the Library of Congress, and Yale University. Linda Robbins, Marion Osmun, Sarah Flanagan, and Gerard Case, all members of the staff at Oxford, were

extraordinarily effective at coordinating, editing, and producing the various segments of each text in the set. Candy
Ruck, Nina de Tar, and Phillis Molock expertly typed reams
of correspondence and manuscripts connected to the project.

I would also like to express my gratitude to my colleagues
who edited and introduced the individual titles in the set.
Without their attention to detail, their willingness to meet
strict deadlines, and their sheer enthusiasm for this project,
the set could not have been published. But finally and ultimately, I would hope that the publication of the set would
help to generate even more scholarly interest in the black
women authors whose work is presented here. Struggling
against the seemingly insurmountable barriers of racism *and*
sexism, while often raising families and fulfilling full-time
professional obligations, these women managed nevertheless
to record their thoughts and feelings and to *testify* to all who
dare read them that the will to harness the power of collective
endurance and survival is the will to write.

The Schomburg Library of Nineteenth-Century Black
Women Writers is dedicated in memory of Pauline Augusta
Coleman Gates, who died in the spring of 1987. It was she
who inspired in me the love of learning and the love of literature. I have encountered in the books of this set no will
more determined, no courage more noble, no mind more
sublime, no self more celebratory of the achievements of all
Afro-American women, and indeed of life itself, than her
own.

A NOTE FROM
THE SCHOMBURG CENTER

Howard Dodson

The Schomburg Center for Research in Black Culture, The New York Public Library, is pleased to join with Dr. Henry Louis Gates and Oxford University Press in presenting The Schomburg Library of Nineteenth-Century Black Women Writers. This thirty-volume set includes the work of a generation of black women whose writing has only been available previously in rare book collections. The materials reprinted in twenty-four of the thirty volumes are drawn from the unique holdings of the Schomburg Center.

A research unit of The New York Public Library, the Schomburg Center has been in the forefront of those institutions dedicated to collecting, preserving, and providing access to the records of the black past. In the course of its two generations of acquisition and conservation activity, the Center has amassed collections totaling more than 5 million items. They include over 100,000 bound volumes, 85,000 reels and sets of microforms, 300 manuscript collections containing some 3.5 million items, 300,000 photographs and extensive holdings of prints, sound recordings, film and videotape, newspapers, artworks, artifacts, and other book and nonbook materials. Together they vividly document the history and cultural heritages of people of African descent worldwide.

Though established some sixty-two years ago, the Center's book collections date from the sixteenth century. Its oldest item, an Ethiopian Coptic Tunic, dates from the eighth or ninth century. Rare materials, however, are most available for the nineteenth-century African-American experience. It is from these holdings that the majority of the titles selected for inclusion in this set are drawn.

The nineteenth century was a formative period in African-American literary and cultural history. Prior to the Civil War, the majority of black Americans living in the United States were held in bondage. Law and practice forbade teaching them to read or write. Even after the war, many of the impediments to learning and literary productivity remained. Nevertheless, black men and women of the nineteenth century persevered in both areas. Moreover, more African-Americans than we yet realize turned their observations, feelings, social viewpoints, and creative impulses into published works. In time, this nineteenth-century printed record included poetry, short stories, histories, novels, autobiographies, social criticism, and theology, as well as economic and philosophical treatises. Unfortunately, much of this body of literature remained, until very recently, relatively inaccessible to twentieth-century scholars, teachers, creative artists, and others interested in black life. Prior to the late 1960s, most Americans (black as well as white) had never heard of these nineteenth-century authors, much less read their works.

The civil rights and black power movements created unprecedented interest in the thought, behavior, and achievements of black people. Publishers responded by revising traditional texts, introducing the American public to a new generation of African-American writers, publishing a variety of thematic anthologies, and reprinting a plethora of "classic texts" in African-American history, literature, and art. The reprints usually appeared as individual titles or in a series of bound volumes or microform formats.

The Schomburg Center, which has a long history of supporting publishing that deals with the history and culture of Africans in diaspora, became an active participant in many of the reprint revivals of the 1960s. Since hard copies of original printed works are the preferred formats for producing facsimile reproductions, publishers frequently turned to the Schomburg Center for copies of these original titles. In addition to providing such material, Schomburg Center staff members offered advice and consultation, wrote introductions, and occasionally entered into formal copublishing arrangements in some projects.

Most of the nineteenth-century titles reprinted during the 1960s, however, were by and about black men. A few black women were included in the longer series, but works by lesser known black women were generally overlooked. The Schomburg Library of Nineteenth-Century Black Women Writers is both a corrective to these previous omissions and an important contribution to Afro-American literary history in its own right. Through this collection of volumes, the thoughts, perspectives, and creative abilities of nineteenth-century African-American women, as captured in books and pamphlets published in large part before 1910, are again being made available to the general public. The Schomburg Center is pleased to be a part of this historic endeavor.

I would like to thank Professor Gates for initiating this project. Thanks are due both to him and Mr. William P. Sisler of Oxford University Press for giving the Schomburg Center an opportunity to play such a prominent role in the set. Thanks are also due to my colleagues at The New York Public Library and the Schomburg Center, especially Dr. Vartan Gregorian, Richard De Gennaro, Paul Fasana, Betsy

Pinover, Richard Newman, Diana Lachatanere, Glenderlyn Johnson, and Harold Anderson for their assistance and support. I can think of no better way of demonstrating than in this set the role the Schomburg Center plays in assuring that the black heritage will be available for future generations.

CONTENTS

Introduction by Gloria T. Hull   xxix

Editorial Note   lv

Alice Dunbar-Nelson: A Chronology   lvii

NOVELETTE

A Modern Undine   3

POETRY

Rainy Day   75
A Common Plaint   75
A Song of Love   77
Summit and Vale   77
A Little Bird Sings   78
The Lovers   78
The Gift   79
Sorrow's Crown   79
Still from the Depths   81
Violets   81
To the Negro Farmers of the United States   82
The Lights at Carney's Point   82
I Sit and Sew   84
You! Inez!   85
To Madame Curie   85
Communion   86
Music   86

Of Old St. Augustine   87
Snow in October   88
April Is On the Way   89
Forest Fire   91
Cano—I Sing   92
The Proletariat Speaks   93
Little Roads   95
Harlem John Henry Views the Airmada   96

NEWSPAPER COLUMNS

From A Woman's Point of View   105
Une Femme Dit   130
As In a Looking Glass   200
An Editorial: The Ultimate Insult   278

ESSAYS

Politics in Delaware   283
Woman's Most Serious Problem   287
The Problem of Personal Service   293
Facing Life Squarely   297
Big Quarterly in Wilmington   302
Brass Ankles Speaks   311

INTRODUCTION

Gloria T. Hull

One senses in practically everything that Alice Dunbar-Nelson wrote a driving desire to pull together the multiple strands of her complex personality and poetics. Yet this desire seems to be undercut or subverted by an opposing—and perhaps ultimately more powerful—ambivalence (I want to say schizophrenia) that makes W. E. B. Du Bois's racially "warring bloods" and Virginia Woolf's female "contrary instincts" look simple. Dunbar-Nelson spent her life assiduously writing herself both into and out of her literary "fictions," using conventional concepts of form, genre, and propriety that (given her lack of creative genius) bound her to divisiveness and inarticulation. This scenario becomes all the more complicated when one remembers that it was played in a late-nineteenth-, early-twentieth-century world where social conditions and the literary establishment made authentic self-definition (as persons and artists) extremely difficult for black women writers.

Dunbar-Nelson began her life as Alice Ruth Moore on July 19, 1875, in New Orleans, Louisiana— marked from the beginning by the mixed white, black, and Indian of her Creole ancestral strains.[1] This mixture endowed her with reddish-blonde baby curls and a fair enough complexion to pass occasionally for white when she was an adult intent on imbibing the high culture (operas, bathing spas, art museums) of the Jim Crow United States society, which was just as committed to her exclusion. Evidence suggests that—a feeling of shame about some circumstance(s) of her birth notwithstanding—she preferred her mixed racial appearance and sometimes looked down on darker skinned blacks, especially if they were also less educated and refined. (Skin color and status were often connected in those early postbellum times. Many progressive colored people believed that the best way to prove their worth was to be as little black as possible, black being equated with narrowness and limitation.) Nevertheless, Dunbar-Nelson fought for the rights of black people in a variety of individual and organizational ways ranging from the women's club movement, to the Dyer Anti-Lynching Bill, to financially aiding, from her own shallow pocket, young charges at the Industrial School for Colored Girls, which she helped to found. She was generally active on behalf of women, motivated by genuine feminist instincts and the available avenues for sociopolitical work. Making a living also occupied and preoccupied her. She was a teacher, stenographer, executive secretary, editor, newspaper columnist, platform speaker, and campaign manager.

All of this reminds us that Dunbar-Nelson perforce wrote in the interstices of a busy existence unsupported (except for one brief period) by any of the money or leisure traditionally associated with people of letters. Doggedly determined to be an author, she plied her trade, often too facilely, hastily, opportunistically, and without revision—carried forward on the flow of words that came quite easily for her. Interestingly enough, she called all of her writing "producing literature," in a humorously ironic leveling of forms and types. But just as ironically, her status is lowered since the more belletristic genres of poetry and fiction are more valued than the noncanonical forms—notably the diary and journalistic essay—that claimed so much of her attention.

Dunbar-Nelson began her career early. As a daring young

author "just on the threshold of life," she published *Violets and Other Tales** in 1895 when she was barely twenty years old. A potpourri of short stories, sketches, essays, reviews, and poetry, this volume is interesting and promising juvenilia wherein the budding writer tries out many voices. Even this early, some of her lifelong characteristics are evident: wide reading and love of books ("Salammbo"); catholicity of intellect ("Unknown Life of Jesus Christ," "Anarchy Alley," "Ten Minutes' Musing"); alienation from her own autobiography and mundane experience; Creole materials and themes ("Titee," "A Carnival Jangle," "Little Miss Sophie"); competence in many genres; use of standard lyric themes; a leaning toward the romantic; ambivalence about woman's concept of self and proper role in the emerging modern world ("Violets," "The Woman," "At Eventide," etc.); a felicitous prose style; and a tendency to pay obeisance to literary and social proprieties. Summarizing the work in this way suggests that it is most profitably read as a precursor of later work, or consulted in retrospect for its revelations of Dunbar-Nelson's roots.

Dunbar-Nelson's second book, *The Goodness of St. Rocque and Other Stories* (Vol. 1, WADN), appeared four years later. Thus, the only two volumes of her own work published during her lifetime (which have kept her writings marginally accessible to later generations of scholars and readers) were printed at the very beginning of her career—before the turn of the century and before books by black writers ceased to be novelties during the "New Negro" era. Therefore, Dunbar-Nelson, in her way, helped to create a black short-story

---

*Included in Volume 1, *The Works of Alice Dunbar-Nelson,* hereafter cited as WADN.

tradition for a reading public conditioned to expect only plantation and minstrel stereotypes. Her strategy for escaping these odious expectations was to eschew black characters and culture and to write, instead, charming, aracial, Creole sketches that solidified her in the then-popular, "female-suitable" local color mode. In the words of one contemporary reviewer, these are

> delightful Creole stories, all bright and full of the true Creole air of easy-going . . . brief and pleasing, instinct with the passion and romance of the people who will ever be associated with such names as Bayou Teche and Lake Pontchartrain.[2]

In part, this sprightly description of the book is accurate. One thinks, for example, of "Titee" (a story that was printed first in *Violets* and then here, with a revised, happy ending). The colorful young hero with a tender heart is eventually rewarded for his self-sacrificing faithfulness to an old derelict as he roams the bayous and canals. Further, the surfaces of all the stories so coruscate with South Louisiana flavor that they give an impression of superficial charm and pleasantness. Yet the truth of the matter is that this apparent brightness is belied by situations of sadness, loss, death, and oppression.

In a story not found in *St. Rocque* ("On the Bayou Bridge," Vol. 3, WADN), Dunbar-Nelson describes the Bayou St. John:

> In its dark bosom many secrets lie buried. It is like some beautiful serpent, langurous, sinister. It ripples in the sunshine, sparkles in the moonlight, glooms in the dusk and broods in the dark. But it thinks unceasingly, and below its brightest sparkle you feel its unknown soul.

Her stories work in this way. Looking upon them (too) closely, "you would shudder because you feel what lies beneath the brown waters." In *St. Rocque*, the dark Manuela resorts to a voodoo madam to vanquish her blonde rival in romance; Tony's wife is beaten and kicked out on the street; Annette gives up her operatic ambitions after being misled by the fisherman of Pass Christian; dire economic want forces M'sieu Fortier to sell his beloved violin; Athanasia's story becomes yet another "broken-hearted romance" by the Bayou St. John; Sylves', a young Cajun man, is brought back to his fond Maman and fiancé Louisette dead in his coffin after working a winter in Chicago; and thus one could continue.

Beyond these plots, one notes that Dunbar-Nelson is inclined to write about difference—for example, Catholic versus Protestant, Anglo versus Creole. Grandpère Colomes is shamed when "his petite Juanita, his Spanish blossom, his hope of a family that had held itself proudly aloof from 'dose Americain' from time immemorial," smiles "upon this Mercer, this pale-eyed youth." More deeply still, one encounters disturbing tropes of enclosure (the veil, the closing door) which subtly critique female confinement and lack of options. Polysemous texts like "Sister Josepha" (Vol. 1, WADN) and "The Locket" (published outside of *St. Rocque*; Vol. 3, WADN), quasiconventional convent stories, further indict the patriarchal oppression of young girls. Obviously, for the readers of these tales, suffering was romantic—as it has often been taken to be, especially when the sufferer is someone other than oneself.

After *The Goodness of St. Rocque*, Dunbar-Nelson continued to mine Creole materials, but went far beyond the ostensibly safe mode of that volume. The undercurrent of "dark-blooded passion" hinted at in *St. Rocque* erupts into the murderous heroine of "On the Bayou Bridge," whose "long fingers" wind themselves around her abandoning lover's neck "like steel cords." Anglo prejudice becomes overt racism in "Nat-

alie" when Olivia's mother opposes the friendship of her
white daughter and the brown maiden Natalie, who has been
treated before this incident with "supercilious indifference"
or "contemptuous patronage." Most significantly of all,
Dunbar-Nelson stops dealing with the Creole as a racial
monolith and addresses the specific dilemma of the black
Creole who has immediate or identifiable Negro ancestry.

"The Pearl in the Oyster" is one such story, but "The
Stones of the Village" is weightier (both stories appear in
Vol. 3, WADN). Young Victor Grabért's childhood has been
blighted by his ambiguous racial identity. His loving, but
stern, old West Indian grandmother forbids him social inter-
action with the youngsters on his street (whom she vehemently
calls "dose niggers").

> It had been loneliness ever since. For the parents of the
> little black and yellow boys resenting the insult Grandmére
> had offered their offspring, sternly bade them have nothing
> more to do with Victor. Then when he toddled after some
> other little boys, whose faces were white like his own, they
> ran him away with derisive hoots of "Nigger! Nigger!" And
> again, he could not understand. . . . [A]ll the boys, white
> and black and yellow hooted at him and called him "White
> nigger! White nigger!"

Furthermore, Grandmére forces him to cease speaking "the
soft, Creole patois that they chattered together" and learn
English, the result being "a confused jumble which was no
language at all." This "confused jumble," this silence—
linguistic, racial, psychic, and emotional—determines his
entire life.

A chain of circumstances cuts off Victor from his past, and
he becomes a highly successful lawyer and judge, marries

into a leading (white) family, and fathers a fine son. Yet the fear of racial exposure torments him and eventually ends in psychosis, madness, and death. He dies apoplectically, about to address a political banquet, imagining that the men who crowd around to help him are "all boys with stones to pelt him because he wanted to play with them."

In this story, Dunbar-Nelson handles complexities she never touched any place else. Certainly, she is treating the popular Afro-American literary themes of the "color line"— that is, passing—and the "tragic mulatto" from the unique vantage of the Louisiana black Creole. That this troubled subject has autobiographical resonance is clear when it is compared with an essay she wrote around 1929. Entitled "Brass Ankles Speaks" (Vol. 2, WADN), it is an outspoken denunciation of darker skinned black people's prejudice against light-skinned blacks told by a "brass ankles," a black person "white enough to pass for white, but with a darker family back-ground, a real love for the mother race, and no desire to be numbered among the white race." This brass ankles recalls her "miserable" childhood in "a far Southern city" where other schoolchildren taunted and plagued her because she was a "light nigger, with straight hair!" This kind of rebuff and persecution continued into a Northern college and her first teaching job:

> Small wonder, then, that the few lighter persons in the community drew together; we were literally thrown upon each other, whether we liked or not. But when we began going about together and spending time in each other's society, a howl went up. We were organizing a "blue vein" society. We were mistresses of white men. We were Lesbians. We hated black folk and plotted against them. As a matter of fact, we had no other recourse but to cling together.

And she states further that "To complain would be only to bring upon themselves another storm of abuse and fury."

This essay was as close as Dunbar-Nelson ever got to revealing feelings about her own racial status as a "yaller nigger." She tried to publish it, but would not or could not do so under her own name, and the magazine editor refused to print it pseudonymously. "The Stones of the Village" is, likewise, as close as she ever got to turning this kind of personal and cultural confusion into art. One notes, though, that in the story, she uses a male rather than a female protagonist, thereby making it easier to write and keep at a safer distance from herself.

Uncollected stories such as this one are serious, potentially threatening. Consequently, they did not sell easily and many were never published. During the years (1898–1902) of professional authorship when she was the lesser known, female half of the Dunbar writing duo, one of the concrete perquisites of her position was sharing the literary agent Paul Reynolds. Her letters to him show that she kept him supplied with a steady stream of material, much of which came back to her. Those stories of hers that "some of the leading magazines of the country regularly print[ed]"[3] tended to be fluffy romances, often with local color backdrops. To Bliss Perry of *The Atlantic Monthly*, she proposed expanding "The Stones of the Village" into a novel. In an August 22, 1900, reply, he offered his opinion that at present the American public had a "dislike" for treatment of "the color-line." And "Stones" remained in manuscript. Knowing more of these previously unpublished stories would certainly have modified our simple generalizations about Alice Dunbar-Nelson.

This becomes even truer when two other of her stories are considered—"Elisabeth" and "Ellen Fenton" (both appear in

Vol. 3, WADN). With ten additional works, they were to be included in a volume, *Women and Men,* which Dunbar-Nelson projected sometime around 1902. Elisabeth is a thirty-year-old single woman who abruptly finds herself alone in New York City needing to make a living: "I am too old to think about marrying, and too young to go to the poorhouse. . . . Too ugly to be attractive, and not ugly enough to make a living in a sideshow." Her efforts to find a job prove "a lonely struggle, lonely and hard" and the one she finally secures "paid little." Here Dunbar-Nelson begins to explore the psyche and life of an ordinary, post-Victorian working woman. Elisabeth is not rich. She is not a Creole exotic. She is not exemplary in any way.

Ellen Fenton, likewise, wakes up one morning and finds herself unaccountably dissatisfied with her forty years of living: "Something was whirling within her, an indefinable feeling that she too, wanted to say aloud . . . 'I don't want to do the same thing; I want to do something different.' " She has been a model wife and mother, a civic inspiration, but now she begins to brood and change until she makes a startling discovery:

> She had always been a woman, who in addition to the multiple cares of her household and public philanthropy, to use the cant phrase, "lived her own life." She was discovering now that the term was a misnomer. The average woman, she found, who "lives her own life," in reality, lives others', and has no life of her own.

Today, this reads like an early formulation of "the feminine mystique"—and indeed would have been had Dunbar-Nelson stuck with her gender analysis and not "universalized" the issue by also giving Ellen's husband Herbert a parallel mid-

life crisis. Similarly, she sidesteps original exploration of
Elisabeth's dilemma by turning her story into a happily-ever-
after romance. In both cases, her "modern feminist realism"
(a phrase Alain Locke used in commenting upon Georgia
Douglas Johnson, Edna St. Vincent Millay, and Sara Teas-
dale)[4] is wrenched into submission and never fully realized.

This realism burgeons into urban naturalism in *The Annals
of 'Steenth Street* (Vol. 3, WADN), another projected volume
of short stories. These stories build on the experience Dunbar-
Nelson gained doing settlement work and teaching on New
York City's East Side in 1897–1898. 'Steenth Street is her
"Main Street," located around 87th between Second and
Third Avenues, underneath the El with the East River in
view. The protagonists of these tales are Irish ghetto youth
whom the reader comes to know as they appear throughout
the collection—Abe Powers, James Brown, Scrappy Franks,
Dobson, Hattie Gurton, Della Mott, Lizzie Williams, Gus
Schwartz. Perhaps Dunbar-Nelson saw these narratives as
juvenile fiction, a possibility that is suggested by the fact that
one of the two stories from this set that were published, "The
Revenge of James Brown," appeared as a Methodist Episcopal
Church young people's story in 1929. Again perhaps, this
fictional vehicle may have been chosen because it helped to
present the harsh social criticism inherent in the selections in
a more harmless guise.

The denizens of this neighborhood live hard lives. Money
is short or nonexistent, the next meal is a daily problem,
parents are alcoholics, and drunken fathers beat their step-
daughters. In the midst of all this, a guy must save face with
the gang, a girl needs a dress for the ball of a lifetime, a
rival wins favor for peanuts, and women like Mrs. McMahon

pick up the pieces when the makeshift foundations crumble. Dunbar-Nelson sees with analytical clarity the female lot. When Belle finally kills her deserving husband ("Witness for the Defense," Vol. 3, WADN), 'Steenth Street celebrates:

> For so long had woman-kind in this particular section of the world quietly taken its beatings, gone without food or fire or light, while its better half found all three with amusement and jollity thrown in at McEneny's on the corner; . . . for so long had the survival of the strongest been the implacable law that now when one woman had broken the bonds of custom and established the right to live and to kill too, there was great rejoicing. The women stood about in doorways and halls and discussed the event with avidity. Emancipation was in the air.

Dunbar-Nelson is also sensitive to the plight of the children. Abe Powers ("The Downfall of Abe Powers," Vol. 3, WADN) writes to the mission matron:

> "Dere Miss Morton, I beat Mr. coller an put him out becos he talked too much an i dont see why we has to be bothered when our mothers is drunk an if you will plese forgive me an let me come to the [Christmas] tree i will be gode. . ."

The stories are about oppression. The idea of difference, which always interested Dunbar-Nelson, becomes here class difference. This she uses, I am sure, as a signifier for race. The vocabulary of racism is unmistakable in Miss Tillman's language ("Miss Tillman's Protege," Vol. 3, WADN) when she breathes raptures about adopting little Hattie: "Such a dear, sweet, patient face. She'd look lovely in a dear white apron with her hair smooth sitting at my feet in my study." When Mrs. Morton reminds her that Hattie may have "family ties, and a mother," she counters, "it's absurd. These people are very different from us. I thought you knew that from your long experience with them."

The kind of transmutations occurring in these stories is further suggested when they are compared with Dunbar-Nelson's comments in a January 23, 1898, letter to her fiancé Paul. She reported a visit to the home of one of her students, where she found a German woman married to a "shiftless, dirty Negro" who drank, beat, and neglected her and the children. They were about to be evicted from two smelly, squalid rooms, had no coal, no food, a nursing baby, a toddler with chicken pox, etc. The scene gets shifted straight into the 'Steenth Street fiction, with only the "shiftless, dirty Negro" bleached out. Why? One reason is that Dunbar-Nelson did not wish to portray this type of black person. Other reasons may relate to marketing conditions, her authorial psychology, and the tricky *why*s and *wherefore*s of her literary passing game. ("Hope Deferred" [Vol. 3, WADN] is an exception in her fictional corpus.)

Nowhere is the sense of passing greater than in her specifically autobiographical stories, those few pieces where she takes herself and the details of her experience as material. It could also be said that nowhere would the need for camouflage be as crucial. Yet one wonders what Dunbar-Nelson thought she could have been concealing. Any of these stories published under her own name would have functioned like public monologues to a voyeuristic analyst. This accounts for her use of a pseudonym and also for the fact that at least one of them reads more like a therapeutic piece of personal catharsis than a work she intended to publish.

Three stories (Vol. 3, WADN) fall into this category— "Mrs. Newly-wed and Her Servants," "The Decision," and

"No Sacrifice." Interestingly, all of them reflect her relationship with Paul Laurence Dunbar. "Mrs. Newly-wed" does so in an innocuous manner, since it is a doleful tale of a freshly married young wife reciting to her amused but sympathetic friend the problems she has had with a long roll of unsatisfactory female servants. She is Alice as Mrs. Paul Laurence Dunbar, after the couple set up housekeeping in Washington, D.C., casting herself into yet another role. "The Decision" and "No Sacrifice" are barely veiled accounts of Alice's courtship and marriage with Paul. Here is a trove of accurate information about their meeting through a magazine, becoming impulsively engaged before Paul sails overseas, Alice's mother's disapproval, their romantic passion and stormy public fights, his bouts with alcohol, her refusal to visit him on his sick bed, and all the rest that made their union romantic copy for scandalmongers. A reader familiar with the relationship peruses these stories for clues to answer the questions of what went wrong and why Alice so obdurately refused to be reconciled.

This aspect of the works aside, their next most striking feature is the way that Dunbar-Nelson has made the narratives racially white. Mrs. Newly-wed recruits her help from the "camp," "that disreputable part of the town just below the Sixth Street hill where a lot of colored folks have congregated." When he is intoxicated, Burt Courtland's eyes are "red-streaked across their blue." Gerald Kennedy is a "Greek God" with "chestnut hair" whose emotional face "flares crimson." Furthermore, wealth abounds. Burt has built Marion a "great, dreary new mansion," the couples "jet-set" like Scott and Zelda Fitzgerald, rich uncles die leaving behind their millions. This lavish flow of dollars calls to mind Dunbar-Nelson saying that play money figured so prominently on stage in black drama because the real thing was such a scarce commodity in actual life (a circumstance that was true for her until the end of her days). Seemingly, too, for Dunbar-Nelson, white equalled rich (or was it that rich equalled white?)—unless fate landed one on 'Steenth Street.

So much of these stories is fact-based fantasy ("No Sacrifice" was written as a "True Story") that it is hard to think through (and beyond) this component—and in the works themselves, images of falseness and illusion are prevalent. Ultimately, these texts reveal the author's attempt to write about herself—but from deep within limiting psychic and formal structures.

Dunbar-Nelson rounded out her short-story career with snappily written pieces in the newly emerging American detective genre. It is not surprising that she would find this "hard-boiled" tradition attractive since the no-nonsense, rational "tough guy" was one of her private personae—and also because she often tried her hand at whatever was new and modern and promised financial reward. A vacationing private detective lays the foundation for the surprise ending of "His Great Career," while "Summer Session" shows us Mr. Terence McShane nabbing the criminal (a white slavery perpetrator) and then winning the girl, to boot. Both stories are slick, well-made; but there is no evidence that they were ever published (Vol. 3, WADN).

Dunbar-Nelson wrote many stories not included here in *The Works of Alice Dunbar-Nelson* and, at her death, left behind both typescripts and holograph drafts. From the publication of *Violets* through the early 1900s, short stories received her most concentrated attention. And as late as 1928, a newspaper article reported that she "considers her short stories her most representative work."[5] Certainly, taken as a whole, this fiction is impressively various and surprisingly complex.

Dunbar-Nelson also tried longer fiction, writing (or partially writing) at least four novels—*The Confessions of a Lazy Woman* (ca. 1899, cast in diary form); *A Modern Undine* (ca. 1901–1903; Vol. 2, WADN); *Uplift* (1930–1931, intended as a satire of an insincere black woman who professionally represents the race; Dunbar-Nelson destroyed the manuscript because of dissatisfaction with it); and *This Lofty Oak* (1932–1933, the extremely long, fictionalized biography of her friend, Delaware educator Edwina B. Kruse). While she was writing *Uplift,* she derisively referred to it as "the Great American Novel," indicating, I think, both her desire to pen that national classic and her knowledge that she was incapable of doing so.[6]

Of these works, *A Modern Undine* is the most satisfactory and most fully realized. It exists as a seventy-nine-page, typed manuscript that can be justifiably considered an organic novelette since it is Dunbar-Nelson's first, complete draft (stretching plots to standard novel length was always one of her problems). We know that she added some now-lost pages because a professional opinion she received in 1903 objected to the ease with which the heroine finds her lost husband.[7] *Undine* tells the story of Marion, a decorous, self-centered, introverted, prickly-sensitive, twenty-four-year-old Southern woman. From a home made lively by her mother and hoydenish sister, she marries Howard, a Northern businessman who falls in love with her despite her aloofness. Mistakenly thinking that Howard is having an affair with a poor girl in the town, Marion retreats even further into paranoia and obsessive mothering of their crippled son. Everything climaxes at once. The truth about the affair comes out; Howard's business fails in the general crash and he has to flee charges of embezzlement; he and Marion for the first time in their lives speak frankly about their feelings, with Howard openly criticizing her narrowness and self-centeredness. Reading this, one is somehow drawn into the rather strange tale, becoming irritated with Marion's almost-total withdrawal from feelings and the world, sympathizing with Howard, and so on. The psychological dimensions are strong (reflecting Dunbar-Nelson's lifelong fascination with this field).

However, the key to understanding this novelette lies in its title. In folklore, an *undine* is a "female water sprite who could acquire a soul by marrying a human being." But if her lover proved unfaithful, she would have to return to the sea.[8] Marion is this spirit. When we first glimpse her on the night she meets Howard, she is standing on the edge of a breakwater with the sea surging at her feet "in a low monotone of life and death." The second time we see her, she gazes "out at the sea," seeming more than ever "in her curious detachment from her surroundings" to remind Howard of "a vestal set apart from the rest of mankind, awaiting mysterious voices from heaven." Water references and the sea motif continue, especially at critical points in the plot. When she first discovers what she thinks is her husband's infidelity, Marion's fainting is imaged as "the darkness and roaring of the sea clos[ing] over her head." After her baby dies, she directs her mother to "bury him by the sea . . . perhaps it will sing to him the same songs it has sung to me."

Further, in these folkloric terms, Marion's "becoming human" through the vicissitudes of love and marriage is emphatically focused. That she is warped is symbolized in the deformity of her child, who was maimed in her womb when she fainted, and of whom she is jealously possessive. During their climactic argument, Howard rebukes her for fancying herself "too superior to come out of the clouds long enough to touch the vital human things of this world," and tells her that getting involved with charity work "would have made [her] seem more like a human being." Humanity first flares in her when she waits to accuse Howard of visiting his paramour: "A cold, deadly fury was stirring at her heart, becoming more passionate and human at every instant that Howard stayed in the house." At the end of their encounter, "for an instant she felt again strangely aloof from the whole scene, apart and out of the disaster which threatened her whole life, but only for an instant." She has entered the realm of human love and sorrow, in a novel which affirms both.

A Modern Undine reflects the fact that Dunbar-Nelson, an astrological Cancer, loved the sea—and rhapsodized about it in her diary:

> But the water! . . . Weeks I dreamed of it. . . . No inconvenience too great for the love of it. . . Lovely, luxurious, voluptuous water.[9]

Deeper still, the work reveals her connection with myth, the mystical, and the spiritual. Her daily living evinced an awareness of meta-realms of experience beyond the visible world which was rooted in her mother's Obeah beliefs and enhanced by her own attention to the spiritual arts. This seems to be the level of reality she is adumbrating here—and is the only time this mystical consciousness is specifically developed in her literary work.

On a completely different plane, it can be noted that, more than once, Dunbar-Nelson wrote about an uninvolved female. *The Confessions of a Lazy Woman*—ultimately a rather silly work—features a heroine who strives (and she really has to work at it) to do absolutely nothing. Dunbar-Nelson was just the opposite, what she herself once described as "another too-busy woman." Might this imaging of idleness and withdrawal be wish fulfillment of a more significant kind than that represented by the material wealth of her romances? It may be that these figures represent—simultaneously—a longing for and a critique of female passivity/inactivity/worldly isolation (they don't even read the newspaper). As a critique, they present the feminine ideal elevated to the satiric nth degree of foolishness.

Thinking in this way raises the comparison between Dunbar-Nelson and her female protagonists. Not one of them is even remotely like her. Unfortunately, when she tried to transcribe her own self/body in the autobiographical romances, the attempts were unsuccessful at best and disastrous at worst. None of her heroines are black—no Iola Leroy or Megda or some other figure to carry us forward to Helga Crane or Janie Starks. One wonders, if they had been black, could Dunbar-Nelson have done a better, or different, job with them? A black woman like herself on the printed page in 1915 would have been a sight to behold. What she did (and did not do) with *Uplift* and *This Lofty Oak* suggests that black women's lives (her own and others') were too real to be fiction—as she understood fiction to be in those largely premodernist days. And there was simply too much that she did not want to say about herself. All of this is, of course, speculation; Dunbar-Nelson did what she could and we can try to understand and appreciate that, even as we wish for more.

What she was able to achieve in prose outweighs her poetic accomplishments although, ironically, being taken as a poet has helped immensely to keep her reputation alive. Dunbar-Nelson was not driven to write poems and did not focus on the genre. When asked by an editor for a poem in 1900, she confessed to being short on poetic inspiration and added,

"Mr. Dunbar tells me that I average one poem in six months, and that there will be none due for several weeks to come." [10] If anything, Paul's estimate is a bit high when spread over her lifetime of writing.

By and large, Dunbar-Nelson's poetry (included in Vol. 2, WADN) is what it appears to be—competent treatments of conventional lyric themes in traditional forms and styles. Her signature poem, "Violets," is the apogee of this type. A few others stand out for various reasons. "I Sit and Sew," wherein a woman chafes at her domestic role during wartime, seems feminist in spirit. "You! Inez!" appears to be a rare eruption in verse of Dunbar-Nelson's lesbian feelings. "Communion" and "Music" were probably (like "Violets") selections in a no longer extant *Dream Book* commemorating her illicit affair with Emmett J. Scott, Jr. "To Madame Curie" and "Cano—I Sing" are strikingly well executed. "April Is On the Way" is a confusingly complicated work about a rape (or attempted rape) and lynching. "Forest Fire" shows Dunbar-Nelson trying to modernize her technique during the Harlem Renaissance years of experimentation. "The Proletariat Speaks" reminds one of her consciousness about difference and class contrasts. "Little Roads" contains a pun on "Fay," the name of the woman with whom she was romantically involved when she wrote it in 1930–1931. "Harlem John Henry Views the Airmada" is an "epic of Negro Peace" complete with a black protagonist and slave spirituals.

Though Dunbar-Nelson's poetry improves markedly from her juvenile verse to the mature work of the 1920s, her gifts—which were more discursive than poetic—were not geared in that direction. Furthermore, her essentially romantic conception of poetry caused her to reserve it for intense emotion and other special occasions. Yet it was one more way that she proved herself a writer and solidified her stature as such.

This same statement can be made about her drama, with the clarification that her interest in this genre may have been keener. From her girlhood in New Orleans, Dunbar-Nelson participated in amateur theater. She was also an avid play (and movie) goer, and she wrote and directed plays and pageants for school and community groups. In the Afro-American community, skits and plays for class night programs, for Christmas and Easter church celebrations, and for club fundraising attractions have always been important. Thus, this form was very much a part of Dunbar-Nelson's personal and cultural background. It also suited her often dramatic (not to say theatrical) temperament.

Furthermore, the early twentieth-century black cultural debates often eddied around the drama. The explosion of dark faces on Broadway (notably in the musicals of the 1920s) was paralleled by the development of serious drama in predominantly black colleges (Howard University in Washington, D.C., was a major center) and the proliferation of plays about blacks by famous white playwrights (Eugene O'Neill's *Emperor Jones* was perhaps the most celebrated). At the same time, Oscar Michaeux and a few others were pioneering the race film and black movie making. Something of this ferment can be picked up in Dunbar-Nelson's newspaper columns. It was a time of intense pronouncements about the proper portrayal of the Negro on stage. A 1928 newspaper article uncovers Dunbar-Nelson adding her bit to the current dialogue:

> [Dunbar-Nelson] believes that the stage is the best medium for exploiting ourselves; that we must break away from

propaganda per se and the conventional musical comedy that starts on a plantation and ends in a cabaret, and present to the American public all phases of Negro life and culture.[11]

This contextual grounding of her plays in black life probably helps account for Dunbar-Nelson's use in them of identifiably black characters, settings, and situations (which is unlike her fiction). Then, too, this would have to be the case if she had any intention at all of seeing them performed. The same 1928 article also mentioned that she "preferred" writing plays (though one cannot fathom what that really means, given her literary record) and had done "a number" of them for "amateur producers." Her extant works for her Howard High School groups are obviously designed for the educational and moral edification of the students. Something like the *Club Ritz-Carlton*, a cabaret show that she staged for the Wilmington, Delaware, Elk Daughters, can only be conjectured about. Her most well-known and probably most acted play was *Mine Eyes Have Seen* (Vol. 3, WADN; publication in the *Crisis* helped its visibility). There is no evidence that the others included here (Vol. 3, WADN) were ever mounted.

Question: What kind of black folk does Dunbar-Nelson present in her racial plays? On the whole, they are all recognizable types—as dramatic characters are traditionally wont to be. In *Mine Eyes*, Lucy is the gentle, patient sister who takes care of her two motherless brothers; Cornelia Lewis is a conscientious settlement worker; Dan is the older brother literally crippled by racial prejudice. *Gone White* (Vol. 3, WADN) highlights Allan Franklin Cordell, a light-skinned, young, educated black man determined to compel potential employers "to admit that a Negro can be as good or better an engineer than a white man," to "ram their damn prejudice down their throats." Granny Wimbish moans spirituals, and Anna Martin is as long-serving as Lucy. Blanche Parker, Allan's aunt, strikes a more original note. Frankly (even immorally) pragmatic, she puts Allan through college (by dressing hair in her own beauty shop), then counsels him to pass for white and maintain his white wife, family, and position, and—if he must—"love" his brown-skinned Anna on the side. Though mostly poor, the characters are decent, respectable, and above all, well-spoken. There is no dialect here, no comedy, as Dunbar-Nelson tries to live up to her call for a broader, more realistic Afro-American drama.

The fact that these plays treat controversial topics helped Dunbar-Nelson achieve more intense effects. *Mine Eyes* argues for blacks to support World War I, but presents the glaring contradictions. When Chris is drafted, he asks, "Must I go and fight for the nation that let my father's murder [by whites] go unpunished? That killed my mother—that took away my chances for making a man out of myself?" And in *Gone White* when Anna comprehends what Allan wants, she "speaks through clenched teeth":

> You are offering me the position of your mistress. . . . You would keep your white wife, and all that that means, for respectability's sake—but you would have a romance, a liaison with the brown woman whom you love, after dark. No Negro could stoop so low as to take on such degraded ideals of so-called racial purity. And this is the moral deterioration to which you have brought your whole race. White Man! Go on back to your white gods! Lowest and vilest of scum. White Man! Go Back!

The Author's Evening at Home and *Love's Disguise*, a silent film scenario (both in Vol. 3, WADN), round out the view of Dunbar-Nelson in the dramatic media. The first work, really a 1900 playlet, is a slick piece that capitalizes on her relationship with Paul. The credit line in *Smart Set* read "By Alice Dunbar (Mrs. Paul Laurence Dunbar)" and suggested a real-life genesis for this comedy about an author in his library who cannot write because of his disruptive wife and mother. *Love's Disguise*—with its extreme portrayal of duality—is simply an instance of Dunbar-Nelson's flirtation with silent filmscripts. Eventually, she gave up the notion and concentrated her talent in forms more feasible for her.

This completes the survey of Dunbar-Nelson's work in the canonical genres. She also did a large amount of other writing that is just as important. In it (her essays, for example), she is as relentlessly racial as she is nonracial in the fine genres, suggesting, of course, that her concepts of genre-reality-race were rigidly stratified. Furthermore, it is in this nonbelletristic work that she truly inscribes herself. Nowhere is this more evident than in her diary, which she kept during 1921 and 1926–1931. Here she allows herself to star, center stage in all her complexity and beauty. Even though no excerpts are included in this collection because this journal is easily available, it is an indispensable portion of her works.[12]

The "real" Dunbar-Nelson also "stands up" in her newspaper columns, playing the role of the urbane journalist—a pose that superbly suited her as individual and artist. This liberating stance permitted her to be as contrary and self-contradictory as she wished. A mobile, moody thinker, she could say one thing on Saturday and something completely different the next week. The column form likewise allowed for variation in length and emphasis ranging from one-liners and snippets to full-scale, expository essays. In any case, Dunbar-Nelson consistently spoke out "from a (black) woman's point of view" (as she did, too, in essays such as "Facing Life Squarely" [Vol. 2, WADN] with its memorable obser-

vation that "the spectacle of two or three ordinary Southern
white women sitting down to talk with several very high class
black women" does not represent racial progress worth "sobbing with joy" about). However, what she wrote was definitely not a typical "woman's" column devoted to narrowly
defined feminine concerns.

Even after sixty years, her weekly pieces are very readable
and engaging—which is praise indeed for writing produced
as ephemera. The intellect, wit, protest, sassiness, iconoclasm,
racial pride, feminism, and humor that one yearns for in her
fictional heroines can all be found here. These columns have
to be read to be appreciated, and some of their impact is
cumulative (like the diary). In her April 10, 1926 "Une
Femme Dit" (Vol. 2, WADN), Dunbar-Nelson repeats an
accolade:

> Mrs. Myrtle Foster Cook, the charming and gracile editor
> of the National Notes, the official organ of the National
> Association of Colored Women, says that this column is "as
> delectable and refreshing as a cool lemonade after a hectic
> day."
>
> That is delightful praise. Should one be too modest to
> reproduce it? Not so. Modesty went out with the corset, the
> pompadour, long skirts, lined dresses, the knitted petticoat,
> the merry widow hat, the lisle stocking, the chatelaine bag,
> and the fleur de lys watch pin. Indeed, so much is modesty a
> lost art, that one is almost tempted to repeat the entire
> paragraph from the National Notes. But lingering phases of
> reluctance, delicate and obscure, forbid. We rise and make
> our best bow in the direction of Kansas City

—while "we" blow our nails and polish them on the bodice
of our dress, in that stage business of self-satisfied modesty
whose verbal approximation is "ahem." Mrs. Cook is backed

up—though in sexist fashion—by Eugene Gordon, who wrote this of Dunbar-Nelson in a 1927 *Opportunity* magazine "Survey of the Negro Press": "In my estimation there are few better column conductors of her sex on any newspaper. I should like to see her on some influential daily where her unmistakable talents would be allowed full exercise."[13]

"Une Femme Dit"—which began as "From A Woman's Point of View," and which shows Dunbar-Nelson at her best—was written for the Pittsburgh *Courier* from February 20, 1926, to September 18, 1926. "As In a Looking Glass" (Vol. 2, WADN) appeared in the Washington *Eagle* from 1926 to 1930. (Dunbar-Nelson also wrote another column, "So It Seems—to Alice Dunbar-Nelson," for the *Courier* from January to May 1930, but this series betrays some diminution of verve and interest.) In these columns (of which the selection in Vol. 2 represents only a small part), Dunbar-Nelson shines as literary critic, political analyst, social commentator, race theorist, humorist, and stage and film critic. During this age of print journalism and rising syndicated chains, when newspaper work was a man's profession, Dunbar-Nelson felt that pressure but excelled nonetheless.

It is unfortunate that this writing, which contains so much of her creative energy, is so underrated as art. Valorizing these texts is the most radical example of the re-reading of Alice Dunbar-Nelson which I hope this edition of her works will foster.

NOTES

1. For a fuller treatment of Alice Dunbar-Nelson's life and more information about her writings, see the chapter devoted to her in

Gloria T. Hull, *Color, Sex, and Poetry: Three Women Writers of the Harlem Renaissance* (Bloomington: Indiana University Press, 1987). Some material in this introduction is taken from this source.

2. Pittsburgh *Christian Advocate*, December 21, 1899.

3. "Mrs. Paul Laurence Dunbar, Wife of the Colored Poet and Novelist," Chicago *Recorder*, August 4, 1902.

4. Alain Locke, "Foreword" to Georgia Douglas Johnson, *An Autumn Love Cycle* (New York: Harold Vinal, Ltd., 1928), p. xviii.

5. Newspaper clipping, no name, July 4, 1928. From the vertical file of the Schomburg Center for Research in Black Culture, New York City.

6. Dunbar-Nelson's diary for 1930–1931 charts her writing of *Uplift*. See Gloria T. Hull (ed.), *Give Us Each Day: The Diary of Alice Dunbar-Nelson* (New York: W. W. Norton, 1984).

7. J. N. M. (?) to Alice Dunbar-Nelson, July 16, 1903. For this "expert opinion," Dunbar-Nelson paid five dollars.

8. Information taken from William H. Harris and Judith S. Levey (eds.), *The New Columbia Encyclopedia* (New York: Columbia University Press, 1975), p. 2822.

9. Hull (ed.), *Give Us Each Day*, p. 325.

10. The New York City *Chute* (?), May 1900.

11. Unidentified July 4, 1928 clipping from the Schomburg Center vertical file.

12. Bibliographical data cited in note 6 above.

13. Quoted as an epigraph to Dunbar-Nelson's February 25, 1927, "As In a Looking Glass" column.

EDITORIAL NOTE

Bibliographic information for Alice Dunbar-Nelson's published work, when known, is noted at the beginning of each text. Unpublished manuscripts can be found in the Special Collections of the Morris Library, University of Delaware, Newark, Delaware. Prior to this present edition, R. Ora Williams helped to make Dunbar-Nelson's work somewhat more available in her *An Alice Dunbar-Nelson Reader* (Washington, D.C.: University Press of America, Inc., 1979). She also published "Works By and About Alice Ruth (Moore) Dunbar-Nelson: A Bibliography" in the *CLA Journal*, XIX, No. 3 (March, 1976). Both of these are useful references.

For this edition of Dunbar-Nelson's works, it was clear that her two published books should be reprinted. In selecting the other works, I used the criteria of autobiographical and literary interest, artistic merit, and representativeness, while keeping in mind the space available. Including the 595 typed manuscript pages of *This Lofty Oak* did not seem compellingly feasible or worthwhile. Nor did I choose to collect a greater number of her slighter romantic stories. Likewise, high school plays and pageants were not considered important enough for publication, but all of her apparently finished, available poetry is here.

Her articles and essays for outlets like *The Southern Workman*, *The Messenger*, and the *Journal of Negro History* are least represented. Though valuable, they are standard expository and argumentative pieces written in an objective style, which makes them not as vital as Dunbar-Nelson's other

lv

noncanonical work for understanding her life and art. However, what they do sharpen is the dichotomy between the nonracialness of her belletristic genres and the racialness of her other writings. The inclusions from her newspaper columns were probably made most impressionistically (and were also influenced by whether the originals were crumbling or had been photocopied). Given what they are, reading through any runs of them provides very similar materials and insights.

The selections are presented here as Dunbar-Nelson wrote them, with only obvious typographical and spelling errors corrected.

ALICE DUNBAR-NELSON

A CHRONOLOGY

1875	July 19, born in New Orleans, Louisiana.
1892	Graduated from Straight College, New Orleans; subsequently studied at Cornell, Columbia, the Pennsylvania School of Industrial Art, and the University of Pennsylvania, specializing in English educational measurements and psychology.
1892–1896	Taught school in New Orleans.
1895	Published *Violets and Other Tales* (Boston: The Monthly Review Press)—short stories and poems.
1897–1898	Taught in Brooklyn, New York; helped to found the White Rose Mission, which became the White Rose Home for Girls in Harlem.
1898	March 8, married poet Paul Laurence Dunbar and began living in Washington, D.C.
1899	Published *The Goodness of St. Rocque and Other Stories* (New York: Dodd, Mead, and Co.)—short stories.
1902	Separated from Paul Laurence Dunbar and moved to Wilmington, Delaware (he died February 6, 1906).
1902–1920	Taught and administered at the Howard High School, Wilmington; for seven of these years, also directed the summer sessions for in-

This chronology appeared in Gloria T. Hull (ed.), *Give Us Each Day: The Diary of Alice Dunbar-Nelson*. New York: W. W. Norton, 1984.

	service teachers at State College for Colored Students (now Delaware State College), Dover; and taught two years in the summer session at Hampton Institute.
1909	April, published "Wordsworth's Use of Milton's Description of Pandemonium" in *Modern Language Notes*.
1910	January 19, married teacher Henry Arthur Callis secretly in Wilmington. He left the next year for medical school in Chicago. (They were later divorced at some unknown time.)
1913–1914	Wrote for and helped edit the *A.M.E. Church Review*.
1914	Edited and published *Masterpieces of Negro Eloquence* (Harrisburg, Pennsylvania: The Douglass Publishing Company).
1915	Was field organizer for the Middle Atlantic States in the campaign for women's suffrage.
1916	April 20, married Robert J. Nelson, a journalist.
1916–1917	Published a two-part article, "People of Color in Louisiana," in *The Journal of Negro History*.
1917–1928	Published poems in *Crisis, Ebony and Topaz, Opportunity, Negro Poets and Their Poems, Caroling Dusk, The Dunbar Speaker and Entertainer, Harlem: A Forum of Negro Life*, etc.
1918	Toured the South as a field representative of the Woman's Committee of the Council of National Defense.

1920   Served on the State Republican Committee of
               Delaware and directed political activities
               among black women; edited and published
               The Dunbar Speaker and Entertainer (Naper-
               ville, Illinois: J. L. Nichols and Co.);
               drawing on her interests in juvenile delin-
               quency and "abnormal psychology," worked
               with women from the State Federation of
               Colored Women to found the Industrial
               School for Colored Girls in Marshalltown,
               Delaware.

1920–1922   Coedited and published the Wilmington *Ad-
               vocate* newspaper.

1921   August, began her *Diary* and kept an extant
               portion of it for the remainder of the year.

1922   Headed the Anti-Lynching Crusaders in Del-
               aware fighting for the Dyer Anti-Lynching
               Bill.

1924   Directed the Democratic political campaign
               among black women from New York head-
               quarters; August and September, published
               a two-part article on Delaware in "These
               'Colored' United States" in *The Messenger*.

1924–1928   Was teacher and parole officer at the Industrial
               School for Colored Girls.

1926   January 2–September 18, wrote column "From
               A Woman's Point of View" (later changed
               to "Une Femme Dit") in the Pittsburgh
               Courier.

1926–1930   Wrote column "As In a Looking Glass" in the
               Washington *Eagle* (her columns and/or ver-
               sions of them were also syndicated for the
               Associated Negro Press).

1926–1931   Resumed and kept the remaining extant portions of her *Diary*.

1928–1931   Was executive secretary of the American Friends Inter-Racial Peace Committee, which entailed much travel and public speaking.

1930   January–May, wrote column "So It Seems to Alice Dunbar-Nelson" in the Pittsburgh *Courier*.

1931   Included in James Weldon Johnson's *The Book of American Negro Poetry*.

1932   Moved to Philadelphia, after Robert was appointed to the Pennsylvania Athletic (Boxing) Commission in January.

1935   September 18, died of heart trouble at the University of Pennsylvania Hospital. She was cremated in Wilmington and her ashes eventually scattered over the Delaware River.

NOVELETTE

A MODERN UNDINE *

CHAPTER I

It was in the still quiet of a summer night that Marion met
Howard. The sea surged at her feet in a low monotone of
life and death. The heavens, a deep blue bowl, glistering
with white points of gems, bent over the earth in an embrace
of enfolding tenderness. The night was full of a thousand
sounds and a thousand silences. The sea sobbed, the crickets
whispered, the crickets shrilled; a night-bird sang somewhere
afar, heart-breaking notes that rose and fell with the cadence
of the sea. Above the minor treble of the little feminine
sounds, boomed the hoarse call of an alligator in the bayou,
like the deep-toned bass motif in an organ fugue. There
would come an instant hush over the clamor when the waves
seemed to soften their tone, the shrill-voiced insects would be
silent, and the bird and the bayou king let the reverberations
of their notes die away into the forest. Some wave breaking
against the pier with more force than the others would start
the silence into sound again, and the trees and the water and
the voices of the night would sing their songs aloud unto the
white diamonds of the skies.

There was no moon, but the stars cast dim shadows on the
ground, and the waves were aflame with phosphorus. It spread
a sheet of silver to the horizon; it leapt in forked tongues
from the dash of a wave against the breakwater; it crawled in
sinister lines over the wet sand.

Marion stood on the edge of the breakwater, and stared

* Written between 1898 and 1903.

curiously down at the shining sands below her. They had been dancing within the house, and she had fled alone into the night. She felt a presence beside her and turned to meet Howard.

"Is it not beautiful?" he asked, with a kind of breathless wonder at the glory of the tropical night.

"I don't know," she answered hestitatingly. They had been introduced but a moment before she left the room, and she was not quite sure that she enjoyed his evident following of her into the sea-garden.

"It is wonderful, wonderful—" he continued. "Up my way now," he added, with an amusing provincialism, "we never see anything like this."

"I think I prefer a moonlit night," she said critically, putting her head on one side.

He was very much in earnest at once, eagerly impetuous to prove her wrong.

"Oh, but you shouldn't, you know. You can have a moonlit effect anywhere, in any climate, and at all times. It is decidedly commonplace, but this—why, this is something one has to come to the South for."

She laughed lightly and turned to go in. She did not care much for the discussion, and the man was a bit forward, she thought. He touched the fringe of the little shawl she wore and said pleadingly, "Oh, don't go in again. That room is so hot and there are so many people there. How can a person feel in such crowds? Do you like crowds?"

"No, I think I do not," she answered slowly, "but it seems that one cannot escape them nowadays. The world is full of people and they are always in the way."

"Think of a mob of men and women dancing on such a

night," he protested vigorously. She surrendered herself to his mood.

"But if they were not dancing," she said with a quiet little inflection of amusement, "they would be out here—in a crowd—descanting upon the—er—scenery."

"Was that a pun?"

"A what?"

"A pun, scenery, you know."

"Oh, scenery? What—why—oh, no, I hadn't noticed it. No I never make puns."

There was absolutely no trace of humor about her now. She seemed to have withdrawn into herself suddenly, and to have become once more the "strait-laced, high-bred young lady of a last century type" which Howard had mentally dubbed her when he had been presented to her.

They walked slowly along the edge of the breakwater. The mood of the night was upon him and he talked recklessly, like a man whose brain is loosed from its everyday thrall of commonplace into a realm of fancy and poesy. The noisy stillness of the deep-hearted night had caught his soul. Unconsciously, too, the woman by his side was inflaming his imagination.

"No wonder you Southerners have such poetic souls," he rambled on.

"I don't talk of mine," she assented. He listened eagerly. He had been generalizing. She had struck a personal chord in the conversation that emboldened him.

"You don't talk of yours because —because—" he bent toward her.

"The music is beginning," she said indifferently, "We must go in."

Above the noises of the night, the notes of a waltz from the cottage nearby rose and fell in a lilting cadence, and the tinkle of the mandolins drowned the night-birds' call from the forest.

CHAPTER II

Although Howard had been disconcerted and not a bit puzzled by Miss Ross' sudden coldness, he was nonetheless persistent in his attentions to her. Because he had occasion to come South for a business trip, he argued, that was no reason why he should not enjoy all the courtesy offered him. Miss Ross was not one of the offerings, to be true, for she held herself strangely aloof when all the others about him were eager in welcoming him into their little circle. He might have felt himself flattered by her aloofness as a special mark of attention toward him, had he not noticed that she preserved the same attitude toward all around her; her own sister even was sometimes included. She seemed to have a detached quality of mind that looked on at others' enjoyment, and in a vague way, enjoyed too, but with a mental reservation, as it were. He began to study her with the same impetuous eagerness that characterized all his actions, but he could not determine whether she was indifferent, or held herself superior to her surroundings. It did not occur to him to consider her as merely sensitive.

He had grown quite confidential with Emmie, the sister. She was a frank girl with an unconventionality that was apt to be startling. Although old enough to know better, she sustained a reputation as a sort of *enfant terrible* of her set.

Emmie enjoyed it, and rather went out of her way to invent situations wherein she could figure with a more startling than dignified effect.

She sat in a hammock one day some time after Howard's first experience of the little town's hospitality at the dance. She swung herself to and fro violently, talking meanwhile in short, jerky sentences.

"You know—I like you—I was telling—the girls the other day— I'd chum with you."

"Indeed?" said Howard, amused, but watchful of the door whence Marion might emerge at any moment.

"I know you're looking for Marion this minute," she continued, still vigorously swinging, "but she isn't coming out now. We've had a scrap, and she's reading off her mad. I'm swinging mine off."

"I shouldn't think either of you would ever 'scrap,' " rejoined Howard politely, trying to suppress a sigh of disappointment.

"Oh, gracious me, yes. I wouldn't live in the house with a person I couldn't row with. Life would be too unbearably dull to mention. I have stated rows about stated things at regular intervals, and if I should miss one of them, I'd be like a cow who'd lost its cud—wild for something to chew on."

"Cow is good," commented Howard.

"Now Sis," said Emmie, reflectively allowing the hammock to slow down, "is perfectly lovely to quarrel with. She doesn't say a word, just gets redder and redder and bites her lips. I started downtown this morning to see if I could find an asbestos towel for her to wipe her face on. Plain cloth would simply have dropped into charred bits. We quarrelled about you," she added, stopping the hammock with one foot, and putting her head on one side to observe the effect of her words.

"About me?" Howard sat up in earnest, and stared hard at the girl, "Why—why—what—"

"Yes, I merely remarked, quite casually, you know, that you were a pretty good nice sort of young man, and that if you hadn't any serious objections, I'd marry you, meaning first to propose, of course. Sis seemed to think that I'd march you off to the altar willy-nilly, without telling you first where I was going. You see, no man will propose to me and I have quite serious objections to being an old maid, and I must propose myself, it seems. I had singled you out, but Sis seems to object to you as a brother-in-law."

"Perhaps she objects to me generally," laughed Howard, but there was an anxious note in his voice.

"Oh, I don't know, I didn't go into details. She said it was time for me to be serious occasionally, and when I said I was never more serious in my life, she got red, began to chew her lips and took up a book. I came out here to swing myself into a calm frame of mind."

"Miss Emmie," he said with much gallantry, dropping on one knee, "will you be mine? I cannot live without thee."

"Rise, Sir Knight," she cried, "you may die for me—"

"Emmie," said a quiet voice in the doorway, "what are you doing now?"

Howard sprang to his feet in confusion. Although he knew that she understood the mockery of the scene he felt that even in play he could not bear her to think him disloyal to her. He had never thought the word disloyal in this connection before, and he recalled it to himself with a little thrill of sentiment. Disloyal? That presupposed a condition of love on his part and of acquiescence on hers. Emmie's laughter roused him.

"You look as if you are ashamed of me," she cried merrily. "Think, Sister, I have had my first proposal of marriage, and he repents already. This is the twentieth century with a vengeance, when a gallant gentleman proposes to a lady, and grows regretful at once. I accept your offer. Congratulate me Marion. You are to have a brother-in-law. How do you feel about it?"

She was jumping up and down excitedly, laughing breathlessly, like a child who has made a discovery, whirling her sister about like a teetotum, and swinging the empty hammock in an exuberance of spirits. She was a big, healthy girl, brown-haired, brown-eyed, rosy-cheeked, hoydenish. Marion drew herself gently from her sister's rough grasp and smiled indulgently.

"You are very fortunate, dear," she said quietly, and would have passed off the gallery into the sandy garden walk, but Howard put forth a detaining hand.

"Miss Ross, don't go. We haven't arrived at that stage yet where we must be alone all the while. Stay and help us get used to each other."

She seated herself obediently on the step of the gallery, and gazed out at the sea, blue and sparkling in the summer sunshine. Howard, leaning against the railing, gazed down at her and became absorbed in the pure profile turned away from him. More than ever, in her curious detachment from her surroundings, did she remind him of a vestal set apart from the rest of mankind, awaiting mysterious voices from Heaven.

Emmie prattled along unceasingly, like a gusty little summer rain pattering on tin roofs. Marion was absorbed in the sea and Howard was absorbed in Marion. A group of girls came up the garden path, noisy, chattering, white frocked, with the inevitable Southern sun-bonnets. They seized upon Emmie and bore her away with them down the village street. She was a prime favorite with them. Marion they saluted gaily, but with a curious mixture of restraint and deference, which always pleased, while it amused Howard. They moved lightly out of the garden and Marion looked after them with a little half sigh.

"I hope I am not keeping you from your friends, Miss Ross?" Howard asked.

"Oh, no," she replied, "they didn't want me, they never bother about me. I am not gay and bright—like Emmie."

He was surprised at the unconscious revelation of herself in the sentence.

"I supposed you didn't care about—er—all that sort of thing."

"No, no one does suppose so. I don't know why, but from a child, people have always taken it for granted that I don't care for pleasures and the joys of life like other young people, for I am really not so very old," she smiled up at him pathetically.

"No, not much more than twenty," he said, his pulses throbbing at his own audacity.

"I am twenty-four."

"Dear me, I feel quite an ancient personage beside you. I am seven years your senior."

"One is an old maid in the South at twenty-five," she continued, "but I have been one all my life. I dance, everyone grants me that much, and I suppose I have my share of partners; after that, I must be quiet and orderly and mind my p's and q's. It would shock the whole town if I should break into a laugh louder than a whisper."

"They pay you the highest possible compliment," he reassured her soothingly, "they have set you apart from them as a superior being."

"Thank you, but it is very much of a bore to be set apart as a superior being, when one knows that there isn't anything superior about one's self."

At that moment Mrs. Ross came out on the gallery and threw herself into one of the big rockers. She was a little, plump, fussy woman, whom you thought at first sight would prove tiresomely energetic, but who, upon further acquaintance, proved almost tiresomely apathetic.

"Where is Emmie?" she asked fretfully, after greeting Howard with unnecessary effusion.

"She went down to the post office with the Girton girls and Adele Hutchison."

"I wish Emmie wouldn't be running around in the hot sun; she knows she's subject to malaria, and it's always a great strain on me to have her ill. I should have thought, Marion, that you wouldn't have let her go."

"You know I couldn't have kept her home, Mother, any more than you could, if I had tried. As a matter of fact, I didn't try."

"No, I suppose not. You think Emmie ought to do as she pleases no matter what I have to go through in granting her whims." She rocked herself noisily to and fro; then strolled off the gallery down to the summer house over the breakwater's edge. Mrs. Ross' method of locomotion was a never-ending source of wonder and admiration to Howard. She gave one the impression when she started to walk that she was going off at a rushing gait, so breathlessly and hurriedly did she begin, but at the third or fourth step, she settled into a slow languid stride, that was graceful, if surprising.

Marion turned her attention again to the sea with apparent

calm, but a red spot on her cheek betrayed some inner agitation. Howard watched her profile for a few moments, then he said suddenly, "Marion, will you marry me?"

She sprang to her feet and threw out her hands with an appealing gesture.

"You mustn't," she panted, "you mustn't say that. I—I— you know, I don't like that kind of joking."

"But I am not joking," he answered impetuously, following her and taking both hands in his own. She had retreated to a corner of the gallery that was overhung with a trellis of honeysuckle. It was a dim, fragrant, secluded bower, safe from the gaze alike of the village street, and the many windowed house. He pressed both of her hands tight in one of his own, and with the other formed a barrier between her and possible escape.

"I am not joking," he persisted, bending over her eagerly, "I mean it with all the soul that a man possesses. I love you, you little misplaced Priscilla, can't you see I love you? You know it, you must have known it that first night I followed you out on the breakwater and we watched the phosphorus of the sea together. I have been wanting to tell you for a month; I should have waited longer, I know, but I simply could not."

"A month?" she laughed nervously, "why, you have only been here a month."

"Is that all? Never mind. It is the whole lifetime of happiness to me. I must have wanted to tell you that first night then, for I singled you out from all the rest as a white lily in a garden of roses. Marion, you *must* say yes."

She looked at him in her peculiarly abstract way as if trying to generalize his emotion, then a dimple flashed in her cheek and she cried softly, "For shame to say such things to me when you are already engaged to my sister."

He dropped her hands and turned away petulantly, "How can you play with me now, Marion? Don't, don't, I am in earnest, terribly so."

Her face became grave at once, "I could not leave Mother and Emmie alone," she answered softly. "They would be very lonely. Since Father died, we have clung together—this house is very big and dreary—it would be cruel to leave them alone. They are very dependent upon me."

"Nonsense," he cried, brushing her objections away impetuously. "If Emmie took it into her head to marry, do you suppose she would stop to consider that you might be lonely without her? That's a foolish notion of self-immolation. It is very sweet and very thoughtful in you, little sweetheart, but it is not weighty enough to stop me. I need you more than they do; and they have had you all their lives. It is my turn now, and I am going to insist that my claim is recognized."

"You take it quite for granted that I love you," she said. There were signs of a timid half-surrender in her manner, and Howard followed them eagerly.

"Of course I do. You must love me. You will, if you do not already. My own love is so overpowering that it must compel a return. Marion, you will say yes, I know you will eventually, but say so now, won't you?"

"Let me think it over. You are so cyclonic; you give me no time in which to catch my breath. I—I—cannot answer you now."

"Oh, yes, you can. If you want time to think it over, you can say yes now. Say you will, Marion. You will never regret it through any action of mine. Say yes, dearest."

She leaned her head back into the fragrance of the white and gold and green of the honeysuckle vine, and looked him full into the eyes. There was a moment's breathless silence between them, a mere pause between heartbeats, as it were, but for Howard it was as if all eternity hung in the balance awaiting Marion's decision. She gazed into his eyes with her own, far-seeing, clear, searching, as if to pierce into his soul for the truth of his words. He met her gaze calmly, confidently, his own eyes burning into hers with a passion of pure desire that made her gaze drop confusedly. Her hands locked and unlocked themselves nervously; her head dropped forward slowly, slowly, her lips parted, but framed no words, though there was acquiescence in every line of her slender figure. He caught her tenderly in his arms and turned her face up to his.

"Marion?" he questioned eagerly, whispering as if he feared to break the spell.

"Yes," she breathed, and dropped her crimson face upon his shoulder.

As he kissed her, he felt a sudden shrinking of her whole being, as if already her soul were closing in upon itself after its brief surrender.

CHAPTER III

Emmie was radiant at the prospect of a wedding.

"We have had nothing but funerals and business failures for so many years," she declared, "that a wedding will be something of a pleasant rarity in the family. My, what a mustering of the clan there will be! You don't know what a dreadful responsibility I will have on me to keep them apart, for half of them don't speak to the other half, and as soon as they will see each other they will want to begin to settle century-old differences of opinion," she sighed and shook her head ruefully.

"Why not have a quiet affair, and let the 'clan' stay peaceably it home?" suggested Howard.

"My dear brother-in-law-that-is-to-be, I have to live in this town after Marion and you are gone, and I propose to end my days in comparative peace and quiet. Such a wedding as you suggest would ostracize Mama and me as completely as if a tidal wave had swept us into the sea. No, we must go right on to the bitter end."

It was the week after Marion's surrender, and Howard found that he must leave the little town. He could no longer plead the slow progress of the business that had brought him thither, for the insistence of the telegrams from home warned him that he must think of his and Marion's future. He was for taking her home with him at once, and pled volubly with Mrs. Ross to prove to her the absolute necessity of such a course.

"Just as if Marion were not the one most concerned," put in Emmie, after listening patiently with her mother to a passionate discourse from Howard. "She won't go now, you know it, and you can just go on home and come back after her when a decent interval of trousseau making has elapsed."

She had been at first tearful at the prospect of losing her sister, then joyful in Marion's apparent happiness, then mock-heroic in her upbraidings of Marion for stealing away from her her first and only lover. With characteristic promptness, she had begun preparations for her wedding at once. Mrs. Ross wept a few conventional tears, and accepted the congratulations of her friends with passive equanimity. She realized that Marion was making a good match. Howard was a man of the world, of good connections; well known by name in all respectable society, with a business and an income that could place Marion far above the common herd.

"If you only do as well, Emmie," she said with a motherly sigh of solicitude.

"I? Never will marry now. Only chance I had gone, and taken from me by my own sister. Going in a convent as soon as I get her safely off my hands."

Marion watched the preparations for her wedding with a curious noninterest. She could not bring herself to feel that it was she for whom all this bustle and preparation was being made. She had held herself aloof for so long, taking part in life in a merely general way, that now she could not realize herself the central figure in any movement. She was passive and acquiescent, but offered no suggestions, nor made any alterations in anything submitted to her for approval. Dutifully, she went up to the nearest large city with her mother and Emmie and bought the customary things that a bride must have, and dutifully, she submitted to the ordeal of dressmakers and seamstresses and milliners. Howard wrote her every day, long, eager, passionate letters. He was refurnishing Edgewold, his home for her, and he lingered over details of picture hangings and upholstering with a minuteness that must have shown how thoroughly his heart was in his labor of love. Marion seldom spoke of him. She had shut him up in the ark of her soul, and brought his image forth only on rare occasions, when the host-bell of her being told her that the hour of sacred seclusion had come. She too, wrote every day, shyly, blushing and trying to hide the paper if anyone came upon her suddenly. Her letters were short, full of half-conscious revelings of herself here and there, like bits of poetry in an old-world prose tale. She had no news to tell, save of Emmie and her mother, for the little summer colony was deserting the sea-village, and the days ran one into another, evenly, monotonously. She described her frequent visits to the city, but she could not bring herself to tell the reason of their frequency. She seldom spoke of the sea in its wonderful transfigurations from storm to sunshine, and Howard was vaguely disappointed. He had thought that the stillness of her nature was that which often comes to those upon whom the sea has cast its glamour and solemnity and he had hoped to find in her some of the reflex of his own poetic temperament. But, perhaps, he reasoned, like everything else that she felt deeply, she could not bring herself to speak of it. She never wrote him a love letter; he was not disappointed in this. He had not expected it. It was enough that she wrote him something every day.

She sat by the window of the sewing-room one day, gazing idly out over the sea. All about her buzzed the voice of bustle and preparation. The dressmaker and the seamstress, her mother and Emmie argued and debated, fussed and fumed over trivial details of her gowns. They had been fitting her, and she still sat, resting a moment, with her bare white neck and shoulders exposed. Mrs. Hare, the dressmaker, was an old friend and servitor, and claimed as her privilege conducting the whole business of fitting out Marion's wardrobe. She fussed about the girl with the coarse officiousness of womankind at an approaching marriage. Suddenly, she saw in Marion's bosom the protruding edge of an envelope, and pulled it out with a cracked laugh of enjoyment.

"That's love for you," she shrilled, "that's what I like to see."

Marion snatched the letter from her with a low cry of anger. A slow flush spread from her cheeks and brow to her neck and bosom and she rushed out of the room brushing aside Mrs. Hare in her haste. Emmie surveyed the dressmaker with disgust.

"I should think you'd have better sense," she said scornfully, "as long as you've known Marion, to do anything so senseless as that."

"Emmie, do put a bridle on your tongue," said her mother. She was rocking herself vigorously, sewing in the meanwhile with exasperating deliberation on a bit of a lace collar.

"Oh, bridle nothing. As hard a time as we have had to get Marion to take even a passing interest in her wedding, for Mrs. Hare to do such a stupid thing." She flung herself out of the sewing-room, banging the door violently behind her.

Marion's room was directly below the sewing-room, its windows also facing the sea. As Emmie opened the door in response to her faint answer to the knock, she did not turn from her position by the window. She was still undressed, the letter in her hand.

"Marion dear," said Emmie going up to her impetuously, "that old Hare hasn't a bit of sense, so you mustn't mind her, you know."

"Yes," she answered absently, "Emmie, listen." She opened the letter and turned the pages as if to find a particular passage. It was the first time that she had ever shown the least symptoms of confiding her love in her sister, and Emmie gave a little gasp of astonishment as she settled herself in the window seat and prepared to listen. Howard described, in his usual boyish riot of language how the trees in the gardens at Edgewold were decking themselves in autumn hues, putting on their most gorgeous gowns to welcome her arrival; how the most brilliant flowers of the year were flaunting themselves by the roadside and garden paths to wave a welcome to her, and how the poor summer flowers, sad and ashamed, because they could not see her when she would come, were drooping and dying with sorrow and disappointment.

Emmie listened with clasped hands and radiant face. When Marion had finished reading, she arose and hugged her rapturously. "Oh, Marion, Marion, how perfectly beautiful that is, isn't it?"

"Do you think so?" asked Marion reflectively, "I thought it sounded—er—rather—high-flown, perhaps. Those things aren't really so, we know that, so why say so?"

Emmie shook her head doubtfully, and a sudden pity for Howard swept over her, but only for an instant. Loyalty to Marion quickly became the usual dominant note in her nature, and she dismissed the subject with an abrupt toss of her head.

"Come on, Marion," she said, rising with a little sigh, "they need you again for fitting upstairs."

"I am not going," Marion's tone was decided and harsh. "That woman can never put her hands on me again."

"Oh, but Marion," pleaded Emmie, "don't mind her. She doesn't know any better. It was coarse, I know, but she really meant no harm. Come on, you must get your things ready."

"Not unless you get another dressmaker."

"Now you know that's impossible. Mrs. Hare's been engaged for the entire work. Don't be silly, Sis."

"Oh, I know I'm silly, and all that, but Mrs. Hare can't fit me again."

"What are we going to do? She must do your work."

"Fit the things on you. We are about the same waist measure, aren't we?"

"That will never do, you'll look dreadful in some of them, I know."

"I won't look any worse than I usually look, I suppose.

That's the only alternative I can think of. I'm not going upstairs, Emmie, you may rest assured of that."

She was taking a dressing sacque out of the wardrobe as she spoke, and putting it on with an air of finality, seated herself at the desk and began to write. Emmie stared at her with a look of hopeless resignation, and went slowly out of the room. Even the faint show of interest Marion had evinced in her own wardrobe had entirely waned now and no amount of inducement could shake her from her apathy.

The townspeople declared that it was a beautiful wedding, and unhesitatingly and truthfully gave all the credit to the younger sister of the household. It was early autumn, still summer in their home, and Emmie had made the best of the natural beauties of the Spanish moss and palms and orange trees, so that Howard could not repress a cry of delighted surprise when he saw the old-fashioned house transformed into a Southern forest with its suggestion of sadness in the festoons of moss. Emmie had mustered the "clan," and was striving with blunt tact to "keep them from scratching each others' eyes out at the first opportunity." She had deftly relegated Mrs. Ross to the background, for that lady after a vague bustle or two, had subsided into a hysterical slowness that was maddening and effectually blocked all proceedings. As Emmie phrased it afterwards, she had so much to do in looking after them all that she was almost late at the wedding. She was maid of honor, and "it would have been dreadful to have missed my only chance to go to the altar," she said breathlessly. Howard had a vague memory of bridesmaids, Emmie's friends, rather than Marion's; of a church full of people and a host of his wife's relatives, who shook him by the hand with characteristic warmth of manner; of Marion, spirituelle in a mist of white tulle; of the tedium of the

Church of England ritual; and the sense of relief he felt when his best man assured him that he had gone through with it without being more of a donkey than most men under the same circumstances. He had brought Holt Towneley with him "to take care of him" as Emmie said. Towneley was an inoffensive young man with yellow hair, whom the girls first snubbed, then adored. For fifteen years he and Howard had abused and maltreated and loved one another, and while Holt felt that his friend was making a fool of himself in marrying, he was good enough not to say so more than once or twice a day.

The wedding was over finally and Marion and Howard sat facing each other in the stateroom of the sleeper.

"Well, it's over," she said with a sigh as she laid aside her hat and gloves.

"No, dearest, it has just begun," he said. He bent over her with a kiss that was reverential and holy, and even as he did so, he noticed with a pang the quick compression of her lips as his own touched them.

CHAPTER IV

It was Mrs. Wilton's day at home, and her little drawing-room was filled with chatter and rustle of silk-lined tailored gowns. Mrs. Wilton stood beside the tea-table where Mrs. Agnes Hunt presided and surveyed the scene with some pride. She was proud of her Thursday afternoons, justifiably so, as Lawrenceville had never known such an innovation until she came thither and set it agog with one innovation after another. It was as provincial a town as a metropolitan suburb can be, and prior to Mrs. Wilton's advent, a church social had been

the height of its feminine dissipation. Lawrenceville was a
circumscribed village with a passion for self-improvement
and a corresponding lack of knowledge as to the best means
of attaining it. It had a sewing circle, a civic committee, and
a Mother's Club, but it remained for Mrs. Jack Wilton to
introduce the intellectual dissipation of a bona fide Woman's
Club, which grew and throve and rented a club room and
went into the National Federation. After this feat, Mrs.
Wilton might well have rested on her laurels, but not content,
she introduced the dissipation of the five o'clock tea into the
town, now ready for any form of metropolitan gayety.

Had there been any doubts of Mrs. Wilton's social preem-
inence, this would have settled it at once. Her Thursday
afternoons were looked forward to with eager interest week
after week by the feminine contingent of Lawrenceville.
There was pride in the hearts of the women as they flocked
about her tea-table; pride of a very different sort from that
which they experienced as they attended the club meetings.
This was something exclusive, something metropolitan, something which stamped them as the elect, set them apart from
the hoi polloi, as it were. Mrs. Wilton had pruned and
scanned her list very carefully before issuing her first cards.
Not for worlds would she have allowed the wives of the small
tradespeople of the town to have appeared in her drawing-
room that day. She confined herself very strictly to the wives
and daughters and sisters of those whose duties took them
rushing into the city every day, with the exception, of course,
of the town officials, who were always social lights, and the
principal of the High School. Mrs. Wilton had set for herself
the Herculean task of raising the intellectual and social
atmosphere, and she was not going to make any blunders at
the outset, or confound the one with the other.

She was aided and abetted in all her schemes by Miss
Hunt, a young lady with a wide range of conventional
accomplishments and a limited mentality. Miss Hunt worshipped Mrs. Wilton as only very young women can worship
those who are several years their senior, and Mrs. Wilton
alternately leaned upon Miss Hunt and ordered her around.
Mrs. Legdon, the wife of the mayor, completed the trium-
virate of feminine Lawrenceville. Mrs. Legdon, however,
was not always so gently acquiescent to Mrs. Wilton's ca-
prices, and had once had a fit of anger at that lady which
lasted over one of the Thursday afternoons. It resulted in
nothing more formidable than a call for the organization of
a Friday evening Euchre Club, to which Mrs. Wilton was
formally invited. She had at first glowered, then hesitated,
then capitulated. The club was organized and conducted
peacefully, and Lawrenceville breathed easily again at the
averting of the threatened social calamity.

There were evident signs of a mild excitement pervading
Mrs. Wilton's drawing-room on this particular Thursday
afternoon. There were more fresh toilettes than usual, and
more than once as the portieres parted to admit a newcomer,
a hush of expectancy fell upon the chattering groups and
anxious eyes turned towards the door.

"Have you seen her?" asked Miss Hunt of a red-haired
young woman in a pale green silk shirtwaist.

"Where? Here? No, it's my opinion that she won't come,
either."

"Oh, I hope so," chirped Mrs. Legdon. She did not drink
her tea, but put a lump of sugar in her mouth and set the
cup down untasted. "It would be too bad to disappoint Mrs.
Wilton, and quite unwise, too."

"I don't think she cares about the unwisdom of the thing,"

said the red-haired girl sourly. "I don't think she cares about us or our teas. She thinks she is a bit above poor little Lawrenceville."

"What has she done to you, May?" asked Miss Hunt, laughing so that she scattered drops of tea on the cloth from the mouth of the teapot.

"I called on her," returned May with astonishing frankness, "and she sent down word that she was sorry, but she was engaged at the time. When I went out, I looked up at the library window, and she was sitting there, calmly gazing out over the tops of the trees. She met my eyes too, and did not even take the trouble to draw away from the window or look embarrassed or confused. I knew it was she because I had seen her out driving with her husband."

The laughter which followed this speech was suddenly hushed as Mrs. Wilton's butler announced pompously, "Mrs. George Howard!"

Marion paused on the threshold as she felt twenty-five pairs of eyes fastened upon her. She had heard the burst of laughter and the sudden silence which followed the announcement of her name and she felt instinctively that she had been the subject of the laughter. For an instant, she stood, a slow, deep flush, suffusing her cheeks, and her head went up, and her lips compressed with angry pride. But the greeting which she gave her hostess, who advanced with pompous rustling of brocaded silk to meet her, was coldly gentle and gracious, and self-possessed, at strange variance with her flushed checks.

Howard surveyed her that night with amusement as she sat opposite him at dinner. "Well, now that you are fairly launched into the seething vortex of Lawrenceville society, what do you think of it?"

"I don't know," she answered slowly, "I think they were laughing at me before I entered the room to-day."

"You are too sensitive, sweetheart," he answered gently. "I am only just finding that out now. What possible reason could they have for laughing at you?"

"I don't know, I didn't stop to think of that. It merely seemed to me that they were laughing at me just before I entered the room."

Howard sighed and devoted himself to his soup in silence. He knew Marion well enough now, after three months with her, to know that no amount of argument and pleading and reasoning with her could convince her that she was mistaken. He fancied too, that he knew how she must have entered the room. He had seen her proud, shy, repelling of all advances made toward her, until his heart had ached for her. He was beginning to understand her attitude of detachment from the world, and the more he saw of her, the more he wondered at his own temerity at daring to speak to her of marriage.

"Fools rush in where angels fear to tread," he murmured into the soup.

"Yes?" she queried.

"I was only thinking aloud, dear. I suppose you heard the usual gush about your soft, Southern speech and gentle Southern manners and dusky eyes and raven hair, and all that sort of thing?"

"No, I haven't," she said, looking up in surprise. "Who would dare say such a thing to my face?"

"That's true, who would? But Lawrenceville is nothing if not daring."

"And then, I haven't all these things at all. The only thing that is characteristically Southern about me is my indolent temperament. Emmie and I both went to school all our days in Connecticut, you know."

"I suppose you will join the New Era Club, and the Friday night Euchre and all the rest, and try to outvie Mrs. Wilton's At-Homes?"

He said it half jokingly, but there was an eager note in his voice that did not escape her. She looked up in surprise.

"Oh, no, why should I? I don't care for that sort of thing at all. You know I never bothered at home."

He flushed with disappointment and chagrin. He was proud of her, her looks, her style, her carriage. He had felt a boyish satisfaction in watching the sensation she created during their three months honeymooning abroad, and he delighted in noticing the glances that followed her as she passed through streets and hotel corridors. He had never yet, however, mastered the quick thrill of disappointment that went through him when he saw how coldly she repelled all overtures of friendship. He had hoped that she would take an interest in Lawrenceville. The place was small and pro-vincial, disgustingly so, at times, but it was his home, and it would be hers, and he had wanted her to shine here above and beyond the other women.

"I know Lawrenceville is a poor little place," he said slowly after a brief period of silence, "but forty minutes to New York isn't so bad, and the people are really quite decent sometimes."

"Oh, yes, they are both quite nice, town and townspeople, but you know, George, I never cared for people, because, I suppose, they don't usually care for me."

With that declaration, he must fain be content.

Marion entered upon her housekeeping duties quietly, and thoroughly, with all a Southern woman's inborn mastery of the tiniest detail of homemaking. Howard had placed a small retinue of servants and a generous private bank account at her disposal. If she missed the kindlier, cheerier atmosphere of her own home in the colder, more formal one of her husband's, she made no complaint, nor did she seek to introduce a new element about her. She accepted conditions passively, but made no change in her mode of inner life or thought. She was the same cold, white lily, transplanted to another garden, it is true, but unaltered in a single line or pose or droop of petal or leaf.

"I don't think she enjoys anything—but Emmie's letters," said Howard irritably to himself one day.

Emmie's letters, indeed, were overflowing with fun and vivacity. The house by the sea had become too lonely for her and the mother, and they had gone to the city to winter, "staying around at various members of the clan, until they get too disagreeable when we move on to the next branch," she put it. She had danced to her heart's content, and announced that Mrs. Ross was contemplating a low-necked gown. "Before she does that, I shall hustle her home, however," she wrote reassuringly. She had had two "real live" offers of marriage, both of which were very tame affairs and had caused her no thrills whatever. She announced that she was deeply impressed with an artist, a Leonard Hobbes— "think of an artistic temperament with that name!"—who was respectable, quite, in the daytime, and only did his artistic business in his off hours, when he was not at his bank. He had given her a tea in his studio, and she had decided to say yes if he ever proposed, because he was a "real dear."

"I wonder if Emmie will ever marry?" said Marion, after reading one of her letters aloud.

"I hope not," said Howard slowly, "I hope not. It would spoil her. She is too nice a girl to be spoiled."

His wife gazed up at him with wide, questioning eyes. "Do you think marriage has spoiled me?" she asked.

"Great God, no, I wish it had," he muttered bitterly, and left the room.

Marion gazed into the fire after he had gone. It was the first time there had ever been a hint of disapproval in his tone toward her.

"I wonder what he meant," she said slowly, her lips tortured in a pitiful curve, "I wonder what he meant."

Howard was back at her side the next instant, and caught her passionately in his arms.

"Marion, darling, forgive me, forgive me. I—I—didn't know what I was saying. Forgive me, won't you?"

She made no reply, and his arms encircled an inert form. He strained her to him closely, covering her compressed mouth with passionate kisses, uttering reassuring words of endearment. Marion made him no reply, but long after he had gone, she sat gazing into the fire, muttering, "I wonder what he meant?"

CHAPTER V

Lawrenceville was held in the vise-like grip of a long, dreary winter. It was a year when the monarch of frost and ice and snow had extended his realm far into the Southland, and Emmie wrote letters full of pitiful tales of the suffering she saw about her in her new home. She had been married to her artist-banker now for four years. The first visit that Marion had made home after her marriage had been to see

Emmie led from under the arch of palms in the little village church by the sea by the radiant and grateful Mr. Hobbes. The stork had visited Emmie twice, making her "do the duty of the entire family," as she put it. Mrs. Ross spent her summers still in her own home, where Emmie and the little Hobbes visited her. Her winters, she spent visiting "the clan" and Emmie. Visitations they were, rather than visits, but it was the only thing to do, and the clan was large enough for her to divide her time into comparatively short visits to each. Emmie, in addition to the rearing of her two small Hobbes, keeping house and attending to the proper giving of studio teas, had gone in for charity, and was maintaining a little mission among the alley Negroes. Marion smiled indulgently over her letters, alternately enthusiastic over her work or depressed for lack of means to do more good, and sent her occasional generous cheques.

Howard was interested in Emmie's little pet schemes, and lent a willing ear to her appeal for aid. He had once suggested timidly that his wife might undertake a similar work in Lawrenceville, but she looked so astonished and disgusted at the idea that he had hastily apologized.

"Not that I meant you to go into slum work, you know," he said, "but I thought if you had some interest, some diversion outside of your home duties— A woman comes so little, comparatively, in touch with life, that unless she takes up something else, she is apt to grow narrow and circumscribed. Even a woman's club, with all its pettiness, is something to be desired."

Marion gazed at her husband with a calm questioning look.

"Do you think me narrow, circumscribed?" she asked.

There it was again, the old irritating personal note which

she struck in every conversation; which she had sounded the
night they had talked by the phosphorescent waters. The most
impersonal appearing woman, she was unable to get beyond
her own ego, unable to see any allusion save through the
medium of her own self-consciousness. He sighed the sigh
of a man who has had a sore spot pressed again and again,
and did not reply.

"I suppose I am narrow, and all that," she said, flushing
slowly, "but I simply cannot help it. It is my nature, and
one cannot change one's disposition. I never could be interested in things like Emmie, and other people. It's entirely
too much trouble."

He made no reply, and the habitual silence fell between
them.

One day, the trees and electric wires and vines hung heavy
with the burden of ice that an all-night sleet storm had
weighted upon them; the streets were like the glass pavements
in fairyland; the scintillant lights of the prisms of ice struck
sharply upon the eyes and dazzled them into quick tears that
as quickly froze on the face and lashes. It was the stern hand
of an iron giant laid on the throat of pulsing life.

Howard alighted from his train and looked about in
surprise not to see the sleigh awaiting him at the station. He
reasoned that they had deemed the road too bad to bring out
the horses, and shaking himself as does a dog about to plunge
into water, he started away for home at a brisk trot. He was
enjoying the warmth of the glow that spread over his limbs
and feeling glad that the sleigh had not met him, when he
heard a low cry and turning quickly, saw a woman prostrate
on the ground a few yards behind him.

He was at her side in an instant, picking her up, steadying
her, gathering her bundles together, uttering reassuring words,
making solicitous inquiries about her.

No, she was not hurt, she said, and thanked him prettily, the while her eyes started with tears.

"But you are hurt," he insisted, holding her tenderly by the arm, "let me call a depot sleigh for you."

"Oh, dear no," she said in a half frightened manner, looking up into his eyes so piteously, that he desisted at once. But he took her bundles from her and tucked her arm into his own.

"At any rate," he said cheerfully, "I am going to see you home."

"It isn't necessary at all, indeed, Mr. Howard, it is not. I am quite all right, and I live such a distance from your home. It will be too much out of your way for you to go all the way with me."

So she knew him then? He smiled down at her indulgently.

"You have the advantage of me, quite. You can call me Mr. Howard quite glibly, but I cannot say Miss—Miss—"

"Grace Weaver," she answered shyly.

"Miss Weaver, then. Well, far or near, I am going to see you to your gate, for you are not to be trusted out alone. There, didn't I tell you so!" She had slipped again and lurched heavily against his protecting arm.

"You should be sure-footed, like me," he said playfully. Then with a sudden breaking of distress in his voice, "Why you haven't any overshoes on, Miss Weaver, really, this is very foolish of you. You should not do it in this weather."

"Yes, I know," she assented, with a laugh, "it was very silly in me." But he knew that the laugh was forced, and he knew too, from the hot wave that swept over her face and the tremor of her hands in their shabby woolen gloves that she had no overshoes. He felt the shiver of her small figure pressed close to his side, and groaned under his warm clothing for the cold that he knew she was suffering.

With the paternal solicitude of the large landowner in a small town he asked her questions and with a child's frankness, she told all about herself. There were four girls and a brother in her home. She was the eldest and worked in a department store. All the others worked too, even the brother, who tended furnaces and did chores after school. The mother kept house and sewed when she could. The father had died a few months ago; she was still in mourning for him. Yes, he had been sick a long, long while and the mother was still tired from the long strain of nursing. She was going to try to keep Bob, the brother, and the youngest sister in school as long as possible.

"How old are you?" asked Howard suddenly.

"Oh, I'm quite old, I am nineteen," she said, with a sudden air of maternal gravity that looked ridiculous on her pretty child's face.

"So old? No wonder you are tottering and falling," he replied merrily. They had reached the house by this time, and he handed her up the steps with all the grace and deference he could show. "Take care of yourself, Miss Weaver, and I wish," he added with a sudden seriousness, looking her full into the eyes so that she knew he had seen through her pure farce, "I wish you would not forget your overshoes to-morrow. You should never be without them."

"I'll try not to," she said simply, with a little catch in her throat.

It was sleeting and blowing hard when he reached home at last, and Marion stood in the hall worried and anxious as he entered.

"I'm so sorry dear, the stable clock was slow, and John was late going to the station to meet you. When he got there you had gone. He says he drove up Main Street hoping to overtake you, but saw no signs of you anywhere. How could he have missed you? And what a time you have been getting here!"

"Yes," he said quietly, "it is very bad walking." He made no further explanation, and if she felt the reticence in his manner she gave no sign. He was usually frank and open with her, and he often wondered if she knew to what extent he lay bare to her calm gaze every detail of his daily life. He wondered, too, if she would know or suspect if he should begin to hide from her. He doubted that she would. He could not tell whether her seeming ignorance of the difference between deceit and frankness arose from lack of interest in him, absolute faith in his probity, or an extreme of selfishness that did not care what happened away from her gaze so that the conventions were observed and her own life left unruffled.

He looked around at the daily service on the dinner table; the swift, silent butler, the perfectly served meal, and thought with a little pang how one tiny bit of all this luxury would comfort the thin little girl he had taken home; how the price of one bit of silver might save her health and perhaps her life by giving her suitable clothing. He groaned at his own helplessness. What could he do to help her? He racked his brain to think of some scheme. Charity, always before a large, vague word with him, had suddenly acquired a definite, concrete significance, and a difficult one, too. They were all at work, so he could not help there; he did not own the house, so he could not take the burden of rent-paying off their hands. He was silent, absorbed, even moody throughout the meal. Marion, however, did not seem to notice. She had been reading a new novel, and she was interested in telling him the plot. Several times he was on the verge of stopping her to tell her of his adventure with Grace Weaver, and to ask her help in devising some means to give the child some comforts, but checked himself each time. She would not understand. She would want to send a check at once, a liberal one, perhaps, and then think her duty and responsibility in the matter ended.

The next day, Howard sent for Bob Weaver to come to his office in the city, and the next day a new functionary, in the person of this same Bob in a uniform and buttons, became a part of the machinery of his office. Bob was fifteen years old, it was time for him to stop school and do something more than chores and depend upon a frail girl to support him through the High School. So he told the boy sternly, and the buttons and uniform proved an able supporter of his words.

Howard had solved the problem. It was comparatively easy to send comforts, and little luxuries even, to the mother by the boy, little things which must inevitably benefit Grace. He had never stopped to analyze his feeling for the girl. She was not of his class and analysis in such a case is superfluous. He knew he liked her, perhaps as one likes a helpless, pretty child; he was sorry for her and he wanted to help her, beyond that, his imagination went no further. It was sufficient to him that his little pet scheme of charity was not a failure.

One day Howard came into the office and found Bob with red eyes and blubbering mouth. He was a fat, bulky-looking sort of boy, and tears and a dirty face did not improve his personal appearance.

"Well, well, well, what's the matter?" Howard queried not unkindly, for the boy's fat figure was such an embodiment of woe that one forgot its ungraceful proportions.

"It's now—it's Grace—now she's sick!" wailed Bob.

"Sick? Grace sick?" he felt a sudden clutching at his heart and a chill dread passed over him like a breath from a spectre.

He visited her house sometimes, not often, for when he went, he was apt to be overwhelmed by a profusion of blessings from Mrs. Weaver and a pretty, confused little murmuring from Grace. In the Weaver household, he was regarded in the role of an amateur Santa Claus, and while it was not altogether displeasing to his vanity, he feared too much of it might not be wholesome.

"Not so very sick, I guess, Bob," he said cheerily, as much to reassure himself as the boy. "Just a touch of grip, I guess. This bitter winter has been very unhealthy."

"No, no, no, t'aint' dat a-tall," sobbed the boy, "de doctors axed Ma what Pa died of, and Ma threw her hands up an' scremed, an' I know he means as Grace's got consumption."

Howard stared at the boy with unwinking unseeing eyes, while Bob broke into fresh wailings.

Grace with consumption! That pretty fragile, flower-like thing to be dragged slowly through torturing days and weeks of agony with certain death at the end. It was horrible, incredible. He wheeled his chair suddenly around and dropped his head upon his outstretched arms upon the desk, and man and boy in the greatness of their sorrow, forgot the surging, seething, hard hurry of the world without and around the office.

That afternoon Marion picked her way daintily down past the station about two hours earlier than Howard was due to arrive. It was cold and raw and damp, although the skies were blue and the sun bright. The awaking breath of spring blew athwart the cold face of winter. Underfoot, it was slushy and disagreeable. She was going to the village store on an imaginary errand. She could as well have telephoned from her little den, or have sent one of her servants or have ordered out her carriage, but she told herself that she must walk a-plenty now, must walk every day, rain or shine, she needed it. She said it to herself with a little self-conscious glow of exultation and a shy, happy heightening of her color. An express from the city thundered in, and she stopped near a group of village idlers to wait until it went on that she might cross the tracks to the store. A familiar form swung off the train and started up the street in the direction opposite her home. It had its head bent, figure set and a dogged, determined expression about its whole body.

"George," she whispered, "where can he be going?"

He had not seen her. He did not seem to see anybody, but went on, brushing aside whatever might be in his path.

"There's Mr. Howard," said one of the men near her. They too, had not noticed her. "Wonder where's he going up that way this time o' day?"

"Goin' to Weavers most likely. Grace Weaver's down with consumption like her father. You know he sets a heap o' store by her; allus up there, an' that Weaver boy works in his office."

The train thundered on its way, and Marion stood staring stupidly across the track at the village store. Where was she going? Oh, yes, but it was of no consequence now. The sun and sky had grown gray and ugly and commonplace like the mud underfoot. What was the use of walking anyway? She hailed a passing depot carriage and sat upright, with wide, unseeing eyes as she was driven home. She did not know how she paid the man and got into the house; she remembered trying to go up the stairs before the darkness and roaring of the sea closed over her head, for before the outstretched hand of the butler could catch her, she had stumbled partly up the staircase, striking heavily against the newel post as she fell.

CHAPTER VI

Marion lay very still and white and indifferent while the quiet bustle of nurses and doctors went on about her. She heard the hushed whispers and the long painful silences which followed and each sound or silence wrung her heart with an exquisite misery. She knew the sounds that she should have heard; the little laughs of wonder and surprise; the little coos of the women over the never-ceasing marvel of marvels. It was absent from her room and she knew why.

The nurse leaned over her bed anxiously straining her eyes to see Marion's set lips.

"My baby," said the mother.

"It will be brought in soon," soothed the nurse.

Oh, why delay it any longer? Did she not know? Why seek to hide from her the truth?

They laid the child in her arms at last. It was tiny and frail looking and wrapped and re-wrapped in bundles of flannel. She hugged it to her breast fiercely, straining it to her heart, and covering its small, almost inanimate face with angry, passionate kisses.

"Madam, Madam," remonstrated the nurse, "indeed, you must be careful," and she essayed to take the child away.

Marion held it all the closer in her grasp, "No, no," she whispered, "it's mine. It is my own, no one's else. You can't take it from me. It's mine."

She was growing excited, and the nurse let her alone. She had not seen Howard, had not asked for him, and now when

he came in and hung eagerly, tremblingly over her bed, she
turned away from him coldly.

"Marion," he said, his voice tremulous with love and
delight, "Marion, is it really you? And is this little spark of
life ours? Our own, Marion, can you realize it?"

"It is mine, my own," she answered sullenly.

"Mine too, Marion, mine too. It is a divine bond between
us, darling, is it not?"

She winced at his words but made no reply.

Several months ago, Howard had come in that bright, cold
day from his visit to the sick girl, and found Marion upstairs
in her bed where the frightened servants had carried her. She
had not been able to leave her room since. At first, her life
was despaired of; then the life of the unborn, quickening
little thing beneath her heart. In all the dreary months that
followed, however, she had made no outcry; had said no
word of accusation or complaint to Howard. She had borne
the pain without a murmur, without a sign of distress. Her
locked lips seldom parted, save to utter a word of thanks to
her attendants. But in the grim silences of the nights, she
clenched her hands and cried out in pitiful whispers to Heaven
to take her away; to end her suffering; to put out the flickering
spark of her poor life which stood between what she fancied
was Howard's happiness. She had none of the self-effacement
of the Puritans, nor yet did she feel that she had any right to
encumber the earth or to reach out after the happiness which
is the divine right of every human being. She had stood aside
and looked on at life as a spectator for so long that it had not
occurred to her that she had her own part to play in the
drama.

She had scarcely spoken to Howard since that day. He had
been all that any woman could have wished, in devotion,

lover-like attention, care and watchfulness. She seldom opened her set white lips in his presence, but her eyes haunted him with a vague accusation in their depths, so that in the nights, he, too, lay awake and searched his soul for the reason for her changed mental attitude.

Howard had essayed at first to win her confidence, to make her lean on him in her helplessness. With the first intimation that he was to be the father of a human soul, he bowed himself humbly, as at a most holy altar, and worshipped as men only worship once or twice in a lifetime. The doctor told him on the day after Marion's fall, and he hurried at once to her room, shaken to the very foundations of his soul.

"Marion," he cried, falling on his knees beside her bed, "Marion, did you know it?"

She looked at him coldly, "Yes I knew it a month ago."

He wrung her passive hands in his, "And you could keep it from me? Ah, but that was cruel in you, Marion. You would never have had that fall had I known, Marion dear. I would have made everyone watch your every movement. How could you keep it a secret, Marion?"

"I thought you did not care," she answered indifferently.

"Not care? Not care? Did you not know how my heart was bound up in the wish? Could you not see how my soul cried out for a child? Marion, you do know. You must have understood after all these years. Could you not see how envious I was of Emmie? Oh, I should have been the happiest man in the world to have shared your sweet secret with you at first, to have hoped and feared and prayed with you from the beginning. Marion—Marion—"

Something in her face checked him. He rose slowly and went out of the room, dazed, wondering, miserable in his new happiness.

Marion lay and looked at the ceiling with hard eyes, "Extravagant and insincere, as usual," she muttered, "I thought he had outgrown all that."

It was because of his love for the girl, Grace, she thought. He was hiding something from her and strove to cover his sin by loudly declared expressions of love and newly awakened tenderness. She set her lips in a grimmer line than ever and steeled her heart the harder against him in her pain.

Mrs. Ross had been sent for, it being a tradition that every woman needs her mother with her at the coming of her first-born. That lady bustled into her home, then trailed leisurely up to her daughter's room, where she sat down upon the bed and burst into tears, rather perfunctory ones they were, to be sure, but the situation demanded tears, and Mrs. Ross was never the woman to fail to rise to the demands of an occasion.

"My precious girl," she sobbed, "how could you be so careless? Only to think of it, and Emmie has been so fortunate, too."

Marion regarded her mother with sarcastic amusement.

"I'm glad you came, Mother," she said.

"Glad? Well, you ought to be. If you only knew what a dreadful time I had getting off. Emmie would pack me off willy-nilly at once as if you were dying. I wanted to wait and get me some new gowns, I do hate to come tearing into a strange place with not a decent rag to my back, but Emmie stood and shrieked at me as if I were perfectly deaf, 'Gowns, gowns! What do you want with gowns when Marion might be dying!' Emmie has so little respect for a person's feelings. She would have come with me, I tried to persuade her to, you've no idea how dreadful it is travelling alone these days. No one has any consideration for a lady, the commonest people are right on equal footing with one." Mrs. Ross was quite warm at the recital of her woes and fanned herself vigorously.

"It would have been too bad to have dragged Emmie away from her home just now," assented Marion.

"Yes, she's quite busy, and the baby's very fretful and exacting. I do hope, Marion, when yours comes you will have it decently trained so a body can live in the same house with it in peace."

"Perhaps it never will come, Mother," said Marion slowly, and under her breath she prayed God that it might not.

Her mother gave a little shriek of dismay and fled from the room to call the nurse.

Mrs. Ross' advent into Lawrenceville was the signal for a tea in her honor given by Mrs. Wilton. Although that lady had never forgiven Marion for her indifferent attitude towards the social life of the town, she relented sufficiently to entertain Marion's mother. "It would be too bad," she said to Miss Hunt as they discussed the invitations, "to have the poor, dear soul come all this distance and be shut up in that great, dreary house with that dreadful sick daughter of hers, and not know anything of our little circle here."

Miss Hunt perfectly agreed with Mrs. Wilton, and thus Mrs. Ross was tead and entertained at luncheon; made and received calls and drove about the country; attended lectures at the club room and went into New York for the opera. She enjoyed herself to the full, while Marion lay with the lines about her lips becoming grimmer and grimmer and the sear in her heart becoming deeper and deeper.

Meanwhile, Grace Weaver hovered between life and death for weeks, but with the coming of the warm days, she had risen from bed and moved about the house, frail and hectic shorn of her pretty brown curls, with great pathetic eyes that seemed to look through the world, ahead into infinity. In the madness of that day when Bob had sent him tearing into Lawrenceville on the early train, Howard had almost blurted out to the sick girl, foolish words which he might have meant only at the time. In his pity he might have fancied that he cared for her more than as a pretty, trusting child, but when he had gone home and found Marion too, at death's portals, the strong, true love of his life asserted itself, and Grace as a woman was forgotten. Grace as a child, as an object of charity was in his mind constantly. There was no comfort or luxury that she did not have. The same physician who attended Marion cared for her. Howard placed Mrs. Weaver beyond the need of toiling so hard for mere existence that she might devote more time to the care of the girl. But since that one day he had never put his foot in their house. He could not find the time to leave Marion's side. All the latent mother-love which is in some men's hearts, he had expended in his efforts to make Grace's life easier, and then he cared no more.

His nights, he spent with Marion. Below the impenetrable mask of bitter reserve he could not hope to pierce, yet heroically, devotedly did he serve her, patiently did he strive to interest her. In his despair he racked his heart for some reason for her grim silence. Perhaps it was her suffering; perhaps he had not tried to understand her in their earlier years together, and he had let the golden opportunity for penetrating into her soul pass by. He blamed himself bitterly, and strove to do penance at her side, the while he worshipped her as one would worship at the shrine of the Virgin.

The boy was three weeks old and Marion had never seen it undressed. They brought it to her and laid it in her arms and she gripped it fiercely while it drank at her breast. No one had ever told her anything, but she knew with the quick, sympathetic intuition of the mother-heart. Between her and the little, frail, whining, red thing already existed a bond of love and misery such as Howard had dreamed might exist between him and his wife, but which is possible only between man and woman when the woman is mother to the man.

She was out of danger, the doctors said. She would be well and strong and walk again. Howard covered his face with his hands and shook with sobs of relief when he was told. Marion turned her face to the wall and cursed the fate which kept her unwilling and unwelcome in the world. Then one day she turned to her mother with sudden vehemence, "Mother, have you bathed the baby, yet?"

The question was like a spark to tinder. Mrs. Ross was volubly indignant at once.

"Of course not," she panted, "they won't let me. As if I were not the child's own grandmother, too. I am ordered around, put out of rooms and hidden from as if I were the veriest stranger. There are some rights to which I am entitled, and I should think, Marion, that you would see I had them."

Marion sighed a sigh of inexpressible relief, "Let me have my son alone first," she said, smiling reassuringly at her mother. "Then you may have him, Mother, but let me be first."

"Stuff," sputtered Mrs. Ross, "sentimental nonsense. I'd expect that of Emmie, but you always had more sense, Marion."

She sat by the window in her low easy chair looking out on the belated summer landscape. The flowers flaunted their last gorgeous hues in the gardens, and the trees showed tinges of crimson and gold on the edges of their leaves. The world was in a riot of happiness for the fulness of harvest time and the joy of the golden days. She could hear the chatter of the squirrels, and the call of the children out from school playing in the field on the right of the house. Everywhere was the sap of life and love pusling save in her own chill heart, and even there some sort of life was stirring faintly in response to the little life throbbing in the next room. The nurse came and laid the child on her lap and busied herself about the room.

"You may go, Nella," said Marion.

The girl started and looked at her anxiously. "Indeed, Madame," she said timidly, "I—I—don't like to leave you alone. You may need something, you know."

"If I need you, I can ring," Marion's tone was authoritative. "Tell Mr. Howard to come to me in ten minutes."

When the door had closed on the nurse Marion tore at the wrappings and skirts on the child. With nervous, trembling fingers she unpinned and drew down his little flannels until he lay bare and tiny on her lap. At the last garment that she tore off, she caught his little form up to her heart and rocked to and fro in an agony, stifling the cry that would have been wrung from her lips at the tiny, bare, twisted limbs. She had known the child was maimed, but how much, how little, or in what way she had not dreamed. No one had told her; she had divined it and confirmed it by their silences at her bedside. She laid the child on her lap again and stroked his little deformed legs, moaning over him inarticulately, as an animal might moan over its wounded offspring.

"You are like my life, baby," she sobbed, "maimed and warped and imperfect, and yet all I have."

She heard Howard's step at the door, and hastily threw a covering around the child. When he entered the room she had it wrapped in her arms on her breast, rocking to and fro calmly.

He was all eager love at once.

"God bless you, Marion," he said, dropping on one knee before her, "to send for me so that we might be alone together with our boy."

She looked at him curiously for a moment, then laid the little form in her lap again.

"I sent for you," she said, and her voice sounded far away in her own ears, while her lips were numb, "I thought you might want to know, I have just known myself, positively—and I could not be cruel enough to let it come to you in the presence of others."

Howard rose and leaned over her chair, surprised and dazed.

"Know—what?—Cruel? What do you mean, Marion, tell me."

She made no reply, but quietly withdrew the covering from the child again. Howard looked and started back as if a blinding flash had come before his face. He threw his hands up as if to ward off a blow, but Marion's voice, incisive and cold made him take them down again.

"Look good, George. I want you to see well."

"Great God, don't ask me to see, don't ask me to look. I can't—can't bear it. Why had this to be?"

He bent over the child, touching its little limbs, sobbing low pitiful sobs as a woman might have done. The baby, too, began to cry and Marion snatched it from him, fiercely guarding it against her bosom, and hushing its cries.

"I wanted you to know," she said coldly, as she wrapped it in its blanket and put its lips to her bosom, "for it is your fault."

"My fault," he cried, stretching out his hands to her appealingly, "my fault? Oh, Marion, darling, don't say that. How could it be? Perhaps it is so, perhaps it is, but how did I do it? How have I sinned? Tell me, Marion."

"No, you should know. If you do not, let it be sufficient for you to know that it is your fault."

"Marion, Marion—" he began, but the door was flung violently open and Mrs. Ross entered hurriedly, followed by the nurse, tearful and expostulating.

"Marion, I overheard the servants say that that child is a cripple and when I asked this girl, she refused to tell me. Now I demand—"

She paused suddenly at the sight of Howard's set white face, and the bitter sneer on her daughter's. Her voice broke, and she held out her arms for the child.

"Let me see, Daughter," she said softly, using the old term of endearment, "I am your mother, let me see."

But Marion strained the child close to her bosom.

"No," she said quietly, "I have showed him once to-day, that is enough. He is mine and I shall keep him to myself. My son does not wish to be exhibited too often, you know. Let it be sufficient for you to know that he is a cripple, Mother. Some other day, you may see."

CHAPTER VII

With the beginning of the hot days of the following summer, Mrs. Ross went home. To Marion's entreaties that she stay and enjoy the cooler delights of a Northern climate, she threw up her hands in disgusted remonstrance.

"Cooler?" she cried derisively. "Now, Marion, I really thought you had better sense. That's merely one of those ideas foisted on unsuspecting Southerners some score of years ago by shrewd Yankee boardinghouse keepers. You know I'll be twice as comfortable at home. Deliver me from the Northern summers as from the plagues of Egypt."

With her going and the departure of the nurses and the cessation of the doctor's daily visits, the house had settled down to its wonted quiet. Wonted and yet unwonted, for the atmosphere had changed in some subtle manner impossible to define, yet felt by every inmate. From his crib in his mother's room little Ross—for Marion had followed the time-honored Southern custom of giving the first-born his mother's maiden name—dispersed an atmosphere of home and love that made itself manifest in the actions of the meanest servant on the place.

He was a tiny infant, but he waxed stronger each day and cried lustily, doubling up his tiny fists with infantile rage; ate heartily, crowed and laughed and developed signs of teeth quite like any ordinary infant. Marion was happy in her child. The grim look of her mouth was softening, and her eyes were less hard and gloomy every day. She had given up her whole life completely to the care of her son. There was no moment, waking or sleeping, when her soul was not wrapped around his life, vibrating with every breath that he drew; trembling when he cried, pulsing with joy when he laughed.

Since that first day she had unwrapped the clothes from his twisted little limbs, she had not allowed anyone to touch him; to bathe or to dress him save herself.

"No," she cried in reply to the nurse's remonstrance, "my son does not wish to be exposed to curious eyes," and Howard had seen that her wishes were respected. Since that day, also, she and Howard had had no further talk concerning the child. He had walked the floor in the bitterness of the nights, and beat his hands together and stormed Heaven with low cries of inquiry. Marion had said that he was responsible for their child's deformity, but no more would she say, although he had begged and prayed and questioned her where his sin had been. At first, he tried to dismiss her words as the ravings of a sick and disappointed woman, but the more he tried to do this, the more the conviction was borne upon him that she had been cruelly, coldly conscious of her words and their full import.

"Marion," he said one day, when the baby was a few months old, "perhaps, while Ross is young, he might be operated upon to—to—straighten his limbs."

"Dr. Neilson has examined him carefully weeks ago, and says the case is hopeless," she said quietly.

"Weeks ago? Marion, why did you not tell me?"

"I did not want to pain you with the knowledge," she said gently.

He looked up in surprise at the unwonted tenderness in her voice and manner. It had been weary months since she had shown even such faint interest in his feelings.

He needed sympathy now, if ever a man did, although he would have been the last one to have suggested it to her. In the heat of the city streets panic stalked abroad day after day with veiled and averted face, and in men's hearts was the chill dread that she would draw aside her veil and stand revealed in all her ghastly horror. The pitiless glare of the August sun beat in the city streets, but no one heeded it, no one cared. Day after day the world of busy men stared at the bulletin boards with set faces and white lips, turning away to groan, "Another bank gone! Another house failed!" The despairing cries of the smaller firms were unheard in the great hoarse roar of the larger ones as the waters of bankruptcy closed over their heads. Out on the cool, green lawn of Edgewold, beneath the low shade of the old elms, Marion played with her child, and felt slowly, slowly the iron grasp of misery lifting from her soul. Daily, Howard, coming home, worried and heartsick beheld them with a new sickening fear in his soul lest each day on the lawn night be the last day they might spend there and call their home their own.

It was inexpressibly happy and restful for him to come in from the turmoil and heat and misery of the city streets and pause at the gate to see the picture which greeted his eyes every day. Marion had had a little basket made for the lawn and in this the child lay and played or slept while she sat beside it and worked and crooned and laughed at his baby gurgles. She kept him in the open air all that she could, for in some way she imagined that her love and care might do what no surgeon could. Several times when Howard had come home, worn to the breaking point, feeling that human strength could endure no longer; that he must turn somewhere for sympathy, the little picture on the lawn soothed and rested him and gave him strength to go out again at night, back to the hot, brilliant city for the hand to hand fight with the gaunt monster of the streets.

Several times he started to tell Marion the danger which threatened them, not in the hope that she would help or sympathize with him, but rather because he thought it cruel to keep her in ignorance of the real state of affairs. But

Marion, always difficult to talk intimately with, was now impossible. Even if she unbent from her cold reserve toward him, it was only to speak of the baby, and any signs on her husband's part toward further intimacy, were promptly discouraged. Sometimes, he wondered if she had not read the papers and found out for herself the condition of the financial world and judged for herself; but if she were interested in anything beyond her child, she showed no sign. She had all the inborn hatred of business details that would come in her blood. Back of her were generations of forefathers who had eaten, drunk and been merry and had known nothing of the whys and wherefores of their splendors and comforts. Small wonder was it then that if the echoes of the ruins crashing around the citadel came to her ears, they were but abstract echoes to her, nothing more, nothing of concrete significance to her or her home.

The hot, dragging summer wore into autumn; the furrows of care and worry in Howard's brow deepened with each succeeding day; the gentle sweetness of Marion's face and manner increased. The unceasing fight with the grim panic spectre was wearing his nerves and his body frail; the continuous happiness with her son, tempered though it was by his deformity, was making Marion into a new, more beautiful, more womanly woman.

In his absorption in his business affairs, Howard had allowed many of his little interests to escape him. Nothing much mattered to him now at any rate. He had thrown his soul into the conflict, and all things of lesser import were as though they had never been. Thus it happened that he had not noticed for several days Bob Weaver was absent from the office. He knew that when he tapped the bell for someone to do his errands, a blue-coated, brass-buttoned boy answered and did his bidding. He had forgotten to look into the boy's face to see who he was. One day, however, in the stress and storm of a busy morning, Bob Weaver came in clad in unfamiliar boy clothes; his face red and swollen and shiny with uncontained grief.

"If you please, Mr. Howard," he began.

Howard looked up, "Oh, yes, why, hello, Bob, where's your suit?" he began and paused suddenly to look at "the buttons who was" to "the buttons who used to be." Then he recalled suddenly, something unfamiliar about the boy who had been serving him lately.

"Why, hello, Bob," he said dubiously, "where—where have you been?"

"Why, Mr. Howard, I ain't been here since last week," said Bob ruefully, "Jimmy's been in my place." Then he swallowed something hard and burst out violently, "Grace's dying!"

"Yes," assented Howard. He had felt that coming as soon as he recognized the strangeness of Bob in the unfamiliar clothes, "Yes, she's dying too, and the little comfort I might have given her in her last days I was too busy to render. Did she want anything at the last, Bob?"

"Yes, sir, she cried to see you. She said she just wanted to hold your hand. But it was five o'clock this mornin' an' Ma said she hated to sen' fer you so early. Now she don't talk anymore, she don't know nobody."

"It will be a miserable memory to me to my dying day," muttered the man, "I'll go in and see her and come back to my work."

There was the fresh tinge of early autumn in the air; the blue haze over the distant low hills; the vivid touches of tree and bush here and there; the flame and flash of goldenrod by the roadsides. Howard noted it mechanically as he sprang from the train and started up the lane toward the Weaver home. "Early beautiful decay," he said to himself and turned into the road out of view of the station.

Out in his basket carriage, swinging and bounding and gurgling his delight at the blue Italian skies, and clutching at the fairy puffs of a bursting milk-weed pod held over his head, went Master Ross Howard down the little lane. Marion was in high spirits over her son's infantile glee. She clapped her hands and called on the nurse to witness his antics.

"See, Nella, see! Is he not a bright child, is he not Nella?"

But Nella spied a familiar form coming toward them up the lane, and she cried out, laughing, too, "Look, baby, look, here comes Papa!"

Marion's face hardened grimly; her lips set themselves in a thin, white line; her back stiffened in an uncompromising rigidity, but she forced her dry mouth to say in a ghastly attempt at imitating Nella's tones, "Yes, baby, here's Papa!" Then she added hurriedly, "Run, Nella, quick to the house. I forgot that I had promised to be at home to Miss Kenton to-day. I'm afraid she will have been there and gone. Tell Wiggins to say to her that I'll be home in a half hour. And Nella," she added, quite naturally, as if it were an after-thought, "you needn't come back, Mr. Howard will push the buggy home."

Nella had turned her back and sped away, not a moment too soon. The Weaver cottage was a few hundred rods away and Howard had entered quickly; his head bent, his manner absorbed, totally unconscious of the figures and the voices below him in the lane.

Marion pushed the buggy a little nearer the house and sat down to wait for his coming out. Before, when she had seen

him bent to his errand in the little cottage, her one thought
had been to hide her misery; to keep it locked in her heart
as a miserable secret. She had not felt that she had any right
and part in life, and it mattered little that she partook or
stood aside. But now, she felt all a woman's, a wife's, a
mother's clamorous want and need of her husband. Perhaps
she did not love him; perhaps she had not forgiven him, but
she demanded her right to him for her child's sake, and she
would brook no abatement of that right. A cold, deadly fury
was stirring at her heart, becoming more passionate and
human at every instant that Howard stayed in the house. She
sat on a stone near by and played with the fluffy balls with
one hand to amuse the child. The other was under the lace
cover, stretched over his form, soothing his twisted little
limbs.

Howard came out at the last, his eyes heavy with unshed
tears, but at sight of Marion, he started forward with a glad
little cry, "Marion, Marion, did you know I was here? It is
good in you—" he began.

She sneered at him, "Good? Do you call it good? This is
the second time I've caught you, George. I had more sense
than before. I thought I'd let you know this time."

He stared at her dazedly. This could not be Marion; this
woman was coarse almost in her speech.

"The second time? Why it's been months—since—Marion,
why do you look at me like that? Tell me, what is it?"

She picked the child out of its buggy and held it in a vise-
like grip against her breast.

"It may have been months ago," she said. She was shaking
like a tempest-driven reed, "but that months ago, see what it
did for my child."

Howard staggered back as if he had received a blow. In

an instant the cruel import of his wife's words were borne home to him. As in a vision, he saw that day that he had hastened to Grace's bedside and then home to find Marion lying as dead from a fall the mystery of which had always baffled him. He threw out his hands appealingly to her.

"It was my fault, Marion, I admit, but ah, it was a mistake, a cruel foolish mistake. If you had but told me—"

"Told you?" She laughed bitterly and loudly, the echoes of her false mirth jarring the deathlike stillness of the lane. "No, I tell you now, and I will tell her. Let me show her her own work." She made as if to brush him from her path. "Where is she?"

He threw his arm quietly, firmly about her waist, "She would not know if you told her Marion. She is dead."

CHAPTER VIII

On the next day the crash came. Marion was seated by the library window, her hands resting idly in her lap gazing out at the encrimsoned maple leaves fluttering softly to the ground. She heard the bang of the front door and the quick steps of her husband as he ran up the stairs and into the library, but she did not turn, although she knew he was standing in the doorway looking at her.

"Marion," his voice was low and quiet, but a something in his tones made her look up in wonderment, "Marion, it has come."

"What?" She was genuinely interested and nervous, a nervousness reflected from his own concentrated and subdued energy.

"The failure, it's all over."

"Failure? What failure? What are you talking about? What do you mean?"

For a moment she thought that grief at Grace's death had crazed him.

"Failure of our firm. It's all gone, gone to pieces, nothing, not a thing left of the wreck. We are ruined, totally, utterly ruined," he sat down at the table and let his head fall on his hands.

"But I don't understand. What is gone? You must explain, I don't understand." She had risen and leaned on the table opposite him, her brows contracted and pained.

"Of course you don't," he rose too and stood facing her, the table, with its gew-gaw outfit of useless writing material between them, "of course, you don't. I didn't expect you would when I told you. I only did so because I thought an explanation was due you for the change in our fortunes."

She opened her lips to speak, but he raised one hand and hushed the coming words.

"Oh, don't talk, don't justify yourself. It was nothing to you that for four months I have worked like a dog, hourly, yes, every minute, oozing out my heart's blood drop by drop to keep a shelter over our heads. It was nothing to you that our daily bread hung in the balance; that any day might see the fabric of my business topple into ruin and we be made beggars as we are to-day. Oh, how my soul has ached all these weeks for one kindly word of encouragement in all the bitter, lonely fight; how my heart has bled for one God-speed one day as I went into town to face the fight. Instead—" his voice broke wearily.

"I did not know, I did not dream—" she began again, but he checked her again.

"Of course you did not, I knew you did not. Yet, whose

fault was it? How many other women in this town, do you suppose are ignorant of the affairs of the world? Are there not newspapers brought to your door every day? Could you not have read and guessed at the struggle that every man was making to keep his head above water? No, wrapped in your own selfishness, immured in your own prison of fancied wrong, you chose to forget that there was a world in which you should have taken your part."

"My baby—" she began pleadingly, but he laughed sarcastically.

"Your baby? Poor little devil, must he be made an excuse for your shortcomings? Your baby? Why, he should have taught you patience and gentleness and perhaps even a passing interest in his father or even in his own bread and butter. Your baby? What, then, was responsible for those five years of indifference and callousness before your baby came? Your baby? Don't hold him responsible, Marion, don't."

Howard's onslaught had been so sudden and unexpected that she had forgotten to be angry; forgotten to arm herself in her usual mask of reserve and latent anger. She was conscious only of a desire to defend herself against his arraignment, to plead her own cause at this sudden and pitiless tribunal that he had set up.

"You misunderstand me, George—" Again he broke in.

"Oh, misunderstand, misunderstand—the cry that every woman raises who is too indifferent to attempt to enter into her husband's life or fancies herself too superior to come out of the clouds long enough to touch the vital human things of this world. Well, granted that I do not understand you, Marion, do you understand me? Have you ever tried to? Have you ever deemed me worthy of an attempt to understand me? Have you ever given me a chance to penetrate into your soul? Have you not shut yourself up like a tortoise in its shell at the first intimation of a friendly approach on my part? You have never given yourself up to me. You have always withheld the best in you. I do not understand you? Great God, who could?"

He leaned against the table, spent with the force of his own words. All the pent-up, unrealized misery of the past six years had suddenly flooded to his lips, and poured forth in a torrent of almost inarticulate words. His nerves were raw, sore to the touch, like a thing flayed alive, and he quivered at the slightest sound of Marion's voice. Perhaps he might have gone to his grave without voicing his grievance, but for this final culmination of misery, the burden of which he had had to bear so long alone.

There was an instant's silence between them, then Marion began slowly, timidly, feeling about for words as one who is not sure of himself. She was humble, apologetic, earnest in her desire to defend herself.

"You know, George, you have not deemed it necessary that I alone should be the sharer of your joys and sorrows. There—was that other woman."

"Its a lie, and you know it," he was white and blazing with anger now.

"I only know what I saw and heard," she went on slowly, "I know that that day last winter—" she paused to collect herself, "I saw you leave the train at an unusual hour. I could not dream what you were doing home so early, and I was glad too, for I wanted to tell you something—something," she caught her breath in a sob, "very dear to us both."

"You should have told me before," he answered doggedly, "it was my right to know."

"—And then I saw you turn off in a strange direction,"

she went on, unheeding the interruption, "even then, I could not dream where you were going, until I heard some men, oh, just common village loafers, laughing over your infatuation for some girl whom they called Grace Weaver. They said you supported the family and had the boy in your office, and then I went home, and fell-fainted, and that is why the baby is a cripple."

She had recited it in a cold, passionless monotone, and now her voice ended in a little gasp. Howard looked at her, his face still steeled and unsympathetic.

"Yes, you told me all that, or practically all that yesterday," he made reply, "but what has that to do with the case?"

"Why, everything," she answered simply. They had dropped into an argumentative strain. Passion and feeling seemed to have died out from both and they were discussing their heart life as coldly and calmly as they might have discussed the grocery bill.

"I don't see it," he said. "Granted that you listened to the idle gossip of some street loafers and accepted their words as a final proof of your husband's disloyalty—rather than give him the courtesy of an explanation, or at best, the benefit of a doubt, granted all that, what has that to do with your indifferent attitude toward me and my affairs in former years? Wait, let me finish. Not that I should want to compel you to do anything that was distasteful to you. You know, Marion, I am not the man to force you in any way, but can you not see how galling it must have been to me to see how apart were our lives; how futile my every effort to draw us together; to weld our lives and hearts?"

She merely bowed her head; she was recalling an expression of Emmie's on the day she and Howard were married, "Love him, Marion, love him well, and give him sympathy, he needs both, and he will be unhappy if he is deprived of them."

"Can you not see, Marion, that it was a dangerous thing to do with a person of my temperament?" He paused and laughed shortly, "It is very effeminate and sentimental, I suppose, for me to talk of 'temperament,' and all that artistic rot, but we all have dispositions, I suppose—and—"

"Yes, that's just it," she broke in, "each of us has his own temperament and mine is an unfortunate one, I suppose, unsympathetic and cold, but you know I could not change it, George; I told you so frequently."

He stared in surprise at her gentle, patient acquiescence.

"It was not because I did not love you, George," she went on, still more gently, "if I had not I should not have cared that day."

He drew a chair near her, forced her into it, and sat down himself, resting one hand on hers, "You will believe me, Marion—" he said.

"Yes," she answered, quite simply, "I will believe you."

He stroked her hand for a moment, then rose and pressed the bell suddenly.

"Pack my bag immediately," he said to the maid who answered it, "I shall take the next express to town."

"Where are you going?" asked Marion in sudden dismay.

"Never mind, we'll talk of that later. I have something more important to speak of now," he resumed his position, and continued calmly as if he had the whole day before him.

"Marion, I was heart-hungry, hungry for some interest outside of business and the eternal office grind. If you had cared for society and had gone in for entertaining, even that would have been something, but you thought Lawrenceville people—"

"Oh, no, I didn't," she interposed hastily, "it wasn't Lawrenceville people exactly, you know Emmie always looked after that at home, I suppose—I lacked initiative."

"Well, you didn't seem to be interested in anything, not even me, you know, and it was dreary here, dear, inexpressibly so. Then I thought perhaps you'd go in for charity or—er—something. Not that I approve of those women whose charity ends at home, but it would have made you seem more like a human being. I could have joyed in your little experiences, and could have been happy in your little interests. But you didn't."

"You should have married Emmie," she said reflectively.

"I didn't want Emmie, and I am sure she didn't want me."

"You cannot deny that I have been interested in Ross," she said anxiously.

"One day I met this child, she was nothing but a child. She was thinly clad, poor, miserable; she fell on the ice. I picked her up, saw her home, and became interested in the poverty and bravery of her family. Nothing more; I was tired of everything, dreary, lonely, hungry, and I turned to the first interest that presented itself."

"You might have interested me in your poor family."

"No, I thought I knew how you would have dismissed the case—with a cheque such as you sent Emmie for her schemes, and a few perfunctory words. They wouldn't have accepted either. That was all there was to it, dearest, merely a little charitable interest in one of our townspeople." He was pleading in an earnest, lover-like way now, and Marion felt herself yielding to his manner.

"When I saw you that day—?"

"Bob, her brother, told me that she was ill, and I went to see her, that was all. I meant nothing. I was sorry for her;

she was a pretty child to me; a pretty, sick, grateful little thing, as all her family was grateful. I did not put my foot into the house again until yesterday."

"She loved you?"

"I did not know it until her mother told me. She—she—died calling my name; she worshipped me. I hardly remember touching her hand. Perhaps it was only gratitude, though."

"She worshipped you, and you did not know it," said Marion reflectively, "and I was sick at heart for love and companionship, too, and the need of a pair of baby arms, and you did not know it. Have I been the only blind one, George?"

"No, no, you have not." He rose suddenly. "It has been like a new lease on life, this talk with you. It is not what I came for, I wanted to tell you some few matters of business—"

"Your bag is ready, sir," said the maid at the door.

"Where are you going?" asked Marion, fear gripping her throat tight and hard.

He looked at his watch. "I have barely time to catch my train. I have taken up my time to talk over other things with you. Don't worry, Marion, everything will come out all right." He was walking to his room as he spoke, and Marion followed him, hastily, watching him with helplessness written all over her, as he bustled about, picking up things here and there to put in his pockets, opening and shutting his watch, pulling at his coat collar, pacing restlessly up and down the floor.

"We went to pieces, all to pieces; it was an awful crash. Not that the echoes will go down to the ages, but it is complete ruin. I—we—well, I guess I kept the firm from failing long after it was legitimately scheduled to go to pieces, and everyone suspects foul play on my part now. I—I—had other interests; they—we—I merged them. You never knew about my business, Marion, so I can't explain it to you. Anyway—" he gulped hard, "they think I have embezzled one set of funds to keep the firm on its feet, and I may be arrested at any moment."

"Arrested!" she gave a low cry of horror and sank on the bed.

"Oh, well, maybe it isn't quite as bad as that. In a few weeks or months it will all be quite clear and the suspicion will be removed from me—but for the present—" he shrugged his shoulders.

"And you are going to run away?" There was a note of scorn in her voice.

"Yes, I suppose that's what you may call it. I haven't the courage to face a simple arrest, for that's all it would mean, nothing more, or even all the misery of a long drawn out investigation. I am as innocent of any wrong-doing in this case as I was in that other. Only, I couldn't stand having the people point me out as the man who had embezzled funds entrusted to him."

"I don't see any difference," she protested. "You are running away; they will call you a coward, as well as a thief." He winced at her crude words, but she went on mercilessly. "Better, far better, to stay here, even if you are sent to prison, and have your innocence proved, since you say it can be proved, than to go skulking away, suspected of everyone."

He paused in his restless moving up and down as if her words were impressing him, then he threw his head up and said decisively, "No, I won't, I won't stay, I can't, I am a wreck, I couldn't stand this last straw. Let me go away, in a few days it will blow over, then I'll come back, and we'll have to start life anew, Marion. We will have to face poverty."

"Poverty!" she rose and laid her hands on his shoulders. "Do you suppose I care for poverty if only your name is left untarnished, but I could not bear—"

"It will be all right," he said breaking from her grasp nervously, "Towneley will keep it hushed until it is straightened out. He will look after you, dear. Don't make it hard for me. I must go. There's money to last—I can't stay to see it all go, the house and everything. You'll go home for awhile—oh, you'll know what to do. I may be a coward, Marion, but that talk we had together has made life seem worth the living again, and I want to fight it out somehow."

It was useless, Marion saw, to attempt to dissuade him. She stood pale, but quiet as he paced the floor.

"You'll want to see Ross, won't you?"

"Of course." She went in the nursery and brought the child just awakened, and crowing, and put it in his arms.

"Poor little devil," he said, "poor little chap. Handicapped already in the race, handicapped, through a wretched, bitter, misunderstanding. You've got to fight it out, boy, and we can't help you. I've got nothing to give you now to start with. Poor little devil."

The baby laughed and clutched at his collar. Howard handed the child to Marion, strained them both to his breast for an instant.

"We understand better, don't we, Marion?"

"Yes," she said numbly. For an instant she felt again strangely aloof from the whole scene, apart and out of the disaster which threatened her whole life, but only for an instant.

Howard snatched his bag and started for the hall, then he

paused and looked back at her wistfully, standing there with the gurling, cooing baby on her arm.

"To-morrow—," he said slowly, "to-morrow, Grace will be buried. I—gave the money for the funeral. Will you—?" he paused.

"Yes, I will go and see her mother," Marion said simply. She was a human soul at last.

"God bless you, Marion," he said, and was gone. She watched him from the window go down the back lane under the elms and maples, then she laid the child on the bed and knelt by it, dry-eyed and silent.

CHAPTER IX

Mrs. Wilton raised her lorgnette and stared hard at the pictures on the drawing-room walls.

"It always seemed to me," she said languidly, "that the subjects were very ill-chosen, and—er—rather typically Southern, you know. I have no patience with Venuses and such unbecomingly nude figures. It isn't just the thing for women to surround themselves with pictures such as should be confined to art galleries and museums where decent people may stay away from."

"She was always eccentric, you know," put in Miss Agnes Hunt.

"I know, my dear, but even eccentricity has its limits. No, I don't think I'll buy anything here. Moreover, the prices are outrageous."

"The house was nicely furnished," pursued Miss Hunt, as she went about touching the tapestries and curtains and hangings, "quite nicely furnished."

"Oh, yes my dear," assented Mrs. Wilton with a bored air as she seated herself on a chair and put out her feet, "but then these Southern women always go in for that sort of thing. The house is quite typical of the woman it—"

"It's typical of good taste," broke in Miss Kenton angrily, "the trouble with most of us, I fear, is that we wouldn't have had the sense to furnish our homes as Mrs. Howard did, nor the money to do it with even if we had had the sense."

Mrs. Wilton put up her lorgnette and stared hard at the audacious Miss Kenton. The lorgnette habit was a new one with Mrs. Wilton, therefore it was excusable in her to use it on all occasions. She attempted to wither the daring Miss Kenton with its magic stare, and failing, laid it down and sniffed.

"Since when did you begin to be the dear creature's champion?" she inquired. "After the way she treated you when she first came I should think you'd forever hold your peace."

"Oh, I've forgotten that long ago," returned the red-haired young lady with unexpected magnamity. "Then it's a shame, now that the poor woman is down and isn't here to answer for herself to have a lot of people going through her house picking her to pieces like crows over carrion."

Miss Hunt shuddered in horror and drew nearer Mrs. Wilton as if she feared an explosion and wished to be near to throw water on the flames. She even laid a restraining hand on the lady's arm. But Mrs. Wilton merely put up her lorgnette again and muttered, "Well, of all fools!"

It was a bleak, drear November day, chill and bitter and gusty. All the morning, Edgewold had been thrown wide to curious visitors for it was the day of the auction sale. They had tramped through the drawing-rooms and fingered the treasures of the curios that Marion and Howard had been at so great pains to collect. They had inspected the kitchen and cellar and laundry; had sniffed at the silver and mahogany in the dining-room; had peered into the drawers of the desk and tables in the library; had trampled ruthlessly into the holies of Marion's own bed-chamber, and gazed at the fittings of the little nursery with unsentimental satisfaction.

Holt Towneley paced the halls and rooms of the house, his hands thrust deep in his pockets; a gloom of despair settled upon his entire figure.

"Beastly business, beastliest I ever did," he growled from time to time. "Wouldn't have done it for my own brother if I had had one."

He had been a frequent visitor to the house in the past five years; he felt almost at home in it. He was grieved and disgusted when he saw its ruthless invasion by the Lawrenceville vandals. Mrs. Wilton and her party passed him on their way upstairs, the elder lady first fixing him with a lorgnetted stare.

"Cats," he growled again, after blushing under Miss Kenton's clear gaze, "nosing around to see what they can spit at. Oh, why did I ever get into this mess?"

The auctioneer had come and his strident voice could be heard in the drawing-room, with the preliminary taps of the hammer. Towneley's heart chilled for the strokes of the hammer came dulled to his ear by the velvet draperies, and it seemed to him as if he had heard the strokes of the gravedigger's spade on a coffin. He followed the crowd that was drifting into the drawing-room, and leaned in a doorway, glooming angrily upon the pulsing, eager, commenting throng.

"Thank God Marion isn't here," he muttered between his teeth.

At that moment, Marion sat in the window of her old room gazing out at the leaden sea and the leaden sky, with a heart as leaden as they and a face as gray and gloomy as the heavy fog which hung over the horizon. The baby lay on her lap, gazing up into her face with a wide, unbaby, almost comprehending gaze. She had fled to her mother a few days after Howard had left. Holt Towneley had come to her at once and helped her get her few things together and leave Lawrenceville. In a sort of dumb misery, she travelled all that night, and it was only the imminent danger of Mrs. Ross' having hysterics in the hall after her arrival that roused her from her apathy.

"And, oh, the papers," moaned Mrs. Ross, when they had gotten upstairs. "They said the dreadfullest things! Did you see some of them, Marion?"

"I never read the papers," said Marion, and a quick shame-faced flush swept over her face as she recalled Howard's bitter words of two days before.

"No, that's true, I acknowledge it isn't a ladylike thing to do, but it was brought to my notice, and I just couldn't help it. To think of your having such a time, and Emmie's life has been so smooth, too. Marion, I verily believe you are cursed."

"Perhaps, I am," Marion assented wearily, and went back at once into her apathy.

To-day, she sat and gazed into the leaden waters before her, while her heart was heavy for the scenes through which her beloved Edgewold were passing. In her mind's eye she could see the unsympathetic gaping strangers passing through the halls and rooms she had loved, peering into the cupboards and closets, commenting on her housekeeping, sneering at the little sentimental touches in her baby's nursery—oh, it was maddening. She gripped the child tight upon her lap, but he made no outcry; he seemed to understand.

The door opened softly, and Emmie slipped in, and leaning gently over Marion, kissed the baby.

"You here, Emmie, when did you come?" Marion half held the child from her as if dreading his first introduction to his aunt.

"Oh, yes," Emmie's laugh was as joyous and carefree as it had been five years before, "I could not resist the opportunity of seeing you and my wonderful nephew, so I just picked up the least offensive of the Tribe, and hopped on the first train hitherward, and here I am!" She extended her arms, turning her form, full of a pretty, matronly charm, about, as if for inspection, and beamed radiantly upon Marion.

"Of course, I can't stay long," she went on, chattering purposely to give Marion time to collect herself, "for the remnant of the Tribe which I brought will soon begin to howl for its kindred spirits, and its kindred spirits will likewise set up noises at poor Len, who is being mother to them while I am here. They won't be long apart. Its a gregarious clan."

Marion had recovered herself, surreptitiously wiped the tears from her eyes, and now regarded Emmie with admiration and pleasure. She reached down into Marion's lap and took the baby tenderly in her arms, making the usual feminine sounds and cries and wonderings over him. But a little spasm of pain contracted her features, and when Marion was not looking, she buried a pair of tear-wet eyes into his little curls of hair.

Emmie's presence in the house acted like a tonic to Marion. She drew herself out of her shell of silence, and as Emmie put it, "acted more like a fleshly being than a ghost." Days passed, and still she heard no word from Howard. Holt Towneley wrote her cherry letters, and sent her money for her needs, saved from the wreck, he said. She puzzled her head for awhile with conjectures as to the means he had employed to save enough for the liberal sums he sent her, for the lawyer's letters said that the ruin was absolute, complete. Edgewold, he said had gone intact to one purchaser, but the money would have to be sunken in the mass of "Blood-money." She used little of the amounts Towneley sent, putting most of it aside against the evil day when there would be no further income. Then she set her brow to think out her future. Something of this she said to Emmie, who promptly vetoed such thinking.

"There isn't any future," she announced. "You and this infant will stay here, and let mother and me look after you both. I'm sure there's enough income from our ancestral estates—" Emmie inflated her chest in the old way and laughed merrily, "to maintain you both riotously. Then, when George comes back, we'll begin to talk about futures."

It was the first time Howard's name had been mentioned between them, and Emmie now spoke it cautiously, feeling her way as if she feared the result. There was an instant's silence, then Marion spoke slowly. "But suppose George doesn't come back?"

"Nonsense," said Emmie vigorously, though a chill dread of the same thing was at her own heart. "Nonsense, why not? He had to go into —er—temporary retirement; it was the only thing to do. If he had been a woman, of course, he would have had to stay and face the situation, but fortunately, the world does not expect such things of men, they are always allowed the alternative of retirement or suicide." She dandled the quiet and solemn little Ross up and down vigorously as she spoke, while the small Emmie by her side laughed and clapped her hands appreciatively.

There came a day, however, when the baby's quietness was too evidently unnatural. Marion laid him on the bed one day, after a vain attempt to arouse him sufficiently to take his nourishment, and brushing Emmie and her mother aside, went out of the house and out to the edge of the winter sea, there to be alone an instant with the sorrowful truth which had been thrust home to her.

She came in again in a few minutes, and joined Mrs. Ross and Emmie in their pitiful vigil over the bed. It was a long and fruitless struggle, a bitter war they and the doctor waged against death for the little sufferer. Once they seemed to gain an inch, then the dark angel pressed them still closer to the wall. Marion set her teeth hard; it was as if she strove with a tangible, personal shape for the possession of her child. She fought bitterly, angrily, and finally, prayerfully, all the mother animal in her keenly awake, and struggling in a primitive way for her mother-rights. The doctor shook his head, but she clenched her hands while her bloodless lips murmured prayers, ineffectual attempts to storm Heaven for aid against the black-winged menace over her child. Emmie and Mrs. Ross turned their heads aside at the last, but she took the child from the bed, holding him tightly in her arms as if to guard him from the death angel's grasp, setting her back against an imaginary wall. It was of no avail, she was pressed farther and farther back, while the shadow of the wings enfolded her and the little life which she had brought into the world, and took it back to the skies to forget its twisted, earthly frame.

Marion gazed long at the tiny form in its little flower-lined coffin.

"They will all say that it is better that you should die," she whispered to the waxen face, "than to live all your days a hopeless cripple, and perhaps, for your sake, it is so, but you are the only thing I ever truly owned, baby, and now—what have I?" She rocked a pair of empty arms and looked down on her breast where a soft head had once lain.

"Bury him by the sea, Mother," she said quietly when she was asked, "perhaps it will sing to him the same songs it has sung to me, and he won't be so lonely without his mother's arms."

Emmie raised her head and stared at Marion in surprise. It was the first time she had ever heard her sister express a love for the sea. "I wonder what George would think of that?" she murmured to herself.*

* The extant manuscript ends here in what is probably Dunbar-Nelson's first draft. She later wrote additional pages that have been lost.

POETRY

RAINY DAY*

What though the rain be falling chill and gray,
A ceaseless dripping from the sad, brown caves?
A tiny bird is singing cross the way.
    Beneath the friendly shelter of the leaves.

The mountain top is sheathed in vapors white,
And o'er the valley hangs a chilly pall;
But through the mists are riding into night.
The robin sounds his loving, little call.

I hear the foaming torrent in its rush.
    And o'er the rocks "It rears in full-grown pride";
Through gray and green of earth, there is one flush.
    A tiger-lily on the grim rock's side,
Life may be drear, and hope seem far away.
But ever through the mist some bird will sing;
And through the dullest, rainy world of gray,
Some bright-hued flower, its flash of promising bring.

A COMMON PLAINT†

    If I could write a tale to-night,
    A tale of thrilling things;
    A spice of love, a bit of fight,

---

* The Elmira, New York, *Advertiser,* September 18, 1898.
†Typescript, probably ca. 1900.

The clink of wedding rings,
The villain's death, and all end right,
If I could write a tale to-night.

My pot is on the fire to-night,
Alas, it needs to boil;
I gaze with would-be seeress sight,
And burn the midnight oil,
Alack, again, I cannot write,
My pot is on the fire to-night.

A check looms large into my sight,
And here, I scribble rhymes;
No editor will heed my plight,
I've proved that scores of times:
Oh, hero, gallant, come bedight,
A check looms large into my sight.

I gaze into the fire to-night,
And build my castles there;
Great mansions, tall, and all alight,
Alas, they turn to air.
Then vainly, I for ideas fight,
And gaze into the fire to-night.

It is no use, I cannot write,
I'd rather dream than work;
Then what's the use, let's take to-night
For luxury of shirk.
Those editors would send it back,
I cannot write, ah, well, alack!

A SONG OF LOVE *

Oh, drink thou deep of the purple wine,
    And it's hey for love, for I love you so!
Oh, clasp me close, with your lips on mine,
    And it's hey for love, for I love you so!
The sea lies violet, deep, and wide,
My heart beats high with the rushing tide;
Was it fancy, beloved, the seagulls cried:
    "Sing loud for love, for I love him so"?

Oh, little boat on the tossing wave,
    Sing loud for love, for I love him so!
Oh, tall pine tree in the shadows grave,
    Sing loud for love, for I love him so!
The little waves kiss the gleaming sand,
I laugh in the sun on the joyful land;
Beloved, one clasp of your strong young hand;
    The world is fair, for I love you so!

SUMMIT AND VALE †

The light hangs over the mountain top,
    But gray and misty the plain;
    The sun's a-glow on eternal snow,
But down in the valley, the rain.

And life is so, the sun a-glow
On the mountains far, while the rain's below.

* *Munsey's Magazine,* July 1902, p. 603.
† *Lippincott's Magazine,* December 1902, p. 715.

A LITTLE BIRD SINGS *

Way out in the grove a little bird sings,
    Out in the young, green trees,
Lilting and trilling with fluttering wings,
    Out in the young, green trees.
He lilts and he tilts and he sways in the leaves,
For the sun is a-shine, and a gold fabric weaves,
And his throat bursts with song, and the blue air it cleaves,
    Out in the young, green trees.

Way up in the sky sounds a great sweet song,
    Oh, heart, in the blue, high sky;
He sings of our love, Oh, 'tis, sweet and long,
    Oh, heart, in the blue, high sky.
All in the trees, a-flower and young,
All in the lore of the heart's quick tongue,
All in the joy of a love well sung,
    Oh, heart, in the blue, high sky.

THE LOVERS †

They are lovers, the winds, that sweep o'er the lea;
He, the strong breeze that lashes the sea;
She the swift wind that sighs through the trees,
Breath of the pines, whose fragrance she grieves;
He strong and salt, with passionate cry,
North Wind and South Wind, lovingly sigh.

* Typescript, probably ca. 1902.
† Typescript, 1902–1909.

THE GIFT*

Like wine, your kisses touch my lips,
Like wine, the blood thrills through my veins;
The honey that the gold bee sips,
The purple draught that foams and stains
Are in your tender, sweet caress;
My heart is yours, I could give less—

I could give less, but all my life
Lies at your feet, to take or no.
    I crave your clasp that shields from strife,
The kiss you gave me, loving so.
I love your breath upon my hair,
    Myself I love—you think me fair.

SORROW'S CROWN†

"A sorrow's crown of sorrow is remembering
happier things"

    In the dead days of long ago
We walked the sun-kissed hill, aye, hand in hand
And knew the perfect love which understands
And asks no words to round its cycle out.
Beside us as we walked the violets bloomed,
Up-springing from the sward in loveliness,

---

*Typescript, 1902–1909.
†Typescript, 1902–1909.

Pressed 'neath our tread or smiling in our hands,
When low we stooped to break their fragile stems.

    In the dead days of long ago
The hand of man had scarce dared yet defile
The hill that raised its crest unto the sun,
And gave sweet thanks because it bloomed afair,
And raised green trees like altar candles high,
Or swung its censers of the deep heart flow'r,
And held two souls that walked in perfect love,
Unmarveling such love could last on earth.

    And now it is to-day,
We walk with sun-kissed hill, our forms apart,
And ever with us walks another form,
Close pressing with firm tread betwixt us twain.
Her face is fairer than the violets' bloom,
And love shines full upon her countenance;
Into your hand her own steals oft anon,
And I, heart-broken, stray apart, alone.

    And still to-day,
The sun-kissed hill, its crest aloft, up-raised
Unto the darkling sky where sorrow broods;
White stones and tow'rs and structures tall are piled,
Where violets bloomed and wild things danced away.

She walks with thee—and yet she too, shall know
The sorrow's crown of bitterness to come,
The jealous guarding of her happy days,
The hoarding of the mem'ry of an hour.

STILL FROM THE DEPTHS*

Still from the depths of a soul unstrung,
Still from the heart by an anguish wrung;
Freed from the dross of an earthly thought,
Touched with a sadness by years unbrought—
My soul to thy soul o'er the infinite way,
My soul to thy soul is calling to-day.

Freed from the power of passion assuaged,
Freed from the depths of self-love ungauged;
Ever increasing its infinite pow'r,
Ever 'tis strengthened from hour to hour—
My soul in earnestness crying to thee,
My soul to thy soul, o'er the infinite sea.

VIOLETS†

I had not thought of violets of late,
The wild, shy kind that springs beneath your feet
In wistful April days, when lovers mate
And wander through the fields in raptures sweet.
And thought of violets meant florists' shops,
And bows and pins, and perfumed paper fine;
And garish lights, and mincing little fops
And cabarets and songs, and deadening wine.

* Typescript, 1902–1909.
† *The Crisis,* August 1917, p. 198.

So far from sweet real things my thoughts had strayed,
I had forgot wide fields, and clear brown streams;
The perfect loveliness that God has made—
Wild violets shy and heaven-mounting dreams.
And now—unwittingly, you've made me dream
Of violets, and my soul's forgotten gleam.

TO THE NEGRO FARMERS OF THE UNITED STATES*

God washes clean the souls and hearts of you,
His favored ones, whose backs bend o'er the soil,
Which grudging gives to them requite for toil
In sober graces and in vision true.
God places in your hands the pow'r to do
A service sweet. Your gift supreme to foil
The bare-fanged wolves of hunger in the moil
of Life's activities. Yet all too few
Your glorious band, clean sprung from Nature's heart;
The hope of hungry thousands, in whose breast
Dwells fear that you should fail. God placed no dart
Of war within your hands, but pow'r to start
Tears, praise, love, joy, enwoven in a crest
To crown you glorious, brave ones of the soil.

THE LIGHTS AT CARNEY'S POINT†

O white little lights at Carney's Point,
    You shine so clear o'er the Delaware;

The Dunbar Speaker and Entertainer, ed. Alice Dunbar-Nelson (Naperville, Ill.: J. L. Nichols, 1920), p. 240.
†*The Dunbar Speaker and Entertainer*, p. 132.

When the moon rides high in the silver sky,
    Then you gleam, white gems on the Delaware.
Diamond circlet on a full white throat,
    You laugh your rays on a questioning boat;
Is it peace you dream in your flashing gleam,
    O'er the quiet flow of the Delaware?

And the lights grew dim at the water's brim,
    For the smoke of the mills shredded slow between;
And the smoke was red, as is new bloodshed,
    And the lights went lurid 'neath the livid screen.

O red little lights at Carney's point,
    You glower so grim o'er the Delaware;
When the moon hides low sombrous clouds below,
    Then you glow like coals o'er the Delaware.
Blood red rubies on a throat of fire,
    You flash through the dusk of a funeral pyre;
And there hearth fires red whom you fear and dread
    O'er the turgid flow of the Delaware?

And the lights gleamed gold o'er the river cold,
    For the murk of the furnace shed a copper veil;
And the veil was grim at the great cloud's brim,
    And the lights went molten, now hot, now pale.

O gold little lights at Carney's Point,
    You gleam so proud o'er the Delaware;
When the moon grows wan in the eastering dawn,
    Then you sparkle gold points o'er the Delaware.
Aureate filagree on a Croesus' brow,
    You hasten the dawn on a gray ship's prow.
Light you streams of gold in the grim ship's hold
    O'er the sullen flow of the Delaware?

And the lights went gray in the ash of day,
        For a quiet Aurora brought a halcyon balm;
And the sun laughed high in the infinite sky,
        And the lights were forgot in the sweet, sane calm.

I SIT AND SEW *

I sit and sew—a useless task it seems,
My hands grown tired, my head weighed down with dreams—
The panoply of war, the martial tred of men,
Grim-faced, stern-eyed, gazing beyond the ken
Of lesser souls, whose eyes have not seen Death,
Nor learned to hold their lives but as a breath—
But—I must sit and sew.

I sit and sew—my heart aches with desire—
That pageant terrible, that fiercely pouring fire
On wasted fields, and writhing grotesque things
Once men. My soul in pity flings
Appealing cries, yearning only to go
There in that holocaust of hell, those fields of woe—
But—I must sit and sew.

The little useless seam, the idle patch;
Why dream I here beneath my homely thatch,
When there they lie in sodden mud and rain,
Pitifully calling me, the quick ones and the slain?
You need me, Christ! It is no roseate dream
That beckons me—this pretty futile seam,
It stifles me—God, must I sit and sew?

* *The Dunbar Speaker and Entertainer,* p. 145.

YOU! INEZ!*

Orange gleams athwart a crimson soul
Lambent flames; purple passion lurks
In your dusk eyes.
Red mouth; flower soft,
Your soul leaps up—and flashes
Star-like, white, flame-hot.
Curving arms, encircling a world of love.
You! Stirring the depths of passionate desire!

TO MADAME CURIE†

Oft have I thrilled at deeds of high emprise,
And yearned to venture into realms unknown,
Thrice blessed she, I deemed, whom God had shown
How to achieve great deeds in woman's guise.
Yet what discov'ry by expectant eyes
Of foreign shores, could vision half the throne
Full gained by her, whose power fully grown
Exceeds the conquerors of th' uncharted skies?
So would I be this woman whom the world
Avows its benefactor; nobler far,
Than Sybil, Joan, Sappho, or Egypt's queen.
In the alembic forged her shafts and hurled
At pain, diseases, waging a humane war;
Greater than this achievement, none, I ween.

* Holograph manuscript, dated February 16, 1921.
† The Philadelphia *Public Ledger*, August 21, 1921.

COMMUNION *

This day I dedicated unto you:
I filled each moment of the time with dreams,
Memories, rose-shot, with irridescent gleams.
And now, I find the hours are all too few,
Too soon the lawns are silvered with eve's dew.
A thousand haunting pictures flit—it seems
My mind's a gracious gallery that teems
With exquisite vignettes, forever new.
O rarest day! Your spirit hovering near,
The pressure of your soul upon my own;
None to disturb, no clamoring, petty task!
Your loved whisper breathing past mine ear.
Yourself denied, what better could I ask
Than to commune with memories alone?

MUSIC †

Music! Lilting, soft and languorous,
Crashing, splendid, thunderous,
Blare of trumpets, sob of violins,
Tinkle of lutes and mandolins;
Poetry of harps, rattle of castanets,
Heart-break of cellos, woodwinds in tender frets;

Orchestra, symphony, bird-song, flute;
Coronach of contraltos, shrill strings a-mute.
Sakuntala sobbing in the forest drear,
Melisande moaning on crescendic fear;
Splendor and tumult of the organs roll,
Heraldic trumpets pierce the inner soul;
Symphonic syncopation that Dvorak wove,
Valkyric crashes when the Norse gods strove;
Salome's triumph in grunt obscene,
Tschaikovsky peering through forest green;
Verdi's high treble of saccharine sound,
Celeste! Miserere! Lost lovers found.
Music! With you, touching my finger-tips!
Music! With you, soul on your parted lips!
Music—is you!

OF OLD ST. AUGUSTINE *

Of old, St. Augustine wrote wise
    And curious lore, within his book.
I read and meditate, my eyes
See words of comforting, I look
Again, and thrill with radiant hope.
"They did not sin, those white-souled nuns of old,
Pent up in leaguered city, and despoiled
By knights, who battered at the peaceful fold,
And stole their bodies. Yet the fiends were foiled,
They could not harm their stainless, cloistered souls."

* *Opportunity*, July 1925, p. 216.

O wise St. Augustine, you give
Great joy to those whose earthly form
Is held in thrall. The soul may live
Unscathed—untouched—far from alarm,
True to its cloistered dream—unspoiled.

SNOW IN OCTOBER *

Today I saw a thing of arresting poignant beauty:
A strong young tree, brave in its Autumn finery
Of scarlet and burnt umber and flame yellow,
Bending beneath a weight of snow,
Which sheathed the north side of its slender trunk,
And spread a heavy white chilly afghan
Over its crested leaves.

Yet they thrust through, defiant, glowing,
Claiming the right to live another fortnight,
Clamoring that Indian Summer had not come,
Crying "Cheat! Cheat!" because Winter had stretched
Long chill fingers into the brown, streaming hair
Of fleeing October.

The film of snow shrouded the proud redness of the tree,
As premature grief grays the strong head
Of a virile, red-haired man.

---

* *Caroling Dusk*, ed. Countee Cullen (New York: Harper and Brothers, 1927).

APRIL IS ON THE WAY *

April is on the way!
I saw the scarlet flash of a blackbird's wing
As he sang in the cold, brown February trees;
And children said that they caught a glimpse of the sky on a bird's
    wing from the far South.
(Dear God, was that a stark figure outstretched in the bare branches
Etched brown against the amethyst sky?)

April is on the way!
The ice crashed in the brown mud-pool under my tread,
The warning earth clutched my bloody feet with great fecund fingers.
I saw a boy rolling a hoop up the road,
His little bare hands were red with cold,
But his brown hair blew backward in the southwest wind.
(Dear God! He screamed when he saw my awful woe-spent eyes.)

April is on the way!
I met a woman in the lane;
Her burden was heavy as it is always, but today her step was light,
And a smile drenched the tired look away from her eyes.
(Dear God, she had dreams of vengeance for her slain mate,
Perhaps the west wind has blown the mist of hate from her heart,
The dead man was cruel to her, you know that, God.)

April is on the way!
My feet spurn the ground now; instead of dragging on the bitter
    road.

* *Ebony and Topaz*, 1927, p. 52.

I laugh in my throat as I see the grass greening beside the patches
of snow
(Dear God, those were wild fears. Can there be hate when the
southwest wind is blowing?)

April is on the way!
The crisp brown hedges stir with the bustle of bird wings.
There is business of building, and songs from brown thrust throats
As the bird-carpenters make homes against Valentine Day.
(Dear God, could they build me a shelter in the hedge from the icy
winds that will come with the dark?)

April is on the way!
I sped through the town this morning. The florist shops have put
yellow flowers in the windows,
Daffodils and tulips and primroses, pale yellow flowers
Like the tips of her fingers when she waved me that frightened
farewell.
And the women in the market have stuck pussy willows in the long
necked bottles on their stands.
(Willow trees are kind, Dear God. They will not bear a body on
their limbs.)

April is on the way!
The soul within me cried that all the husk of indifference to sorrow
was but the crust of ice with which winter disguises life;
It will melt, and reality will burgeon forth like the crocuses in the
glen.
(Dear God! Those thoughts were from long ago. When we read
poetry after the day's toil, and got religion together at the
revival meeting.)

April is on the way!
The infinite miracle of unfolding life in the brown February fields.

(Dear God, the hounds are baying!)

Murder and wasted love, lust and weariness, deceit and vainglory—
 what are they but the spent breath of the runner?

(God, you know he laid hairy red hands on the golden loveliness of
 her little daffodil body.)

Hate may destroy me, but from my brown limbs will bloom the
 golden buds with which we once spelled love.

(Dear God! How their light eyes glow into black pin points of
 hate!)

April is on the way!

Wars are made in April, and they sing at Easter time of the
 Resurrection.

Therefore I laugh in their faces.

(Dear God, give her the strength to join me before her golden
 petals are fouled in the slime!)

April is on the way!

FOREST FIRE *

And I have seen a forest fire;
God, it was an awful thing!
It crept with scarlet tongues,
Fire!
Higher.
It lapped at the soft white rim
Of the dogwood blooms;
It flung orange and black
Scarves to hang in a mocking wrack,

Harlem I, November 1928, p. 22.

That made green leaves shrivel and curl in despair;
Pointed ironic fingers here and there

In the cool caverns of moss,
Turning the gold of foliage to dross,
Till the forest, panting in shame,
Gave its virginal beauty to the flame
That left it a stark, black hag
Stripped
Of soul and beauty and love,
Whipped
By the Forest Fire!

CANO—I SING *

Let others sing in their intricate strophes
        Of sorrow and grim despair
And wail of the snares that beset the race,
        Of the hate that befouls the air;
Let them beat their breasts at the lynching tree,
        And clench their fists at the sky—
My soul sinks, too, but I will not wail,
        I know there's a God on high.

So it's hope again, trust again, sing again,
        A whine is a weakling's plea;
The stars have not changed in their courses,
        The moon still orders the sea.

There's murder and hate in the Balkans;
        There's vengeance in far Cathay;

* *AIPC (American Inter-Racial Peace Committee) Bulletin*, October 1929.

Injustice and tyranny threaten
>Where men and greed have their sway;
They're lynching my sisters in Texas,
>They're flogging my sons on the farm;
But I know that Omnipotence watches,
>That God has a far-flung arm.

So it's hope again, trust again, sing again,
>Step proudly, your face to the skies,
Though the curtain of midnight fold you,
>At the dawning, the sun will arise.

Let despairing youth carve in their cameos,
>Black, lurid, and hellish hate;
Paint a Japanese couplet to emblazon the screed
>That Christ came to earth too late;
'Twas ever the way of the young to forget
>That Love is the one great rule;
Through ultimate tears this lesson is drilled,
>For this God sends us to school.

So it's hope again, trust again, sing again,
>For hate is the wild beast's yelp;
Though the pack of the jungle be at our heels,
>Omnipotent Love is our help.

THE PROLETARIAT SPEAKS *

I love beautiful things:
Great trees, bending green winged branches to a velvet lawn,
Fountains sparkling in white marble basins,
Cool fragrance of lilacs and roses and honeysuckle.

* *The Crisis*, 36, 1929, p. 378.

Or exotic blooms, filling the air with heart-contracting odors;
Spacious rooms, cool and gracious with statues and books,
Carven seats and tapestries, and old masters
Whose patina shows the wealth of centuries.

And so I work
In a dusty office, whose griméd windows
Look out in an alley of unbelievable squalor,
Where mangy cats, in their degradation, spurn
Swarming bits of meat and bread;
Where odors, vile and breath taking, rise in fetid waves
Filling my nostrils, scorching my humid, bitter cheeks.

I love beautiful things:
Carven tables laid with lily-hued linen
And fragile china and sparkling irridescent glass;
Pale silver, etched with heraldies,
Where tender bits of regal dainties tempt,
And soft-stepped service anticipates the unspoken wish.

And so I eat
In the food-laden air of a greasy kitchen,
At an oil-clothed table:
Plate piled high with food that turns my head away,
Lest a squeamish stomach reject too soon
The lumpy gobs it never needed.
Or in a smoky cafeteria, balancing a slippery tray
To a table crowded with elbows
Which lately the bus boy wiped with a grimy rag.

I love beautiful things:
Soft linen sheets and silken coverlet,

Sweet coolth of chamber opened wide to fragrant breeze;
Rose shaded lamps and golden atomizers,
Spraying Parisian fragrance over my relaxed limbs,
Fresh from a white marble bath, and sweet cool spray.

And so I sleep
In a hot hall-room whose half opened window,
Unscreened, refuses to budge another inch;
Admits no air, only insects, and hot choking gasps,
That make me writhe, nun-like, in sack-cloth sheets and lumps of
    straw.
And then I rise
To fight my way to a dubious tub,
Whose tiny, tepid stream threatens to make me late;
And hurrying out, dab my unrefreshed face
With bits of toiletry from the ten cent store.

LITTLE ROADS*

Come, let us go exploring little roads,
Gay, tiny paths, who faltering stray away
From the hard concrete of the main highway
That by its straight white sheen yells speed, and goads
To ruthless rush. But cool, green little roads
Wandering in sweet, lush places—surely a fay
Will lead our eager steps some green-gold day,
When from our souls they slip—speed-burdened loads.

* *The Dunbar News,* Vol. 11, No. 23, March 11, 1931.

O little wistful roads, you beckon me
To green-arched cloisters, hung with lilting note
Of feathered freed ones. Here, clad in leisured coat,
Plunge deep, where haste and time and grinding glare
Forgot. No ultimate aim, speed-folly free,
Let's track these sweet, small roads to their cool lair.

HARLEM JOHN HENRY
VIEWS THE AIRMADA *

Harlem John Henry mused into the sky,
"Beauty must be, must be, else life is dust."
 Outspread white wings that cleave the sullen gray,
 Myriads of double wings, swooping on in threes,
 Darting trilineate, far, near, in threes,
 Twelve, thirty, sixty. And converges now
 A flock of eagles, zooming crescendo roars;
 In threes and twelves, thrice tens, and six times ten;
 Six hundred more make dark the air, and cloud
 That lone sarcophagus commemorative of him
 Who cried in pain of soul, "Let us have peace!"

Beauty must be. But is this threat beauty?
Harlem John Henry hears the sinister drone
Of sextuples of planes. Sings jeeringly—

    "I've got wings,
      You've got wings,
      All God's chillen got wings!"

The Crisis, January 1932.

Lowers his gaze from dun rain-clouds of May,
Where scarring wings insult the quiet of spring,
And laughs aloud at that white pediment,
On whose Corinthian beauty blazons tall
The hope-fraught words that make the Hudson sneer,
And Harlem John Henry rock with mirthless mirth.

Beauty and peace? Beauty and War? Yet no.
Beyond the clouds that drift athwart the wings,
An ancient scene seeps in John Henry's soul.
Above the crashing zoom of mighty sound,
John Henry hears a throbbing, vibrant note—
    "Boom ba boom boom
      Boom ba boom boom
        Boom ba boom!"

Jungle bamboula beats the undertone
To all that fierce hoarse hiss above the sky.
Cruel corsairs of foul, slave-weighted ships;
Deep-throated wails from black, stench-crowded depths—

    "Sometimes I feel like a motherless child,
      Sometimes I feel like a motherless child,
      Sometimes I feel like a motherless child,
        A long ways from home!"

Beauty must be, must be, beauty, not death.
Harlem John Henry shivers. A gusty blast,
March winds benumbing Boston streets of old;
Crispus, the mighty, gone Berserk again,
Cursing his rage at red-coats' insolence,
Smiting a first wild blow for Liberty,
Dying, his face turned to the bullets' spirt.

>"Joshua fit de battle of Jericho, Jericho, Jericho!
>   Joshua fit de battle of Jericho,
>   An' de walls come tumblin' down!

Surcease of weary strife. An infant land
That marched erect to wealth on lowly backs.
Harlem John Henry's soul flowed to the past;
Zoom-zoom, resounding from the lowering sky,
Throbs like the bass-viol in the symphony—

>"Go down, Moses, way down in Egypt's land,
>   Tell ol' Pharaoh, let my people go!"

"Peace will be served by this, this airmada,
For me and mine, they said," John Henry mused.
"We helped build beauty tall unto the skies."
But years ere towers could rise of steel or stone,
Structures that clutched the rocks beneath the sea—
Boom-boom, drum beats of seventy years agone,
Boom-boom, answering the zoom of circling wings—

>"We are coming, Father Abraham,
>   One hundred thousand strong!"

And in the camp fires' glow o'er Wagner's heights,
A thousand black throats hurl their melody—

>"Dey look like men,
>   Dey look like men,
>   Dey look like men of war;
>   All dressed up in deir uniforms,
>   Dey look like men of war!"

Let us have peace! and weary warriors
Echoed the clatter of dropped pen that wrote
Fulfilment of three centuries of hope—

"Sometimes I feel like an eagle in de air,
  Some-a dese mornin's bright an' fair
  I'm goin' to lay down my heavy load,
  Goin' to spread my wings an' cleave de air!"

Who thought of beauty? Money marts and trade,
Argosies on seas, schools, churches, trusts and rings,
Politicians, wealth, cotton, wheat, machines,
Steel tracks, flung spider-like o'er continent.
Harlem John Henry hears a tiny voice,
Piping a thin thread through that turgid roar,
"Get money, get trades, be thrifty, be compliant!"

  "We are climbin' Jacob's ladder,
  We are climbin' Jacob's ladder,
  Every roun' goes higher, higher,
  Every roun' goes higher, higher,
    Soldiers of de Cross!"

Beauty is lost in smugness, sordidness,
Harlem John Henry sights a bombing plane,
Flashing white shafts across the lowering sky,
As back in Ninety-eight there gleamed cruel steel
Of jingo jabs, and little children sang
About a ship called Maine, that sank too soon.
Surging up a red-hot Cuban hill,
A medieval charge in khaki garb

  "There'll be a hot time in the old town to-night!"

Beautiful the feet of them that bring us peace!
Beauty in wings that cleave th' uncharted air!
Zoom-zoom, by threes, by twelves, six hundred more,
Etching their path from cruel past to now.

Harlem John Henry stands with lifted face,
Ruthless star-shells are shattering round his feet;
He staggers through the muck of No-Man's Land—

　　"Singin' wid a sword in my han',
　　　Singin' wid a sword in my han',
　　　　Purties' singing evah I heard,
　　　　Way ovah on de hill,
　　　De angels shout an' I sing too,
　　　Singin' wid a sword in my han'!"

Stumbles again from France and Flanders Field,
Back from the mire and rats and rotting dead,
And that wild wonder of a soundless world,
When death ceased thundering that November day.

　　"My Lord, what a mornin',
　　　My Lord, what a mornin',
　　　My Lord, what a mornin',
　　　　When de stars begun to fall!"

Back o'er the sea and home—that soon forgot,
Lustily singing, as he ever sang—

　　"Goin' to lay down my burden,
　　　Down by the river-side,
　　　Down by the river-side,
　　Goin' to study war no more!"

Now, o'er the Hudson on this day in May,
Circling six hundred wings, sinister, strange.
Harlem John Henry asks, was that in vain?
Beauty and peace? Must beauty die once more,
Slain o'er and o'er in stupid, senseless rage?
But from the throats of all those millions dusk,

Harlem John Henry hears that beauty's cry,
Beauty from pain, triumphant over hate—

   "Great day! Great day! Great day, de righteous
        marchin',
    Great day! Great day! God's goin' to build up Zion's
        walls,
    De chariot rode on de mountain top;
    God's goin' to build up Zion's walls!
    My God he spoke an' de chariot stop,
    God's goin' to build up Zion's walls!
      Great day! Great day!"

NEWSPAPER COLUMNS

FROM A WOMAN'S
POINT OF VIEW

Far be it for women to gloat over the way the sister-hood is attaching to itself the formerly exclusive masculine prerogatives. Not to mention women governors who are in danger of impeachment, there are bandits, bank robbers, embezzlers, female Ponzis, high flyers in finance, and what not. Is it votes for women, sun spots, post-war hysteria, the restless age, or the adolescence of the sex? Short skirts and cigarettes, fancy garters or sheik bobs, and all the rest of the feminine adornment or exposement, whichever happens to be the fad; Turkish women doffing the veil, Chinese women demanding the vote, the Orient donning the habiliments of the occident, Japanese women rolling their own, and college girls demanding smoking rooms, fur coats and chiffon hose; German women demanding the right of their own method of self expression, the youth movement, and the barefoot cult, artists and models dressed in a scant bunch of grapes, modistes threatening Victorian bustles, upheaval, unrest. Whatever is the blatant sex coming to?

So spake Isaiah twenty-six hundred years ago. Listen to his tirade: "Stretched-forth necks and wanton eyes, walking and mincing as they go, and making a tinkling with their feet; the chains and the bracelets and the mufflers; the bonnets and the ornaments of the legs, the headbands and the ear-rings; the rings and the nose jewels; the changeable suits of apparel, and the mantles and the wimples and the crisping pins, the glasses and the fine linens and the hoods and the vails. . . ."

Sic semper the female of the species.

* * *

She had not had time to bob her hair; the babies came too fast. She did not know much about international affairs, and the latest agony story in the howling tabloid was unread by her. Her gingham frocks were comfortable looking and she was able to hold a cooing bit of soft loveliness in the hollow of her arm, while she cut bread and butter for two others clinging to her skirts. Like Werter's Charlotte, when the artists begged to be allowed to sketch her she "went on cutting bread and butter." Nothing marred the serenity of her broad brow, and when the Man came home, it was to a well ordered house and steaming dinner and the understanding smile—all the domesticities that you read about in the old-fashioned novels and see in the hokum movies, and wish that they could exist again as of yore.

Where can you find her? Or is this a picture of two generations ago?

Her name is Legion. She is all over this jazz-mad, radio-crazed hysteric nation. Black and brown and yellow and white, she is to be found in villages and hamlets, in small towns, on farms, on Main Street, in New York and Chicago and Philadelphia and Pittsburgh. North, where she puts galoshes on the children and sends them forth to school; South, where she gives them a stick of sugar cane to appease the hunger of their sweet tooth; West, where they tramp miles across the prairie to the country school house, and in the effete land of the Cod and Bean, where she helps them to scan their Emerson before they pray to the God of the Pilgrim Fathers. She exists by the million, and realizing this, we can lean back and sigh with relief that the country is not going to the dogs any more than it was in the days when the first dauntless maiden had the temerity to leave off her bustle and hoop-skirt, or than England was when the fair maids at the court of Henry the Matrimonialist essayed the awful waltz, as they stood shamelessly and allowed courtiers to place a timid hand about their tiny waists.

No, she's a pretty stable article, woman. But she is not news, because she does nothing spectacular. It is only the abnormal things that get into print—like the old wheeze about the dog and the man and the biting episode, reversed. Comforting thought that. Plenty of mothers, and babies and bread and butter and little noses carefully wiped, and placid ignorance of abnormal psychology. Those women, in the first paragraph, who persist in breaking into print—little iridescent bubbles on the surface, forced up by ephemeral disturbance in the depths. But the depths remain cool, placid, unmoved, eternal. Basic womanhood. The backbone of the world.

* * *

Inhibition. Wonderful thing. When the dog was a puppy, he could not climb over a chair that was laid length-wise across the dining room door to prevent his coming into the room. But he grew into a great dog. And still the chair was laid across the door, and he would come and stand on the other side of the chair, and whine and howl more piteously to come in. He had only to lift his huge paws and step over the chair, but because he had been trained as a puppy to believe that he could not cross that chair, he stayed out in the hall and howled because he could not cross the barrier and enter the enchanted land of food and warmth and tempting smells.

So the man of color. He was told some generations ago,
"Thus far shalt thou go," and he still believes it. He has only
to lift his huge racial might and brush aside the frail barriers
separating him from the outside of things where he has been
relegated, and step into the promised land—but he does not
know that the barrier that seems so huge and real is afer all—
nothing but a few frail lies laid on end, and he looms above
them, and can step over them.

That ancient standard of beauty, for instance. How hard
it died. How many battles had to be fought before that lie
was brushed aside, and the true beauty of color came into its
own.

The French cabinet is changed again. One needs to be a
mental gymnast to keep up with the politics of Paris. If
Liberia or Haiti changed governments one-fifth as often, we
should have learned professors rushing into print to point out
the inherent inability of the Negro to govern himself, due to
his highly hysterical, volatile and unstable temperament. And
so forth.

*   *   *

This poor race of ours is always getting the worst of it. Now
after the stench of the Rhinelander case has died down, we
will have to carry the burden of owning the Artful Alice with
her bared romance and still more bared back, who married
a man so dumb that he thought a girl with a brown skin
father, a black brother-in-law, and a golden body was a white
woman. Though she repudiated her race, it must bear her on
its aching shoulders. Thank Heaven by this time next year,
the whole unsavory mess will be swept away with the crossword puzzle books, and the mah jong sets that we wasted our
good money upon.

*   *   *

If the custom of selecting fair maidens to represent localities and clubs at the annual football classic continues, we may expect a beauty pageant before or after the game, comparable on a small scale to the famous Atlantic City pageant of moneyed fame. Why not? Think of a huge hall with all the golden browns from all the burgs competing for a Lincoln-Howard golden cup? When this beauty pageant is a reality, and the winner of them all bows over her golden trophy—a year or two or three years hence, what fun it will be to tabulate the long list of names of those who "first thought of the idea and passed it on, you know."

January 9, 1926

. . . . . .

Speaking of the unobtrusive woman who does things without undue hooting through the megaphone, I am reminded of Edwin A. B. Kruse, of Wilmington, Delaware. Born in Porto Rico of German and Cuban parentage, she was educated in New England, and came to Delaware to teach in the "down state" schools for colored children. It was not long before she was in Wilmington, in a two teacher school, under a white principal. How she became the principal of that school; how it grew from a two room primary to a two story grammar school; how it was named after Gen. O. O. Howard, who came to dedicate it; how it grew to be an accredited high school, with a faculty from the best universities in the country, and graduates figuring on the roster of colleges north, south, east and west; how at the fiftieth anniversary of the school, educators came from far and near, even though a blizzard was raging, to pay homage to the woman who set the intellectual pace for Wilmington—all these things are not so well known. Miss Kruse is retired now on a pension, and a male principal carries on the work which she set so firmly on its feet, but ever and anon a group of teachers or old grads of the school make loving pilgrimage down to "206" East Tenth Street, where she has reigned in her home for so many years, and carry her a tribute for the work she has done. For nearly half a century colored Wilmington meant Howard High School, which gathered under its wings one of the finest little groups of intellectual men and women in the country—all due to the careful culling and pruning of the doughty principal. To have raised the intellectual standard of a community is no small task, but when you add to that, the enduring monument of a splendid school, and the education of thousands of boys and girls, you have an achievement well worth while, and a life that has been finely worth living.

*   *   *

We have come a long ways in the appreciation of our own, and the realization of our own possibilities. The writer can remember one day in a well known school when, in company with the other students, she helped stage a student musical strike because some visitors from the North asked the students to "sing some of the songs of your own people." It was considered degrading even to refer to the old songs of slavery, much less sing them. And this attitude was by no means uncommon. Colored people felt uncomfortable and self-conscious and humiliated when the old songs were sung, and few were there who saw any beauty in them. And now this book season brings three well edited, authentic, beautifully arranged editions of the "sorrow songs" out in one month, and the Negro public is falling over itself to buy and own them.

*   *   *

So with our standard of beauty. Nordic, vs. Hawaiian. Two little girls sat playing dolls on the porch of a summer hotel where a goodly group of women of the race tilted their rocking chairs to and fro. The little golden skinned child played with a brown skin doll, with shorty curly black hair, wine dark tints in its bisque cheeks, and brown eyes that opened and closed most realistically. The little dusky maiden played with a big blonde doll, all golden curls and pink lace. And she was frankly amused at her little friend's brown hued doll.

"I wouldn't play with a funny looking doll like that," she giggled, "Why it's DARK. Who ever saw a dark doll?"

Mother No. 2 registered fury. What mother could brook an insult to her own child?

"And look at her hair!" continued Mother No. 1, as she smoothed the golden curls of her own child. "Why it's funny stuff, I wouldn't have a doll with hair like that."

Mother No. 2 gathered her insulted brown baby to her outraged bosom and rose in dignified wrath.

"It's not funny," she sobbed. "And if it is, it's hair's heaps better'n yours!" and fled with all the honors of war.

* * *

This was less than fifteen years ago. Yet what Negro mother now would buy her child a Nordic doll in preference to one of the color of its own race? And every little colored girl treasures her little brown doll as the most cherished of her family. It shows progress in racial ideals more strikingly than any one thing that we can notice.

* * *

And have you noticed how the prevalence of the brown doll has tinged the characteristics of the dolls made for little white girls? The so-called "character doll," with the tinted com plexion? The Negro pigmentizes all American life, literature, music, art, dancing, dolls, dress, oratory, law and love. Is it a subtle overtone of brown, or a deep-rooted foundation of the great mother-heart of Africa, reaching out and embracing America?

*   *   *

Now that everybody has about finished rushing into print on the subject of the president's message, and either used up all the italics and exclamation marks praising his utterances, or put the linotypes out of business damning his faint praise, we rise to inquire why does the brother seem to feel that he must have a special paragraph devoted to him? There has never been a Jewish section to the message of the president, nor an Italian, nor Roman Catholic, nor one for the women, nor even the Labor Unions. Why is it that the American Negro always feels somehow that if he hasn't a special paragraph in the president's message, calling attention to his wonderful progress since emancipation (that's about all any president can say, there is nothing else)—if such a paragraph does not appear, somehow the party has slipped up, and the occupant of the White House will bear close watching. But if the obvious group of sentences is tacked on at the end of the annual message, announcing the fact that we have in our midst a Man and Brother, who has acquired some of this world's learning and goods in the past sixty years, and we want to treat him kindly therefore—well, when the Man and Brother reads it, he knows that God's in His Heaven, and all's right with the world, and nothing else much matters. Segregation and scant recognition, and Sweet trials and Rhinelander cases, and exclusion from colleges, and student strikes—nothing else matters. What must be the private mental reaction of the Chief Executive, when he realizes that a supposedly intelligent and modern racial group within the body politic, is standing around, like a child with its finger stuck in its mouth, waiting for teacher to call it by name and praise its sum on the blackboard?

*   *   *

Now they are howling about the danger of the obliteration of the sex line. Humph! Might not be so bad, if, in obliterating it, the single-standard of sex morality took its rightful place in the life of the nation. Time was when any worn out old rake felt cheated and defrauded if he could not marry a pure young innocent girl. But the innocent young thing is learning to demand equal chastity from her spouse to be, and in turn to feel herself cheated and defrauded if she gets shop-worn goods.

*   *   *

Statistics! The root and basis of the speech of the average colored man or woman. Never fails to get an enthusiastic hand. Two sure things an audience of our people will lap up and clamor for more—statistics of the "progress of the race," combined with a running history of the United States per Crispus Attucks, Peter Salem, Fort Wagner, Lake Erie, Jackson and New Orleans, Carrizal, San Juan Hill, and the Argonne Forest. Cheers! Billions of dollars of church, school and home property. Cheers! So many and so many teachers, preachers, doctors, newspapers, banks, insurance companies, etc., etc. More cheers! Everybody looking complacent, with side glances of triumph at the white members of the audience—if there are any.

Number Two. Go for the young people! Wonder what is to become of them. Lambast the movies, and the fact that they (the young folks) probably don't say their prayers nights. Criticize their dress, lip-sticks, rolled hose, boy friends, the

Charleston, and taste in cocktails. Paint the decline and fall of the Roman Empire due to just such a condition. Heavy sighs and groans, with perfervid Amens!

If you want to be a wonderful orator, there are your two speeches. Mix them with some poetry, tear a few stars from the universe, and throw in a moon or a sun, spread plentiful allusions to the Deity throughout—be sure you pronounce "God" in two syllables, with a rising inflection, learn a funny story or two, with a wise crack at the local situation, decry modernity and improvements with one breath, while you howl for progress with the other. Don't forget the old slave grandmother, and the washerwoman of the past generation. Hang a few Croix de Guerres around, and be sure that the old flag never touches the ground. If the occasion and the audience are big enough, you may combine the two formulas, and you will have a surefire howler, that will send your audience rocking into cheers. Try it sometime. Nothing easier.

January 16, 1926

The quality of being able to ignore that which is not agreeable, or that which interferes with whatever preconceived plan is in our minds, either a thesis to be established or a point to be made, is a wonderful accomplishment. And lest the intricate involvement of the preceding sentence be too Hergesheimer-ish for the lay reader, let us say that it is a good thing to know how to ignore unpleasant truths.

All of which thought is brought about by a recent editorial release from the "Lawyer and Banker" and "Southern Bench and Bar Review," wherever that may be. "Sheriff or Coroner?" asks the editorial. And proceeds to attack the recent release of the Inter-Racial Commission on "Mississippi and the Mob." The tone is far better than might have been found in any Southern publication ten years ago, for instance. Deploring mob violence, there is the usual appeal to the law to do its duty by the horrific black rapists. Figures of lynched persons are correctly quoted—doubtless obtained from the nation-wide advertisement of the "Shame of America." Three thousand, four hundred forty-five persons lynched in the United States; 2610 in the South. Of these 2400 admitted guilt.

Now here comes the charming Southern irresponsibility— 2400 admitted guilt. But guilt of what? The inference is made quite openly that these 2400 persons admitted the crime of rape. While correct figures are quoted correctly as to the number lynched, and the number guilty, the crimes for which they were lynched are carefully concealed. The number of women lynched is not mentioned. The less than 2 per cent guilty of rape is not taken into consideration. The 30 per cent only accused of rape is ignored. The crimes of murder, arson, theft, and lesser misdemeanors for which the rope and shot gun and torch were the punishment is glossed over. The figures so carefully collated by Munro Work of the Negro Year Book and the National Association for the Advancement of Colored People are deliberately used to make good the Southerners' thesis that all black men are lynched because the Nordic gorge rose at the thought of the despoiling of the flower of Southern womanhood.

How is one to get the idea over to the world that raping is not the chief cause for lynching? That white men are rapists? That black men are killed for seventy per cent more crimes than this one?

Southern white women look facts in the face, and tell the

truth, when they touch the matter at all. At least more of the truth than Southern white men. Tell any Southerner, north or south, or any Southern sympathizer of the Shame of America. Pouf! Away go facts, truth, everything, and out trots the same old lie, all clothed in new language, fresh words, and modern phraseology. There is no getting over that hurdle of smooth ignoring of the facts in the case. There is no getting past it. There is no breaking it down. You may argue until you are purple in the face—or until your larynx cracks, you are met with that same horrible, smooth, Chinese-like polite lie—"The bestial crime of rape."

Watch for the speeches in the Congressional Record when the Dyer bill comes up in this Congress—if it does come up, if you want to learn a lesson in elimination of that which you don't wish told.

January 23, 1926

The classic remark of the Shah of Persia when asked his opinion of Prohibition in America, "When does it start?" gains new significance, if one studies the advertisements in the daily papers closely. Malt extract. Bottling machines. Rye extract. Wine presses. Barrels. Kegs. Charcoal barrels. And so forth. If not exactly ad infinitum, certainly ad intoxicatem. But it has remained for the very cream of advertisements in this dry and Volsteadian age to be perpetrated. A drug guaranteed to cure drunkenness. Testimonial from poor down trodden wife, who had suffered many beatings at the hand of drunken spouse. Just put a drop in her husband's coffee, and lo, instead of Saturday night beatings, now she goes to the movies, and does a Marathon to the bank Monday mornings. Absolute cure for drunkenness. Just send for sample and booklet of testimonials.

How long has it been since we have seen such advertisements? Seven years. And if we are dry, why do we need such magic cures? If prohibition has prohibited, why do drunken gentlemen still come home Saturday nights and wipe up the floor with their faithful and suffering wives? Can it be— could it be—But no. There is no drinking. God has wiped out the curse of the nation and the advertisement was a mistake. The pressman absent-mindedly mixed up the forms with those of eight years ago. Drawing a deep sigh of relief, we go our way secure in the comforting thought that all law is immutable, and the nation is safe under the wings of the Eighteenth Amendment.

* * *

So the Connecticut klansmen have seen the light, and Arthur Mann, former Kligraph of Connecticut, indicts the whole organization as nothing less than an organization of greed. "It has become a travesty on patriotism," he adds, "and a blasphemous caricature professing Protestantism. It is not only anti-Catholic, and anti-Jew, but absolutely unAmerican and anti-Protestant. It has become, without question, the greatest menace facing our people today."

All of which is long since known to the general public. But I have often wondered how the women klansmen, or shall we say klanswomen, square themselves with their own conscience. For the men organize themselves under the guise of patriotism and racial purity. But the women? What must a klanswoman think, if she thinks at all, or, if she has anything to think with, of the concommitance of violence and mobocracy that follow in the trail of the organization? Or, are they like the women of the mountains of Kentucky and North Carolina and Tennessee in relation to the feuds of their men folk—certain that the violence is right, no matter how they suffer? But the mountain women are born into their feuds and their misery; klanswomen deliberately elect to become a part of lawlessness. Poor white women! One cannot but be sorry for them; they have so much to bear—their own men—the burdens of the white race, and all the other sorrows of womanhood.

* * *

Sessue Hayakawa, the Japanese actor, is defying public Nordic opinion in a new play, not a motion picture, called *The Love City*. Wonder how long it will last? For a white woman prefers a Chinese to a white man—albeit the Chinese is a prince, and the white man her deserting husband. And a Chinese dive keeper kills a white man, who makes too free with his beloved flower, though she had been set to tempt and lure him. It all ends very badly for the Caucasian, though the Mongolians are by no means happy at the end. But just how does Sessue expect an American public to stand for anything that does not end with White Man completely on top, all moral and waving the American flag and race purity, 'n' everything? Sessue must wake up. And if he wants to produce a play showing the conflict of races—and not lose money on it, he must study *White Cargo* and *Aloma of the South Seas* and the *Bird of Paradise*. Remember that ever and ever more must the white man refuse to mingle his blood with brown ladies—on the stage—and always chant a paean of race purity, and the *Star Spangled Banner*, while little brown girl, fades sobbing into the arms of her faithful brown lover, who has waited in mute expectancy in the background until White Man is through with her. No, Mr. Sessue. *The Love City* will not do. It tells the truth. Give the American public anything but the truth. Give it lies that it wants, and it will rise and shout your praises and pour gold into your pocket. Tell the truth and it will crucify you, and throw your rent carcass to the dogs.

*   *   *

Notice how we are getting away from resolutions? Not the
New Year kind that are no sooner made than broken, but the
kind that the Man and Brother was wont to put on paper,
with an air and a flourish of therefores, whereases, be it
resolved? Remember the good old days, when should there
be a grievance, or a condition that seemed to need the attention
of the race, a mass meeting was staged, fiery speeches indulged
in; then the chairman appointed a committee on resolutions,
who retired, and after due deliberation, much sweating of
phrases, and inverted grammar, finally brought in pages of
resolutions, wherein God was patronized, and the rest of the
universe tolerated, while the evil in question was flayed with
much verbosity, and no end of split infinitives? Those were
the days! The resolutions were adopted with cheers, and
everyone went home happy, feeling that the race was waking
up, and now the white man had better watch his step. And
too often everything stopped right there.

We don't have so many resolutions now, and not so many
fiery speeches. And our mass meetings are apt to strike the
note that if somebody hits the Man and Brother, he'd better
hire himself a good lawyer and make the hittee pay for his
little party. And that to hire a lawyer takes money, and that
it is up to the Man and Brother to pay his own bills, and
stop talking about things and ACT! Verily, the world do
move!

They aren't even reading resolutions at funerals any more!

January 30, 1926

. . . . . .

And now we are to budget our days. Mrs. John T. Sherman
called upon all the women of the country, by virtue of her

presidency of the General Federation of Women's Clubs, to observe Thrift Week by economizing time. Days and hours to be budgeted as a safeguard against waste. Which reminds me of the story of the meek little woman who was a witness in a murder case. The prosecuting attorney had established the definite fact of the hour by her averring that she knew it was seventeen minutes of nine because she looked at the clock just before she heard the fatal shot fired, and told Johnny he'd better hurry or he'd be late for school. And she knew it was nine o'clock, when she saw the man getting over the fence, for she stood on the porch and heard the school bell ring, and wondered if Johnny had managed to get in the school house door.

"And can you tell what you did in the intervening seventeen minutes?" asked the Judge.

"It wasn't much, sir. I just did up the breakfast things, swept off the back porch, shook the parlor rugs, took up the ashes in the dining room stove, emptied the ice box pan, wiped off the kitchen shelf, hung up the dish towels to dry, and was just going out in the back yard to carry the milk to the pigs when I saw the man getting over the fence."

Budget time! Can you hear the busy mothers and house-wives all over the land asking the lady president of the General Federation what does she know about saving time, or using it? There's just the difference between her idea of time in the home, and the regular housemother's as there is between the notions of a graduate of Domestic Science who can cook one lovely dish at a time, and that of the mother of a hungry brood, who knows to a minute just when to put on meat, potatoes, greens, pie and hot rolls, so they will all come out just right at the same moment.

Budget time! CAN'T YOU HEAR them snort!

The poor Virgin Islands are contending in court for the right of "Free speech, and a free press, and jury trials to the residents of the Islands." Blended with these inherent rights is a general attack on all the laws of the Virgin Islands, as enacted by the Colonial Councils, and a tale of bitter political and racial animosities.

It was inevitable. The little dark islands, erstwhile happy and contented become a seething vortex of racial prejudice and hatred as soon as the hand of the United States grapples them by the throat. Prohibition here, and no more rum manufactured there. Poverty. Distress. Surreptitious law-breaking. Break down of pride and self-respect. Race prejudice. Setting of brother against brother. Unjust white man's laws, enacted to keep the black man intimidated, and the white ruler in an exalted position. So a trial is brought in the United States Circuit Court of Appeals, and the Negro editor of *The Emancipator* demands of the land of free speech whose flag waves over his native home the right to criticize a policeman for cruelty to an old woman in making an arrest. And the right to be tried by a jury.

Let's see. Did not one Edmond Burke some hundred and fifty years ago argue for the right of the colonists in this country to be tried by a jury? Was not there a big fuss made about that trial by jury business back in the 12th century, and a Magna Charta signed? And there isn't a word anywhere to say that it is only white men who have the right of free speech or a trial by jury—and a jury of their peers.

Poor little Virgin Islands—Virgin no longer, but despoiled.

* * *

The radio, the newest toy, has been put to many strange uses. It has been figuring in novels and songs and stories for some time, and Griffith used it in one of his latest big pictures to

hang a murder case upon. But now comes Florida—quite in
the public eye lately, and broadcasts a lynching. The affair is
staged near a broadcasting station. Northern visitors are called
out of their beds to see the horror, and to taste well of the
sweetness of a murdered man's cries. The microphone records
and transmits the victim's dying moans, and the Floridians
far and near, who are unable to be among those present tune
in on Station S-A-V-A-G-E and have their cup of cruelty
filled to its poisoned brim. Shots come with startling distinct-
ness over the aerials of the listeners-in, and head phones and
loud speakers give out alike the yells and curses of the superior
Nordics who need five hundred to kill one. Poor Nick
Williams, who was so stupid as to speak impudently to a
white shop keeper, albeit that shopkeeper was a woman, paid
the penalty of an indiscreet tongue with his life. But the glory
and grandeur of his death lies in the fact that it is the first
one in the world to be broadcast. And thus is Nick a martyr
to science, and the purity of Nordic womanhood is upheld,
and the superiority of the Nordic male is once more established.

·   ·   ·   ·   ·   ·

February 6, 1926

It is a fine thing to found a school, or an institution, to
conceive, build and establish a thing of brick, stone, mortar
and wood. But when all is said and done, it is evanescent and
must crumble, even as did Ozymandias in the desert. The
real work done is in the building in the lives and hearts of
myriads of people who must pass through the halls, an ideal,
faith, ambition, and in reaching out through the individual
lives into dark and unknown places, and letting the influence
grow in ever widening circles, like a ripple in the water.

It is possible to do this without building a school or

founding an institution. Sometimes the mere presence of some individualities in a community is an influence as potent as that wielded by the head of an institution. Countless lives are reached, and countless hearts uplifted because one person has chosen to live a life of helpfulness.

Such a woman is Violet Johnson of Summit, N.J. She came up from North Carolina to Brooklyn, when she was a slim young thing, and eventually reached Summit, a score or more years ago, and Summit is deeply cognizant of her presence there. Summit is a proud little town in the hills of North Jersey, all rich folks, and commuters, and clannishness and indifference to the poor or the working class. Or so Summit was until Violet began to transform it. Most of the colored people in the town were of the working class, and nothing was being done for them. Girls waited in hotels, or entered service of the very wealthy and their evenings and holidays hung heavy on their hands. There was no colored church; there were no activities among our people. So Violet Johnson rolled up her sleeves and went to work. Recreational activities for girls, a home where they could live and have social life after working hours, a firmly established Baptist Church, and best of all, a changed attitude towards the colored people on the part of the wealthy class has been the result of her years of quiet, unheralded work. She brought to the little town the best that we have and presented them at the leading churches so that the white population—their entire conception of the Negro too often gleaned from the kitchenry—might know and see our contribution to the literature, music and history of America. A deeper respect for the Negro permeated the atmosphere of the haughty little town, and the Negro in the town held his own head higher for having gained the respect of his white neighbor.

To her friends, Summit is Violet Johnson, and Violet Johnson is Summit. So far as we are concerned, she put it on the map.

Of course, she is a club woman, and is one of the vice presidents of the New Jersey State Federation; an indefatigable worker, and a familiar figure at National Conventions. Her activities sweep all North Jersey, and her slogan is "Talk, tell them all about it, let the good word go forth; they need to be told about our work and what we have done!" But, she does not want herself talked about.

.   .   .   .   .   .

Speaking of the distinction between art and propaganda. Until the Negro realizes the sharp cleavage between the two, his position in the world of art will be experimental. Circumstances have made the race keenly alive to the necessity of placing his case before the world. Each and everyone of us is, of necessity, a propagandist. We are forced by cruel challenges to explain, show our wares, tell our story, excuse our shortcomings, defend our positions. And we insist that every Negro be a propagandist. We want our pictures to be painted with an eye single to the exploits of the race. We want our poets to sing of the fame of the Negro. We want our novels, short stories to have a bludgeon, none too cleverly concealed within the narrative, hitting the Nordic and exalting the Negro. We want our singers to appeal for the Negro. We forget that didacticism is the death of art; that when Ariel girds on the armor of St. George, he sinks beneath the weight of the harness, and loses his heaven sent gift. We forget that when Shakespeare dips his pen in commonplaceness and tries to emulate North, he is a mere chronicler, and no creator. And the divine spark of creation is what the world needs, as well as records of those who have had the divine spark.

The real novel about, by and for the Negro will be written only when we can see clearly the sharp cleavage between the work of art and the propaganda pamphlet; when we learn to tell a story for the sake of the artistry and the sheer delight of a good tale, without an eye for the probable effect of the story on the consciousness of the white man.

Batuola for instance.

* * *

An Oxford lecturer prophesies that chemistry will create synthetic man.

As if there were not already plenty of them.

Maybe he means the Robots.

* * *

A college in Baltimore blames radio sets for the loss of pep—lowered efficiency, stupidity in class and general nonscholastic attainments. The president finds the radio an aid to late hours and not an aid to general culture. Headaches and fagged maidens have banished the receiving set from the classic atmosphere. Aerials are down and head phones in the cellar. The president goes farther and would ban the poor radio from the business world. It is easy to pick out the business men who own radios, he says. Their faces tell the story of late hours, and much strain from listening to jazz bands and banquets, and late theatre broadcastings, and picking up of Cuba and Montreal and Los Angeles.

Well, there's some comfort in the reflection that it is the radio which is responsible for the jaded girls. It might have been suppers, jazz hounds, midnight rides, petting parties, novels, cigarettes, hip flasks, ukulele practice or saxophone quartets. Query: Who is to be commended, Prexy for his innocence in placing the blame on the radios, or for his insularity in banishing a modern invention? Or the fair maidens for their sweet childish love for the dear radio, or their cleverness in making poor Prexy place the blame on the loud speaker? It takes a woman to hang the sign in the right place every time.

*　*　*

Speaking of bans. Now it's the Charleston. Humanity is a hysterical animal. Every new fad or fashion at once has its denouncers from the pulpit, platform, professors's chair. It once was a penal offense to bathe every week, and the owner of the first bathtub was looked at askance. Remember the Shifters? Harmless kid prank, where the whole of adolescence all over the country, white, black and otherwise united in one joyous whoop of fun, put on little paper clips, and called themselves Shifters. Nothing to it. Yet the Grownups arose solemnly and denounced them as immoral, and schools banished Shifters from classes. The most innocent thing in the world. Yet sour faced old maids and tight mouthed dessicated men teachers howled denunciations at the merry boys and girls who meant nothing but to have a passing bit of fun. The Shifter died as all fads will die; passed into the limbo where repose the celluloid bows of our youth and the cigarette pictures of your father's boyhood. But not before several hundred clean and withered old souls with suppressed desires and over active imaginations written all over them had licked their lips in anticipation of the downfall of Youth.

Then it was the Dance Marathons and pulpits rocked. Now it is the Charleston. The Y.W.C.A., in Chicago, has started a clinic, where Charleston steppers will be laboratory specimens. Records will be kept of their heart action, fatigue curve, loss or gain of fat, and tape measures of the ankles as they twist and turn.

Some schools have banned the Charleston from their classrooms, and others announce that it may be danced ad lib. Charleston contests are being held, writers rush eagerly into print to prove that the dance was not invented by Negroes, but is the legitimate brain-child of a pure Nordic. Every jazz orchestra throws in the rhythmic lilt of the refrain of the original song into every piece they play. Somewhere, sometime, somehow, the thud of the refrain "Charleston" sounds in the piece. Exhaustive discussions are rife proving that the colored boy or girl does not dance it right, anyhow, there is some inherent reason why they could not get the intricacies of its steps, but the twist is done just right by the "superior" race.

The Negro looks on and listens placidly to all these mental and physical gyrations.

He has been dancing it for five years, and is pretty well tired of it.

Perfectly willing to let Mr. White Man take his leavings from the dance hall, and do as best he can with his undeveloped sense of rhythm.

For it is the history of dance and song in America, that the white man takes up where the Negro leaves off. And just as aforesaid White Man is getting quite excited over his rare discovery the Man and Brother, and Woman and Sister have hied them to fresh fields and pastures new in the musical world.

February 13, 1926

. . . . . .

For centuries the white man has built up a propaganda about that very word *white* that has driven into countless millions of minds a connotation that is about as complete and as subtle a mass of propaganda as can be found anywhere on this globe—or any other, I fancy. Apart from the fact that white robes, white-winged angels, white mansions, and a white-faced God with white hair have been thrust upon the world by the subtle propagandists as the only true and possible heaven, white has been forced to connote correct treatment, purity of motive, high ideals and freedom of spirit. "Treated me white," for example, as the highest method of treatment. "Acted like a white man." "Acted white." "Free, white and twenty-one," as a few examples of the completeness of the propaganda which has filled our books, schools, churches, vocabularies, vaudeville sketches, songs, histories and mode of thought and expression. And the Negro, of course, is just beginning to perceive whither this expression is leading him. He counters with his "Brown," which is doing pretty well, thank you. But he still needs to be on the alert for the man whose highest praise of treatment is that he was treated "white."

* * *

As if it were not enough to dramatize the Ten Commandments, now someone has started an argument about the desirability or undesirability of reading them in school, with all the usual bunk about religious prejudices, the commandments being outworn, and all the rest of it.

When Legislators haven't anything else to do, they jump on the poor teachers about reading the Bible or not reading it, as the case may be.

If someone could just get hold of one of these backwoods solons and make him take charge of a school room for a week, it might be wonderfully illuminating to said solon.

He would find out, for instance, that when Dear Teacher stands up to read the Bible, dear little Johnny and Mary and

Betty and Lizzie and Andy fold their little hands, and their dear little faces go absolutely blank, as do their dear little minds. They oppose to the Word of God a stone wall of impassivity and imperviousness that is complete and absolute. And they have no more idea what Teacher is reading out of the Book of Books than if she were reading Sanscrit.

It is a part of the daily routine; a boresome interlude in the otherwise joyous events of a day that might bring all sorts of possibilities.

Their bright eyes are fixed expectantly on Dear Teacher, to note when she slips her fingers between the Book, and starts to bow her head. Then they chime in lustily with the Lord's Prayer. And they know and she knows that so far as any real instruction goes, it is a mere formula.

Nobody ever learned the Bible by having a few verses read at the beginning of the day—but they did learn a respect for a book which seemed to have the magic effect of getting peace and order and harmony to start off the day.

Now, if the law-makers of the land who get so eager about the matter, really want the Bible taught throughout the land— why, it would not be a bad idea for some of them to learn something about it themselves.

An eminent writer has been running a series of popularizing articles in a well-known weekly on "The Book Which Nobody Knows," bringing the Bible into a condensed form for the benefit of the masses who have grown to like their religious literature pre-digested.

And he does not always conform to the strict interpretation of the narratives, poems and drama of the Book of Books, himself. Some parts of his story are quite askew.

UNE FEMME DIT

The title of this column changes this week. It is to be regretted that it must be done. The writer is a peace-loving soul, with conservative tastes, and getting old enough to dislike change from comfortable well-known conditions to new things. But it had to be done. The title, "A Woman's Point of View" got to be so popular that it cropped up in all sorts of places and the writer found herself reading articles that bore her title, but not her imprint. That is regrettable. There are so many words in the English language, over a half-million, are there not? And so many phrase books. And thesauruses galore. But evidently not accessible to some editors. Am almost tempted to hunt up some of these battered old dictionaries and word books, left over from the crossword puzzle craze, and distribute them to the fraternity of the Fourth Estate. So, the English language not being large enough to accommodate all the female columnists extant, recourse must be made to the French. So—"One Woman Says" in French is the future caption of these burning thoughts.

Let us hope there will be no further need of charge.

Never did like anyone to have a hat like mine. If someone did buy one—even though imitation may be the sincerest flattery—said imitated hat went promptly to the rummage sale—even though to go hatless was the alternative.

* * *

Lulu Belle has come to Philadelphia; has been seen by the surrounding country, and has conquered. By now it is delighting New York.

130

And you can hear a howl go through the country like the wail of lost souls from the Man and Brother and the Woman and Sister over Lulu Belle.

"The worst side of Negro life depicted."

"Why did not Belasco and Sheldon pick out the best types of our race—our Washington and Cleveland and best New York and Philadelphia and Pittsburgh colored people and show them on the stage?"

"Why present the demi-monde and crap shooters, prize fighters, barbers and slum denizens to write a play around?"

"Why scenes in cabarets and saloons and bedrooms, instead of fashionable drawing rooms?"

"It will hurt us with the white people, who want to believe that what Octavius Roy Cohen says is true."

And in spite of all that, *Lulu Belle* is a wonderfully fine piece of production.

And why should a white man do our propaganda for us?

Our so-called "best people," our lovely drawing rooms and high types of men and women are uninteresting. Just as uninteresting as would be a pageant written around—well the Coolidge family for instance.

Lulu Belle, the play, is alive, vivid with color, action, romance, character study. Lulu Belle, the woman, is thoroughly detestable. She has not a single redeeming quality—except her vivid beauty, and the fact that she runs true to form. She is elemental, primordial, the Lilith of the ages, she is, in fact—Carmen.

Edward Sheldon and Charles MacArthur did not go far afield, when they conceived the plot of *Lulu Belle*. They simply took the old story, popularized by Merrimee, and set to music by Bizet, and now lately Russianized under the title of *Carmencita and the Soldier*. The old, old story, as old as the story of Adam and Eve. Transplanted now from Seville and the Pyrenees to Hell's Kitchen and Harlem and Paris. There is no detail of Bizet's opera missing. Lulu Belle swaggers into the noisome, picturesque, teeming streets of Hell's Kitchen, as Carmen swaggers into the streets of the Spanish town. Lulu Belle fights with one of her associate street gamins, as Carmen fights with one of the other girls in the cigar factory. Lulu Belle tempts the virtuous young barber, married and decent, into forgetting his respectability, as Carmen tempts Don Jose, the gentle young officer into forgetting his duty as a soldier. Lulu Belle is faithless to the barber, and he is cognizant of the fact, yet sinks so low that he aids and abets her in her plunder of the victims who come to her apartment in Harlem, even as Carmen is faithless to Don Jose, who deserting the army becomes a smuggler and a thief in her band of smugglers. The infatuated George is deaf to the entreaties of his uncle to return to his wife and suffering family, even as Don Jose is deaf to the pleadings of his erstwhile sweetheart, Michaela, who comes with a message from his dying mother. Lulu Belle deserts George when he is in dire trouble because of his love for her and goes with Vicompte de Viliars even as Carmen deserts Don Jose for the Toreador. And George, the beggar and ex-convict, finds Lulu Belle in Paris, and wreaks horrible vengeance on her, even as Don Jose finds Carmen in Seville, in the hour of her greatest triumph, and makes her pay the penalty of her falseness and cruelty.

There are no details lacking to make the parallel complete. Lulu Belle is superstitious, a believer in dreams and their interpretations, a gambler, who must rub her hands on the hump of her hunchback mascot before she goes into a friendly game of craps, even as Carmen is superstitious and helps the smugglers gamble, and reads her fortune in cards, and interprets dreams.

And neither seems to have a soul. They go from lover to lover with blithe abandon. The preferred man is the last one, and the one with money to spend for jewels. And the age-old law of retribution and compensation finds them both at last and fulfills itself upon their lovely, passionate, false, golden bodies.

Lulu Belle is Carmen, and Carmen is Lulu Belle, and both are ageless, eternal, universal, of no race, no clime, no color, no condition. They are in the jungles, and in the drawing rooms of the most exclusive Nordics. They are white and yellow and brown and black. They have always been and always will be.

So why rise and gibber at Sheldon and Belasco?

* * *

The author and producer probably had no more idea of putting Lulu Belle forward as typifying Negro womanhood than Mr. Stribling had of making Peter in *Birthright* the typical young Negro college graduate. He was an individual, not a type. A reflection of his environment. Even the most ignorant Ku Klux Klanner must know how that Lulu Belle, while a type, is not a typical colored girl, or rather not all colored girls. High schools, colleges, Y.W.C.A., Christian Endeavors, B.Y.P.U., teachers, decent working girls, rural maidens—it is not in these groups that we find the Lulu Belles. Not even the most rabid Negro hater will fail to realize that. We need not concern ourselves about that idea becoming prevalent among our enemies.

* * *

Rather let us look at the beauty of the play. Its sumptuous setting. Its vivid color. Its clash of personalities. Its tropic abandon. Its riot of color and sound. Its frank revelations. Its minute details. The richness of its blending of complexions, frankly natural and beautiful. In some spots the drama is so true that it hurts. In others, it is informative. And one can but marvel at the patient endeavor of the authors and producer to penetrate below the surface of the kind of Negro life which they depict in the play, and present to the audience the results of their painstaking studies.

*   *   *

Of one thing we may be sure—our people will have something to discuss, argue about, get into heated controversies over, write bitter editorials about, denunciatory letters, diatribes from the pulpits, and long-winded papers form Uplift Societies for some weeks. Debates are forthcoming, whether Mr. Belasco means to insult the race, or merely to present a cross-section of metropolitan life. Resolutions—in spite of the conclusion at which we arrived a few weeks ago—will be drawn up, denouncing Mr. Belasco, Mr. Sheldon, Mr. McArthur, Miss Ulric and Mr. Hull for their slander against a race that has always proved loyal to the union, and the saviors of San Juan Hill (not in the play) and the Argonne Forest. We shall hear of Booker Washington and Du Bois, and Harriet Tubman and Lillian Evans, and Mrs. Bethune—all in one wild and hysterical outburst. See if we don't.

In the meanwhile, some of us would like to ask Miss Ulric, How did she find out about that darker brown streak down the middle of the spine of mulatto women?

February 27, 1926

.   .   .   .   .   .

Speaking of this month's Mercury, nearly everyone has had a fling at poor L. M. Hussy, with his "Aframerican, North and South," and since he is down, one kick more or less cannot do any harm. His idea of the isolation of the poor cultured Negro South is a wierd one. Someone should take him gently by the hand and induct him into some of the communities where large numbers of cultured Negroes live— Durham, North Carolina, for instance, or Baltimore, or New Orleans, or Atlanta, or scores of like cities. He might change his ideas of what isolation means. Surely there were never happier or more self-satisfied groups to be found in any race anywhere than those above mentioned, especially in Durham.

But—why should all of us or any of us waste perfectly good time, type, paper, or energry frothing at the pen over what our white contemporaries think or write of us? We will rush into print and assert, deny, asseverate, fulminate, vociferate, and use up the dictionary, the thesaurus, and the encyclopedia with masses of statistics to prove that these statements made by the Nordics are all wrong. And to whom do we prove them? To our own dear selves. For said Nordic never sees our answers, or our papers or our statements. Wouldn't read them if he did. Having flung his bolt, he looks not to see who picks it up.

Someone should offer a prize, since prize awards are in the air for the most effective method of getting our answers over to the other side of the racial stream.

It must be admitted, however, that Hussy's dictum that "Great Cultures come only from assured peoples, from peoples of abounding self-esteem," is a splendid point. Grant him correct; then the African was a great race, a great people, and their art a great culture—or else his axiom is not true.

* * *

H. L. Mencken, the great Iconoclast, and a god of the Iconoclasts, says that the inferiority complex got into everything Booker T. Washington said! That a Negro was almost as good as a white man, was the best he could think. In like manner, this inferiority complex is also in Du Bois, who is more intent on getting Negroes into Pullman cars, or in Kiwanis clubs, than in finding the Negro soul! Wow! Du Bois with an inferiority complex!

*   *   *

Having duly celebrated Negro History Week in the same week with the birthdays of Lincoln, Douglass and St. Valentine, and in near juxtaposition to Washington's and Longfellow's birthdays and Ash Wednesday, let us hope the poor tired teachers will stop to take breath, and let the bewildered brains of their million charges recover from the shock and indigestion of so much knowledge, history, Negrophile history, literature, art and science; so much patriotism, Negro spirituals, cherry tree incidents, Gettysburg speech, Christ on the mountain with the Tempter, Children's Hour and Paul Revere, Second Inaugural, Farewell Address, Roland Hayes, Phyllis Wheatley, Crispus Attucks, Hearts and Flowers, ground-hog day, Frederick Douglass mixed up with Stephen Douglass, the great debater, cupid, the first bluebird, snow storms, soft coal nuisance, end of longest strike in history, and Booker Washington, the Father of his Country; while George swept all over Hampton Institute. That is the way the poor youngsters' brains seem—an omelette of February data. What the little month lacks in chronological length, it amply makes up in historical depth.

Now they are saying that a certain well-known actress has colored blood in her veins, hence her understanding delineation of a mulatto gamin. Well, the accusation places her right in the ranks of the immortals. We claim them all; it is a sign that they have arrived, when we put forth our arresting hand and call them ours—Alexander Hamilton, Robert Browning, one of the Kings of Spain, Warren G. Harding,

Charlie Chaplin, and there are still others. If the Germans can claim Shakespeare, what is to prevent us from claiming everything in sight? It's good politics.

. . . . . .

March 6, 1926

. . . . . .

"Will Uncle Sam Dishonor Our Women?" breathlessly says an esteemed contemporary, anent the marriage bill now up in Congress. Hardly. No one can dishonor a woman but herself, in the first place. She may be insulted, reviled, even raped, but dishonor can not be put upon her, except in so far as she is a consenting party to the aforementioned proceedings.

But—leaving quibbling out of the question—has not Uncle Sam been a silent party to the rape of black women for over three hundred years?

Think it over.

* * *

About this time of the year some folks begin to wear a mysterious and harried look, and to talk in vague terms of income tax blank computations, helpful lawyers, difficulties in establishing exemptions, etc., etc.

And nine-tenths of those who are talking the loudest never had a blank to fill out.

Or an income large enough to be taxed.

And never will have.

But it sounds well to appear to be paying an income tax— even if it is like some of those $1.25 ones that were published last year in the list which we all read so carefully.

Watch out for the four-flusher who "was up all night figuring his income tax."

He might have been up all night, and he might have been figuring, but the chances are, that it was not on what he has to pay to the government, but how he could stretch that little hundred dollars a month to cover rent, groceries, clothes, insurance, shoes, and a trip to the movies on Saturday nights.

March 13, 1926

.　.　.　.　.

The dark nations are having a hard time. Poor little Liberia has been raped on a rubber proposition, and for the first time in its history will have a white minister from this country. Haiti, as usual, is in hot water; the Virgin Islands have had a cross-eyed decision handed down in Philadelphia, which out of its welter of word, affirms nothing, but leaves no doubt in the minds of the readers what the intent of this nation is concerning the freedom of the Islanders. Is it not true that the octopus is a white fish—reptile, creature of prey, what not? Its slimy white tentacles gripping, plunging, exploring, seizing, devouring all in its reach? Yes, surely, it is white.

*　*　*

Lothrop Stoddard has found a mare's nest and cannot count the eggs. He does this once in a while. Now it's the Jews about whom he has made wonderful discoveries and announced them in the March *Forum*. He sets forth a "biological background," which will help them in uncovering the festering sore, of which the editor speaks in the foreward. Said festering sore being the whole discussion of the Jewish question.

For once Mr. Stoddard seems to have struck a fairly accurate, and for him, dispassioned presentment of the racial aspects of the case. Knowing his attitude on the darker races, we can infer that his love for the Jew is purely scientific. Grudgingly he admits what pseudo-scientists vehemently deny, that the ancient Egyptians belonged to the Hamitic race. This is distinctly refreshing. In the light of the unearthing of the Tutankhamen—who must perforce be of Aryan stock, because of his high degree of culture, it is interesting to find one Nordic admitting that the ancient civilization of the Nile was Negroid.

So, Mr. Stoddard admits that the Jews in their sojourn in Egypt acquired Negro blood, which persists to this day, showing in frizzy hair, thick lips and prognathous jaws. And the great genius of a statesmen, Benjamin Disraeli, showed plainly his Negro blood.

Glory be! What great man can escape us.

There is much more that is fascinating in the article, such as inferring that the ancient Philistines had a Nordic ruling class and so forth and so on, but it is well worth while to have had that much of an admission from Mr. Stoddard— that Africa was inhabited by, ruled by and belonged to the Africans.

* * *

By the way, have you noticed that ever since it was discovered that the youthful Tut died of lung trouble, there have not been so many vehement denials of his Negroid descent? That tubercular taint just settled things.

* * *

The gray snow is still piled in the back yard. The sick room from which this is typed is smelly with disinfectants. The furnace abateth not from its labor of furnishing gratuitous whiffs of coal gas, and a minimum of heat. The March winds howl, and spits of snow blow before a furious gale. The colicky baby next door makes nights hideous with its plaintive yowls. The family dog is still in need of a bath. The purple crackles and sparrows, who have fed all winter from the bounty of kitchen scraps, huddle their feathers and chirp plantively but their crumbs and suet are slow coming out to them. The pussy willows in the neighbors back yard are sheathed in ice. Skies are gray, and blue-black clouds before the wind. But—spring is on the way. You can feel it in your grip-laden bones. Your husky breath grows a bit quicker at the thought. If I am not careful, I shall write a spring poem—and then my usefulness will come to an untimely end. Let us go and shake down the furnace!

March 20, 1926

Out in Springfield, Illinois, is another woman who has been doing yeoman service for the children of our race for the past 26 years. Mrs. Eva G. Monroe, of 427 South Twelfth Street, saw her duty and, without any flinching, went ahead and did it. It is an uphill work establishing any kind of an institution, and when you start out looking after orphans only the Lord knows what a rough and thorny road you must travel. How Mrs. Monroe has weathered the storm of the past quarter of a century; how her orphanage has thriven; how her children have grown up, gone through schools, "made good," and returned many a time and oft to bless the great-hearted mother, is a story that some day we hope she will tell herself. For the present, she is too busy keeping the work going, financing it, and looking after her charges to exploit herself. Just another one of those instances to make one continue to have faith in womanhood and Christianity.

* * *

Missouri is famous for its Supreme Court decisions on the subject of the Negro. Its latest dictum is that "the adoption of the Fifteenth Amendment to the Federal Constitution has been the source of more plagues to the body politic than the legends tell us were visited upon Pharoah by the God of Israel." Of course, the whole twelve million of American Negroes in the United States are burning with righteous indignation. But—and here is the pitiful part—what are we going to do about it? Write bitter editorials in all of our Negro papers? Write long and scholarly letters to such white papers as will publish them gratis? Let loose a flood of excellently prepared and authenticated statistics to show that the whole country has been benefited by the passage of the Fifteenth Amendment? Deluge the members of that Missouri Supreme Court with letters from individuals, organizations, scholars, Negroes and friends of the Negro? What good will it all do? The Missouri Supreme Court has spoken. Its decision is recorded. It will not meet to reconsider that decision, nor will it take it back. A precedent has been set— a dictum established. The bitter editorials in our own papers will not be read by the members of the Supreme Court of Missouri, nor by the lawyers of Missouri, Mississippi, Georgia or elsewhere, who might be influenced by this statement. The long and scholarly letters will be read and appreciated by our friends—our enemies, including the Missouri Supreme Court, will not know of their existence. The statistics will meet with a like fate. We can only bolster up our own crushed pride with said figures. No one else will read them, or believe them if they should happen to read them by mistake. The letters that might be written will be put in the waste baskets of the said members of that Supreme Court, or, if they should be read, will be dismissed with a sniff as "nigger impertinence." That's the pitiful problem. And this writer rises to remark that there is no question that faces the Negro graver than just this one—the inability to get our message, propaganda, story over to our enemies. What are we going to do about it? The big prize of the century should go to the Negro or white man who can invent, evolve, or otherwise work out the answer to that problem. In the meanwhile, let's not waste our ammunition—verbal or otherwise—shooting into the air.

．　．　．　．　．　．

We have heard a deal about the quadruple tragedy at Tia Juana. The "sob sisters" had a harvest of hysteria over the matter, and the desperate deed of a father who sought death for himself and his women-folk because of the dishonor of his daughters was responsible for much moralizing, and tears enough to drench the deserts of Mexico. The ultimate in a commonsense view comes, however, from a California paper—the Los Angeles *New Age Despatch*. Near enough to the scene of the tragedy to know something of the details which the Eastern papers failed to chronicle. Says the *New Age Despatch:*

> Tia Juana is in Mexico, a foreign country. It is a notorious resort of gambling, drinking and prostitution. Americans go there to spend their money, knowing where they are going and why. And much of the filthy profit from the dives goes into American pockets. The Mexicans know what the Americans want to spend their money for and prepare for them.
>
> That father who took his daughters into those resorts knew where he was taking them, to dance and drink, and bought drinks for them and his wife. His "proud Southern blood" that made death preferable to disgrace for his women should have asserted itself earlier. He laid his women liable by taking them into such places. And the demand for the protection of "white" women, now so vociferously being made by certain newspapers and writers should have been heard long ago in demands that our government make rules against such free entry of daily caravans of Americans into Tia Juana for the known purposes of carousal.

In other words, if you lie down with dogs, you will get up with fleas. If you carry your daughters into dives in an unspeakably foul border town, you must expect them to be insulted and raped. And to demand any protection from the government, after the damage is done, is cowardly, while the murder and suicide of the entire family is—well, some people are better off when they no longer encumber the earth. Heartless? No. But Mexico is no place for weaklings.

. . . . . .

April 3, 1926

Mrs. Carl Diton, who is always doing fine things artistically for Philadelphia, in presenting the young geniuses of the race to audiences of the Quaker City, under the proper auspices, and in fostering talent other than that of her gifted husband, has recently thrown open her doors to an exhibit of the work of Laura Wheeler, and all Philadelphia went to see and to admire and talk about the work of the young artist.

Philadelphia art critics say that Laura Wheeler excels in portrait painting. "In the landscapes, light is often absent. One does not feel the out-o-doors, the freshness of the air or the living quality of foliage."

But her portraits, and her illustrations are inimitable. Who does not remember those exquisite black and white Egyptian spring dancers on the *Crisis* cover two years ago? And the sombre joy of some of her Negro boys and girls? She gets at the heart of our people, delving down deep below the superficial gayety of the surface to the sorrow-laden heart of a race.

That is why her portrait of the old colored woman, the model of whom lives near the Cheyney Training School, is one of the best things that Laura Wheeler ever did. Since this last year abroad, "Dorothy," and "The French Violinist,"

and "The Arabs of Algiers," and the colorful French landscapes have enraptured the public—but I go back to the age-
old sorrow-lined, calm-after-storm of the aged colored woman.
An epitome of a race. Summing up in her weather-beaten
countenance three centuries of making bricks without straw
under the hissing coil of the whip-lash. Envisioning a future
of a people out of bondage, but still wandering in the
wilderness, listening for the thunders on Mt. Sinai.

Laura Wheeler's portraits have the uncanny faculty of
finding one salient soul characteristic, ripping it from its
fleshly sheath, and flinging it upon the canvas, sometimes
without enough context to disguise it. You sometimes say,
"But that is not just like the person," because perhaps you do
not know or recognize the cross section of soul that Laura
Wheeler has discovered and exhibited in the raw.

For instance, the young brown girl with the tragedy of
unfulfilment in her face. Ambition thwarted. Great haunting
eyes beseeching her chance in a Nordic civilization. Proud,
sensitive mouth, pleading to be called beautiful. The tragedy
of young girlhood, crushed beneath the realization of a wrong
evaluation of beauty in a cruelly standardized civilization. It
grips you, and you turn your eyes away, half ashamed to see
an almost unreserve of tragic grief of the youth of a whole
people.

Laura Wheeler's best portraits have this clairvoyant touch.
And if the artist fails to become en rapport with her subject,
the portrait either is a failure, or is not finished. Lord pity
the person with a mean soul who should come within the
purlieus of her gifted brush.

* * *

This tragic quality of Laura Wheeler's portraits; this intense
interest in subjects Biblical and religious of Henry Tanner;

this profound brooding quality of May Howard Jackson's sculpture; this inate sadness of Meta Warrick-Fuller's work, are sharply indicative of the sincere elevation of tragedy in the artistic life of the race.

We may be a humorous people, but the bitterness of proscription lies so close to the surface that the humor brushes it with a fragile wing. When we think at all, we think in terms of sorrow, and every artistic expression that we have had—literature, music, painting or sculpture—is inexpressibly and profoundly sad, but not gloomy, with

Thoughts that do often lie too deep for tears.

. . . . . .

When grownup folks take to writing bitter things about each other, and indulging in recriminations, either through the public press or in personal letters, they always remind me of little children; boys thumbing their noses at each other, and yelling mixed-up insults, and little girls, switching skirts and yelling "You did!" and "I didn't!" at each other over the back fence, or in front of the paternal front stoop. Sheer waste of time, but then some people must be employed, if not amused, and time may hang heavy on their hands. "Ya! So's your old man!" sounds all right from the under-teenage youngsters, but it sets ill on those who boast of superiority in education and culture.

All this apropos of those big, strong, brave he-males who call each other names and question each other's veracity—in newspapers.

. . . . . .

"Anxious Lover," who has somehow gotten this column mixed up with advice to the lovelorn, writes to ask me if it is the proper thing to send his beloved a phonograph record. The postmark on Anxious' letter is blurred, but I am sure he comes from the far districts of the inner hinterland, where maidens yet thrill at a present from a swain. He should thank his stars that she will be content with a new record for the family phonograph, instead of demanding a five pound box of candy or a quart of pre-Volstead. Now if Anxious can find a record with the wedding march on one side and "O Promise Me" on the other, all will be well. But he must beware the canny salesman who would sell him a double-faced disk, with "Sleepy-Time Gal" on one side and "Show Me the Way to Go Home" on the other.

. . . . . .

April 10, 1926

. . . . . .

You haven't seen any mention of Crispus Attucks in a school history written by Nordic authors, have you? Not yet. The Boston Massacre carefully told in detail, all but the name of the brave citizens who shed their blood.

But for the past two decades the Negro has done a lot of talking about Crispus Attucks. To the credit of the Massachusetts people, be it said that they did erect a monument to his memory, and place it where it could be seen—on Boston Common. And perhaps that gave the impetus to the flair for insisting upon lugging in Attucks in every speech made from the Atlantic to the Pacific and Mexico to the Great Lakes. And the historians began to squirm. A fact so generally talked about must be mentioned in the books else they might lose their reputation for the verities. And then the colored people took to writing histories, and insisting upon this Attucks person. It was very poor taste for the Commonwealth of Massachusetts to erect a monument to him; it just started these Negroes off mixing up colored people with the Fight for Independence.

More and more speeches—more and more histories. Then some talk about a Crispus Attucks Day. The situation was fearfully embarrassing.

But lo! A light broke upon the horizon. The historians found that they could prove beyond a doubt that while it was true that "the first blood of the Revolutionary War was shed by Crispus Attucks"—that he was not a Negro!

Isn't that just splendid! He was an Indian or a Spaniard, or a Portuguese, or a dark Yankee, or a half-breed, or what you will.

But a Negro? A historical error.

Let us draw a deep breath of relief. The supremacy of the white race has been saved, and the courage of the early Continentals rescued from the black man, and placed back on the breast of the proud Puritan. Hurrah!

. . . . . .

The only thing needed now to make the ghetto of Indianapolis complete, as the race-segregation ordinance passed by its council would have it, will be a ton of barbed wire, strung around the prescribed district, guaranteed to keep colored people in, day and night, and white men out at night. Then all will be beautiful.

. . . . . .

Mrs. Myrtle Foster Cook, the charming and gracile editor of the National Notes, the official organ of the National Association of Colored Women, says that this column is "as delectable and refreshing as a cool lemonade after a hectic day."

That is delightful praise. Should one be too modest to reproduce it? Not so. Modesty went out with the corset, the pompadour, long skirts, lined dresses, the knitted petticoat, the merry widow hat, the lisle stocking, the chatelaine bag, and the fleur de lys watch pin. Indeed, so much is modesty a lost art, that one is almost tempted to repeat the entire paragraph from the National Notes. But lingering phases of reluctance, delicate and obscure, forbid. We rise and make our best bow in the direction of Kansas City.

April 17, 1926

That is a good thought that Lester Walton puts forth in his discussion of motion pictures for Negro actors and theaters in the New York *World*. Two thoughts stand out like beacon lights: "The public no longer laughs at a Negro either on the stage or the screen carrying a chicken or watermelon, drinking gin, industriously wielding a razor or shooting craps."

"Negro comedies furnish a virgin field for movie exploitation, but a combination of money and brains is necessary. If big results are to be realized the promoters cannot be in the piker class, and the writers of the scenarios must know the difference between comedy and burlesque."

"Now that we have realized this, it only remains for us to get that idea over to the white producers, writers and actors."

But Mr. Walton, living as he does, in the North, cannot know that it is unfortunately not altogether true that "the public no longer laughs at a Negro on the stage or the screen, etc." The sophisticated public of New York probably does not, but enter any motion picture or vaudeville house elsewhere catering almost exclusively to a Negro patronage, and listen to the loud guffaws of joyous mirth when the minstrel type of Negro appears. Slapstick comedy, of the type which relies upon rolling eyes, fright at the supernatural, cowardice, childish delight in wads of money, razors and dice, still goes big. Decent comedies are needed, not only to delight the intelligentsia, but to educate the submerged ninetieth. Just to see a Negro servant in a white picture elicits howls of delight from the frankly joyous and unrestrained Negro audience.

To some of us who have seen the Negro on the stage for the past quarter of a century, and whose memories of Ada Overton and George Walker and Cole and Johnson and the rest are still fresh, it is with a sigh of relief that some of the newer productions are getting away—oh ever so slightly from the good old blurbs that have held the stage since the days of Billy Kersands.

But even in such sophisticated productions as *Shuffle A'Long Chocolate Dandies* or still later ones, it is painful to see the awful props still holding up the flimsy structures. Witness those awful costumes of Florence Mills. And for instance:

First act on a plantation. Everyone in gingham, calicoes and the leading lights in voiles or Dolly Varden versions of plantation costumes.

Second act, a gorgeous outburst of ballroom finery. Everyone in satins and velvets. Specialties aplenty, and the plot forgotten, while the principals show you just how they can blossom forth in sartorial elegance.

Two leading comedians who cheat, lie, steal and squander wads of stage money, the value of which seems never to penetrate to their dumb heads.

Free and unlimited thrusting into hands of delighted actors of gobs, wads, hunks, bales of money.

(I have sometimes thought that this insistence on the prominence of the money idea is a sort of Freudian complex. Poverty being so prevalent in the race, the Negro realizes his dreams of munificence in his playacting.)

Male quartet which runs all the way from very ordinary jazzing of spirituals to the good work of the Four Harmony

Kings. But somewhere, somehow—relevancy does not count—the ancient member of the cast, in the traditional make-up, shuffle, limp, aching back, red bandanna streaming from pocket, with shaking head will cause that quartet to break into "Old Black Joe." Inevitable. Apparently as necessary as spot lights.

Leading prima donna stepping across the stage, with steps halting by the count, as precise and regular as an untrained church choir trying to keep step to an unfamiliar recessional.

The female members of the cast always talk too fast, too shrill, too chattery. Where, oh where, is the tradition of our soft, beautiful voices? Rarely do they appear in the dialogue of the musical comedies. Everyone seems nervous, too high-keyed, hysterical. That this is a necessary concomitant of musical comedies does not appear, when we remember some of the latest and best successes of the other race, where the best-trained leading women rested the ear with soft speech and gentle utterance:

(I am reminded of Evelyn Preer's exquisite tones in *Salome* and the *Chip Woman*. Of course, she is a common street girl in *Lulu Belle*, and her voice is strident accordingly.)

But even the ingenues of the Negro musical comedies are shrill and raucous speaking, no matter how melodiously they sing.

Standardization—twenty-five years of it, has dulled the edge of the convention of musical comedies produced by our people, as the cheap comedy props of gin, watermelon, crap-shooting, rolling eyes and ready razors have been standardized. If we are to get away from the one, that is, while the lower strata is to be educated into a better comedy sense, the upper strata should be taught to insist upon better plot, more finish in production, less conventional adherence to century

old types, comedy with a modicum of brains, more culture
in the speaking voice, and some attention to little things,
showing a modicum of acquaintance with some of the amen-
ities. Such as, for instance, the hero leaving his hat firmly
settled on his head, when entering the home of his lady love;
the heroine talking with her mouth full, when she is not
doing a comedy stunt; the prima donna scratching her nose
in the midst of an aria. Tiny evidences of a certain lack of
refinement, which grate on the fastidious.

* * *

The Negro theater is at its wonderful beginning; a burgeoning
into a tropic bloom. In another quarter of a century it will
be in the midst of its glory, like the drama of the Elizabethan
age which was a slow process of centuries, flowering almost
suddenly, and dying down almost as suddenly. We are making
a good start, but even the Elizabethans, crude and coarse as
they were, paid attention to all the refinements of their own
day and time, and urged themselves away from the conven-
tionalities of existing stage procedure.

. . . . . .

April 24, 1926

Wise men (and women) change their minds; fools never. It
was asserted that this column was going to sail under a French
flag. That "Une Femme Dit" would be its caption for the
length of its life, and so forth and so on. But Fate and the
painful pronunciation of that magic caption decreed otherwise.
When one in whom you have put trust and confidence from
time immemorial rises and asks you what "Ooon femmy ditt"
means, is it not time enough to weep, and sadly lay aside the
French tri-color and lug out the old stars and stripes? You

could see from the painful grimaces of "I know what this is, do you?" that it was not getting across, but stubbornness gripped us, and we kept right on. As "Little Julia" says, our folks speak two languages, English and profane, and that wasn't profanity. Well, we'll let bygones be bygones. My naturally sweet and gentle disposition, and unruffled temperament never showed to better advantage than it does now. Has it, now tell the truth?

.   .   .   .   .   .

Sat in the closing exercises of one of the Opportunity Schools in a huge auditorium. Colored men and women, nine hundred of them, had been going to school, and hundreds of them had learned to read and write. The star speaker was a man of eighty-four. He had learned he said, to sign his own checks for the first time. Get that, will you? Money in the bank, plenty of property, and yet had always signed his checks with an X. Now that he had gotten a start, for it was a wonderful thrill to sign those checks, and be able to read his own bank book—now that he had started, he thought he'd just go on and get an education, and really make something of himself.

And he, eight-four!

Optimism? Yes. And something better. The spirit of youth in the New Negro, even if he is eighty-four and was just beginning to read and write. For he refused to acknowledge age. The indomitable will that conquers time was there—a quality not so common in our people, who oriental-like, age rather young. But the New Negro is not always to be found among the youthful poets and artists in the metropolis. He may be found in the aged but erect bodies of the back-woods dwellers, or the farmers or the small town denizens. It is the spirit of the age that counts—not the years, nor the artistic achievements.

* * *

Wonders will never cease. When a well-known Atlanta paper, the leading Negro journal in Georgia, finds excuses for Jim Crowing at the Birmingham Sunday School Convention, and suggests that those spirited Negroes who preferred to stay away rather than be insulted, committed a sin against Christ, one cannot be but amazed at the kind of Christianity that editor found in his Bible.

But then we don't live in Atlanta. Perhaps if we did, and our bread, butter, bank, business, political position, patronage, and permit to walk on the streets depended upon the nod of the White Man on Top of Things, maybe we could read in Christ's vigorous religion anything that we were told to put in our editorial columns.

. . . . . .

May 1, 1926

. . . . . .

Speaking of words, "Usonians" comes forward with a sprightly bow in the columns of the *Public Ledger*. Delightful. "American" is vague and includes Mexico, Yucatan, Brazil, the Straits of Magellan, Porto Rico, and Tacna and Arica. There is a lack of definiteness about it. One feels loosely slipping around the Western hemisphere, from Hudson Bay, or Greenland's icy mountains, to Buenos Aires and the Amazon's torrential strand. But "Usonians" locates one within the confines of the Star Spangled Banner. One has then but forty-eight states in which to rove, and must not go beyond Brownsville, Tia Juana or the Everglades of Florida, not to mention the Bay of Fundy or into Vancouver. "Usonians!" Natives and inhabitants of the United States only. And there is an intimate chummy sound about it. Sort of "ussy," as it were. Gets one in a Babbit state of mind, with a Rotary Club trimming. Although, of course, all "Usonians" do not belong to Rotary Clubs, as Dr. Du Bois will tell you.

Still, we accept "Usonians" along with the gallant company of "Scofflaw" and "Pitilacker," and waft it to the last seat in the front row of words.

$\cdot$ $\cdot$ $\cdot$ $\cdot$ $\cdot$

May 15, 1926

$\cdot$ $\cdot$ $\cdot$ $\cdot$ $\cdot$

Now that the Emerson Hotel has insulted Countee Cullen on the color question, let us hope that the unwise will not rush into print and demand that the young poet at once take steps to break down discrimination, insults to the Negro, Jim Crowism, the practice of making engagements with artists without finding out local conditions, and all the other evils of being a Negro.

Mr. Cullen may write another charming little poem on Baltimore, only this time there may not be a saving sense of humor to transmute the black iron of insult into the white gold of poetry.

$\cdot$ $\cdot$ $\cdot$ $\cdot$ $\cdot$

Georgia is redeeming herself. First, the fearless Atlanta clergyman who spoke out at that farcical Birmingham Sunday School meeting; and now the Pulitzer prize award for the 1925 medal for the "most disinterested and meritorious public service rendered by an American newspaper during the year" goes to the Columbus, Ga., *Enquirer-Sun*, edited by the son of Joel Chandler Harris. The paper spoke out in meeting against the Ku Klux Klan, against racial and religious prejudice, against the antievolution law.

To be in Columbus, Georgia, to live there, to be a white Southerner there, and take so fearless and advanced a stand, merits not only the Pulitzer prize for journalism, but the Carnegie medal for heroism.

But there is one thing about a Southerner—when he espouses a cause he espouses it all over. No luke warm damning with faint praise. He rolls up his sleeves and tackles the proposition whole-heartedly, and let the consequences go where they will.

* * *

The North Carolina Inter-Racial Committee has appointed a committee to investigate traveling conditions in the Jim Crow cars, and to insist upon better Jim Crow cars.

TO INSIST UPON BETTER JIM CROW CARS!

Can you beat it?

. . . . . .

My most humble apologies are hereby made to the chain letters which were so anathematized several weeks ago.

I did not write the nine letters demanded by its screed. I ignored the implied threat of dire disaster should I break the chain. I scorned the good fortune that was to be mine if I wrote nine letters in one day and sent them to nine persons. I sniffed scornfully, and said I was not superstitious, and the mails were cluttered enough already with advertisements, soliciting letters, suggestions as to how one might get a pair of silk stockings or a house and lot free, with gaudy invitations to buy Florida real estate and the *Congressional Record*. So I spared Uncle Sam and saved myself eighteen cents and an hour's writing of nine letters.

And the next week I fell downstairs and sprained my ankle and had to pay lots of money to the hospital for an X-ray, and much taxi fare and loss of work, and pain and anguish, and all the things that one can read about in the prayers and petitions against railroad companies. And the worst of it all was, I couldn't collect any accident insurance because it happened at home and not on a street, trolley, bus, railroad, taxi, steamship or hansom cab.

I am not superstitious, but I have the same feeling toward a chain letter now that the late lamented Dr. Sinclair always said he had for a bulldog—not affection but respect.

Don't try to argue with me that I would have fallen down anyhow. It was the chain letter that I threw in the waste basket. That ends the argument.

May 22, 1926

Now that the smoke and dust of battle have cleared away, and the spell-binders, ward workers, directors, political sharpsters, high-ups, senators, congressmen, cabinet officers, women's clubs, sob-sister, repeaters, old-timers, I-knew-him-whenners, big guns and small fry have lain them down to rest after six or seven weeks' strenuous campaigning, the like of which has not been seen since the good old days before the late war—the mere voters can heave a sigh of relief and go about their daily occupations again, and the housewife may clean up the mess of campaign literature, and use the innumerable booklets to light the kitchen fire.

And everybody is saying I-told-you-so.

Those who are on the winning side, with a complacent smirk of triumph, and a "don't-you-wish-you-were-in-my-shoes" air that is irritating, to say the least.

Those who are on the losing side, with a sigh, and an "I-knew-we-couldn't-win-but-I'm-no-quitter" expression.

And those who were caught between the upper and nether millstone of being in the crowd of also-rans, with an "I'll-know-better-next-time" air of resignation.

This game of American politics is one of the jokes of the gods.

*   *   *

When the Olympians want a diversion they stir up a political mess somewhere in these United States, and hold their divine sides in Gargantuan laughter. And the thing that provokes them to the greatest mirth is the colored man and brother in an American three-cornered primary fight.

* * *

He gets so intensely interested. So angry with all who do not agree with him. So het up in argument. So sure that his opinion, influence, work, vote are the last word, and the court of last resort. So important. So busy. So much to do about headquarters. Heavy frowns. A longer stride than usual. Mysterious conferences about nothing. Long seances somewhere. Cryptic utterances in deep bass voice.

In short, the Man and Brother about campaign time is a joy to behold, and a wonder to see.

* * *

Before the Nineteenth Amendment became a part of the Constitution, when poor woman was campaigning all over this land of equal opportunity, the brother opposed to equal suffrage used to howl about woman's place being in the home. One of those irrefutable arguments, like all lynchings being for the crime of rape. You just couldn't get around it, any more than the Negro can get around this later one. Woman had no time for using the ballot. The inference was, as Dr. Anna Howard Shaw used to say, that woman would get up early in the morning, Monday morning, and vote steadily all day, Monday, Tuesday, Wednesday, Thursday, Friday, Saturday and twice on Sunday. There would be no time for washing, ironing, cooking, scrubbing, sewing, baking, wiping the children's noses or getting them ready for Sunday school. Buttons would go unsewed and stockings undarned. It was impossible to convince mankind that because of the extension of the ballot, election laws would be unchanged. That there would not be any time, place or opportunity for woman to exercise the right of franchise uninterruptedly. And the women who were fighting the fight of equal opportunity, used to look at that old argument, and wonder where in the heck it came from, and how they could break it down.

* * *

But since women have been in the game, they have found out where men obtained that conception of the ballot. Right from themselves. They knew all along that it takes them about three weeks to vote, and that for about ten days before election they are not fit for anything else, and they simply judged the poor women by themselves.

* * *

Those of you who have not forgotten the *Silas Marner* you read in school, will recall how all the good husbands of Raveloe for weeks had to go to the Rainbow Inn and spend hours and hours every night, staying late, and going home unchallenged, because they had to discuss the stealing of Silas' gold. Not that any one of them had a single thing to do with apprehending the thief, or even in searching for him. But the mere discussion of the robbery necessitated their constant attendance of nights at the Inn. And the good wives were given to understand that this was men's business, which needed unremitting attention and care.

* * *

Somehow the Man and Brother about election time reminds one of the Raveloe farmers. It is essential that he be about headquarters. He must ask, "Well, how's things?" scores of times a day. He must discuss with profound gravity the outlook for the respective candidates. He must tabulate election forecasts. He must slap other busy forecasters and wiseacres on the back, and with heavy frowns, lay down the law

as to the outcome of the great event of election. He must
recount to whomever will listen just what happened in such
and such a year, and how all the dope of those in the know
was upset at the last moment. He must pay his respects, with
much strong language, to the candidate whom he opposes,
and set forth with great show of wisdom the shortcomings of
the reprehensible individual who dares be on the opposition
ticket. He must acquire pockets-full of literature and distribute it to whomever he can buttonhole. He must assure the
uninitiate of his absolute grasp of facts, and his perfect rapport
with the insiders of the inside of the sanctum sanctorum. No
mere manager of the campaign, no head of a bureau, no
private secretary to the great politician is as busy as the Man
and Brother, who has elected himself as the Great Mogul of
the Negro in Politics.

*   *   *

And at meetings or rallies! Ah! There he does indeed shine with
a refulgence that puts an acetylene torch to shame. He always
has a seat on the platform. Perish the suggestion that he be
in the audience. He is ready to speak at a moment's notice.
But if, perchance, the master of ceremonies, the chairman,
or the toastmaster, if it be a banquet, should omit his name,
or fail to call upon him for a "few remarks," he is in no wise
abashed. For at some time, when the chairman is off his
guard, he will arise unsolicited and get in a speech that for
sheer ego-ness is unsurpassed. Failing this, he will assist the
chairman, by gratuitous addenda. When a speaker or a singer
comes to the platform, he arises and helps them forward by
a gentle pat on the back, and assists them from the platform.
He does all the paging for the meeting, and starts all the
applause, winking at the audience to show them when to
begin and when to leave off.

Try to squelch him.

Canute tried to sweep back the ocean with a gesture. That is the apotheosis of futility. Multiply it by ten and raise it to the n'th power, and you have the futility of trying to squelch the Man and Brother who has elected himself to lead the campaign.

* * *

This is no sporadic picture. This is no fauna indigenous to any particular locality. This is no exaggeration of this particular campaign just over in Pennsylvania. It is a composite of Man, Lordly Man, exercising the right of franchise, and showing poor weak woman just how the Game is Played.

* * *

And the reason why the Olympians hold their sides with Gargantuan laughter is because the Man and Brother is such a non-essential in the picture.

Oh, yes, we know all about the Balance of Power in a crisis, and how our vote always saves the Party, and how we can show our strength, etc., etc., etc., etc. We've made campaign speeches, too, for the past 'steen years, and there isn't a line of the familiar pattern that we cannot fill out and then some. But—

* * *

Remember the Man in the Brown Derby was in Florida this winter? He thought he was crashing into the society of Billionaires, and was getting quite chesty about it. Then when the Society Reporter and Photographer suggested that he pose with Mr. and Mrs. Millionbucks for the rotagravure section of the metropolitan paper, he struck an attitude, swelled up his bosom, and held his cigar at a proper angle. And he showed the proofs to the little wife with great pride and vainglory. But when the paper came out, all that could be seen beside Mr. Millionbucks was the crook of an elbow, where the picture had been cut, and the Man in the Brown Derby cut out.

Get the point?

Or—you know the story of the Ham Actor who got a part in a great motion picture, and went through his pantomime in the best style, and when the night of the First Showing came, invited all his unfortunate brethren who had no parts, to come and see how superior he was to Conway Tearle and Douglass Fairbanks. But in the cutting room the Ham Actor had been sacrificed for the unity of the story, and all he had to prove to his friends that he had been in the play was one foot of film, showing a retreating back.

That's the Man and Brother in the Political Game up to date.

May 29, 1926

Now that the elections are over, the next business in hand is getting all the young folks graduated from grammar, high, technical and professional schools, from colleges, universities and theological seminaries. It is an arduous task, this, that the cynical old world addresses itself to each spring—that of setting the feet of millions of eager young hopefuls into the path of what they call with bated breath—the owners of the feet do the calling, not the feet—what they call with bated breath LIFE. An arduous task and one accompanied with much witticism, stale puns, jokes, sneers, lifting of eyebrows, sob-stuff, slopping over, and what not on the part of the same cynical old world.

But we colored people—or shall I say Race people? Other individuals in the world, apparently being non-Race people, or just folks without any race. At any rate, we people have not yet adopted that air of cynical, blase wordliness when we talk of the graduating of our own youths and maidens. To us, even after fifty years' experience of it, the annual hegira from the upper classes of the schools of our own young people, is an event fraught with wonder, adventure, marvel, and vicarious delight. The spectacle of our own youths standing capped and gowned, receiving mystical parchments at the hands of grave dignitaries has for us a never-failing marvel. We cannot be cynical, we are too much awed. To us it is the vision of a great future, the hope of a frustrated people, the laying the burden of our woes and aspirations on the shoulders of those who will carry on; the handing on the torch to be borne higher up the mountain peak of our racial ambition. The whole race rises, as it were, and lays the accolade on each individual youth who receives his diploma.

This is the right attitude. If it is ingeniuous, let us thank the Lord, who has saved us many a time from being ridiculous. When a people begin to look upon their young folks with cynicism; to be distrustful of their ambitions; to carp at the white flame of their aspirations—that race has already implanted within itself the germs of decay. We still are awed in the presence of the child and the youth who are so much nearer the source of the divine fire. And let us be thankful for that, and drop a little prayer for the poor other people who can see the matter for joking in the loveliness of youth.

* * *

Before Commencement Days come the ever-delightful Field Days. If anyone would say that this nation is going to the dogs, he would do well to hark back a score of years ago, when the practice of the annual field days in schools, colleges, communities and city centers had not obtained to any appre-

ciable extent. And now no hamlet, no school, no community
so backward that does not have its annual Field Day—a day
for healthful sports, for taking stock of the physical well-
being of the young people. How much nearer the nation is
getting to the good old Greek ideal of a sound mind in a
sound body. The growth has been rapid, and has taken its
most rapid strides since the Armistice. The war taught us
that we were in danger of becoming a weak-kneed, spindly
nation, and that if we didn't watch our step we would be
over-balanced in physical development by these black Americans, who have a peculiar fashion of being remarkably well-
built and well-balanced physically. The tremendous impetus
given just plain outdoor exercise, not stunts, but health, and
the annual exposition in the innumerable field days over the
land must delight the gods of fair play, who see in this
movement a tribute, subtle, unknown, perhaps, to the Negro.

. . . . . .

Speaking of money. Much noise is made often about the
waste of money. I would like to rise with the remark that no
money is ever actually wasted, unless it is burned in actual
fire, destroyed by chemical change, buried in inaccessible
vaults, or withdrawn from circulation by some hoarding
miser. If the rich man gives a party and spends thousands
and tens of thousands on it—he may put out his money, give
it away by excessive charges made to him, but someone profits
thereby. The florists, and caterers, and maids and men-
servants, the wine dealers, and haberdashers, and butcher,
baker and candlestick maker, the jewelers, and decorators,
and all the army that go to make up those who cater to the
whims of the rich. If he even chooses to give away five-dollar
or twenty-dollar gold pieces for favors, or as tips to his
menials, they profit thereby, and pocketing their emoluments,

buy houses and clothes, and thus keep the money circulating to the betterment of business and the consequent increase of commerce and the up-bringing of the city's status in the marts of trade. It is a poor sort of Marxism to whoop about waste. There is no such animal, generally speaking. There is diversion of funds—but someone has them.

So this talk about excessive expenditures in campaigns is poor sportsmanship. The mere matter of mailing 100,000 circulars advertising the fact that a candidate is before the people, calls for the expenditure of $1,500—granting that they went for a cent and a half each. And the United States government is the better therefor. And so in proportion does the Western Union and the Postal Telegraph, and the Bell Telephone profit. And the paper manufacturers. And the automobile shops. And John D. Rockefeller pockets the price of gasoline. Why kick? Somebody has the money, and the millionaires who put it up, are thereby saved that much on their income tax.

Some of these days some of these howlers are going to take down their elementary physics off the back shelves, dust them off and re-read that old law about the conservation of matter, and apply it in its strictest sense. Then maybe they will stop grouching.

June 5, 1926

. . . . . .

In spite of the fact that the music of our people is the best in the world, and is the foundation of most of the latter-day classics, there are still those among us who are so benighted as to refuse to see the beauty of the spirituals, and would suppress them for their connotation of slavery and oppression. Of course, everyone has the right to his own point of view, but ofttimes a point of view may be warped by an early prejudice. It does seem too unfortunate to have our friends and enemies of the other race profit hugely in money and fame by that which we cast off as a thing of no moment— just because we are purblind and prejudiced. But let us thank heaven the majority of us are not that bitter against our own beauty.

* * *

Something of this went through my mind as I rode on a bus out into the suburbs. I looked up from the riotous pages of *Gentlemen Prefer Blondes,* because a familiar tune smote on my ear. Someone was whistling, "Every Time I Feel the Spirit." He was whistling it vigorously, with thrills of delight, and appreciation, as if he loved it. He threw in little lilts and runs, and ran in a double note or so. I rubbed my eyes and looked around mystified. For there were but two persons on the bus—the driver and myself. And the driver was a large, rather hard-boiled specimen of Nordic masculinity. He it was who was whistling, "Every Time I Feel the Spirit," as delightedly as if it were the "Prisoner's Song." I could not help but smile at him as I dropped my fare in the box, and he smiled back, as he rang up the fare, and said with hearty delight, "I like that tune, don't you?"

* * *

And then I went up the road where some little girls were playing on the lawn before a school. Someone was at the piano and began playing the "Humoresque." The little girls stopped, listened, cocked their heads to one side, and then with astonishing precision burst into the "Swanee River." For with childish ability to seize on the right thing, they had detected the origin of Dvorak's masterpiece.

* * *

Yes, it would be foolish to refuse to bring to light the precious gems from a mine, because we disliked to remember how the grandfather of the owner of the mine obtained the property.

* * *

Langston Hughes not only wins prizes with his poems—but he can read them. At first one is disappointed when he begins to read. A certain sophomoric note in his voice that is—well—young, too young. Then he gets into the lilt of his verse, and his interest peels off the thin rind of boyishness from his voice, and he chants the verse. A rhythm and swing to the blues, a sonorous chant to the folk songs, an ironic swing to the soberer verse. And you settle back contentedly and say, "He has it—perfect."

* * *

What is IT? You know the swing and chant and sonorous bell-like rhythm to be found only among our own. The chant that Booker Washington's speeches swelled into, when he made his crescendo of climax; the undeniable lilting swing, chant, too, of James Weldon Johnson, when, having stated his case, he begins to hammer home his arguments. The IT that distinguishes the difference between the orator or reader, who feels and dramatizes the situation into the very hearts of the listeners, and the purely intellectual, thin-blooded one who constantly says to himself, "How wonderfully I am speaking!"

Was it Milton, or was it Wordsworth or was it both who said that all great achievements, emotions and deeds are built to music?

The Eighth Grade will arise and tell you that it was Shakespeare in *The Merchant of Venice*, who reminded us of the man who hath no music in his soul being fit for treasons, stratagems and spoils.

And so—it is the music in our race that makes us great artists in other lines.

Let us then arise and thank the God of Things as They Are for the gift of song, and not seek to Freudize it into the limbo of suppressed desires.

For our own is the best that the world has to give just now.

June 12, 1926

. . . . .

The Women's International League of Peace and Freedom complains of misquotations from the press; particularly when some wag suggests that the organization is sustained by the "Garland Free Love Fund." There is just enough half truth in that statement to make denial futile. The Garland fund does help sustain the league, with other worthy causes, but it is ridiculous to call it a "free love" fund—as if the Garland fortune came from indulging in free love.

The bitter disgust of members of the International League for Peace and Freedom suggests how often the Negro is damned by just such half-truths, such glaring mis-statements, and how futile it is to attempt to deny them. Such as, for instance, the classic statement that all Negro women are flattered by the attentions of a white man, no matter what his status.

* * *

The purchase of the Schomburg library by the Carnegie Corporation for the New York Public Library marks an advance in thought of this generation over the last. Not that it is an advanced idea to purchase the library—but the fact that Mr. Schomburg has made disposition of his treasure before his death is a fine thing. His books are priceless. His pamphlets, posters, prints, autographs, mezzo-tints, manuscripts, newspaper clippings—all collected with a rare and unerring flare for just the right and rare bit, representing the result of thirty years' arduous labor, are now to be available to a great public instead of the favored few of Mr. Schomburg's friends. In making this matchless collection available to all students, Mr. Schomburg is looking ahead to the future of history and literature in our race.

If one were permitted to indulge in a feeling of pride at the attainments of another, we should all rejoice at this fine work done by Mr. Schomburg. And the fact that he refused larger sums than the ten thousand offered by the Carnegie Foundation bespeaks a real interest in the race, as he means that the collection shall be for all and not for a few.

Those of us who remember the fine Adger collection and the no less splendid, and in many respects unique collection of dear "Billy" Bolivar, and how they have been lost to the public, will rejoice that a like fate is not for the Schomburg collection. And in making Mr. Schomburg a member of the newly appointed Board of Trustees of the collection, the New York Public Library has ensured a continuance of interest and an intelligent advice for the upkeep of a rare addition to the Americana of the nation.

* * *

South African natives are being pushed to the wall. Their segregation, discrimination against, contempt for and difficulties of living make our life here in the United States look like a paradise. Five and a half million natives against a million and a half whites. And by the passage of recent legislation they may not choose their occupation, much less the place where they may live.

Five to one, and they tamely whine over their wrongs!

. . . .

June 19, 1926

Well, now that Howard University has elected its new president, and the Senate has refused to reconsider the confirmation of James Cobb, we can all draw a deep breath, and settle down to the affairs of the summer. Commencements have done their worst, and our throats need a little rest from hurrahing for Bishop-President Gregg. Everything being all in order for the next cataclysm, we will proceed to sit down squarely and get the next grouch out of our system.

And it's all about that dear old wheeze, that ancient blurb, that moth-eaten howl, that moss-grown alibi of the superior Nordics, and their wail that "your people" cannot agree.

A most excellent and fine gentleman of more than ordinary insight into things Negroid, with a conscientious desire to serve, started me off on this protest, which has been milling over in my soul for more years than one would care to indicate. To quote him more or less verbatim, "That is one thing that I have to complain about with your people, you cannot agree with each other, and you will fight each other."

My jaw dropped. In the twentieth century, too! I protested mildly that perhaps all white people do not agree with each other at all times, and then why should all Negroes agree on every subject at all times, in every place, and under all circumstances?

It was like pouring water over a duck's back.

"You disagree among yourselves," he continued, "so much more than white people under given circumstances."

If I had not had positive assurances of his absolute saneness I might have supposed that he was—well, putting it mildly, temporarily deranged. I swallowed hard, and suggested timidly that politicians, for instance, did not always agree. He was a bit sore on some local political situation, and the subject changed. Fortunately. My poor brain was missing both cylinders, and I could not have stayed much longer without more air than the spacious room afforded.

* * *

There are, roughly speaking, twelve million Negroes in the United States, and the Lord knows how many, many millions scattered over Africa, Australia, Asia, South America, Central America, the East and West Indies and the islands of the sea. Of their diversities of language, tradition, religion, background, culture and what not, it behooves us not to say. But we can confine ourselves to the twelve million in the United States of America.

* * *

Twelve millions of Negroes of all ages, sizes, complexions and religions. Twelve million souls in whose veins, thanks to the white man, run the fires of Spain and Italy, the independence of England and Ireland, the canniness of the Scot, the slow poetry of the Scandinavian, the treachery of the Greek, the methodicality of the German, the passionate desire for self expression of the Russian and the Pole, some Mongolian here and there, some Malay, too, and the low cunning of the Balkans. Twelve million Negroes with the heritage of the bloods named above, not to mention Indian, and a tradition of slavery, for two and a half centuries, during which time, thanks again to the white man, he was taught to hate and despise members of his own race, to tattle, and spy upon each other, in order to safeguard the white man. For the Southern planter knew that if ever there were union among the slaves he was doomed, so he trained them to disunion and disharmony. Yet—somehow, all Negroes wanted freedom and, all who could, fought for it.

* * *

Twelve million Negroes, grown from four million, pitched into a strange and half hostile civilization, and fighting barehanded against fearsome odds. Managing somehow to pile up tremendous assets of property, education, and all the rest of the statistical talk that we all know so well. But they MUST agree. They must never know any difference of opinion. Catholics and Protestants, Methodists, Baptists, Presbyterians, Episcopalians and Seventh Day Adventists, must merge into a common mould and worship Jesus and sing only spirituals. The free thinker, the Unitarian, the pantheist must not be. All must be similar in thought and speech.

Twelve million Negroes must have the same standardized course of action. They must have the same heroes and heroines. If one benighted soul prefers Du Bois to Washington, or vice versa, or one still more benighted suggests that, after all, both are just men, and picks flaws in either or both— holy horrors! "Your people could never agree!"

* * *

The very excellent gentleman who is responsible for this diatribe is not one of those who use that slogan, "Your people cannot agree" as an alibi. But there are many who do. Too many. Whenever the wily politician finds that his feet are being held to the fire on the subject of a pre-election promise of an appointment to some favored position, he digs up two or three candidates for said position, then says unctuously to the anxious delegation, "Well, I might make the appointment, but there are so many applicants that I don't see how I can select one. Now, if your people could only agree on one candidate—"

And the delegation goes away crestfallen, and the word goes out to the brethren that somebody is double-crossing somebody else. And the job goes to a white man.

* * *

Old stuff. Why should there be only one candidate for a position to be held by a Negro? There are usually a dozen anxious and willing white Barkises for every slice of pie or political plum out of the pot. It seems like a tacit agreement that, of the entire race, there is perhaps only one of a mould. Only one man in a city capable of being a policeman. Only one man in the tens of thousands of college graduates of the race capable of holding a Federal position. Inference is that we're fearfully and wonderfully dumb, if after sixty years going to school, college and university, and spending millions of dollars on our education, we can only produce one or two educated men.

* * *

The inconsistency of the stand that "your people do not agree" lies in the fact that Negroes are everywhere and at all times accused of harboring the criminals of the race. And we are always accused of hiding our deepest feelings from the proud Nordics. Of not allowing them to know our reactions in given circumstances. Of drawing a veil between them and us on matters of deep import. Which is true. We are one thing in the presence of the Caucasian and another in our own councils. Yet—"your people do not agree."

* * *

Of course the white people never differ on any subject. That is why we have wars and strikes, and labor unions, Ku Klux Klans, elections, prohibition, campaigns, propaganda literature, religious persecutions, boycotts, comic papers, prisons, Greenwich Village, Peace Societies, Military Colleges, Inter-Racial Committees, lynchings, exclusive society, single-tax colonies, Catholics, Protestants and Fundamentals, the Democratic Party, the G.O.P. and the communists. All these things because the white man always at all times and under all circumstances agrees and acts with commendable unanimity.

* * *

And the poor Negro, who has taken up the white man's civilization, falls into all these various groups—nay, has been forced into them—and has been dared to express his own race consciousness, or to disagree with the findings of the white man historically, or religiously.

Yet—"your people do not agree."

* * *

We admit that we are a superior race, with a civilization dating back before the Ten Commandments, and that our birth on this continent has been but "a sleep and a forgetting." Now, our racial consciousness is alive, alert, vivid. We have unlearned the lesson of the planters and grown to have racial self-respect. We have learned the beauty of the color brown, and the glory of the heritage black. We know the thrill of a faith in a future, and the joy of a glorious and ever-widening horizon of all that goes to make up a racial solidarity. But—we have honest differences of opinion, and if we are honest, we will express them.

Some of us are fundamentalists and some are modernists—and we'll tell the world about it. Some are prohibitionists;

some temperance, and some, plain wet as the ocean. Some of us don't like pork chops, and some of us are vegetarians, and some of us despise spinach and poached eggs—and we hope not to have to go to jail for it.

Some of us like jazz music, and some of us are fond of Verdi and Wagner, and some of us don't care a rap about the later musicians, and don't see anything to rave at in Galli-Gurci. Some of us see beauty in the Cubists and some prefer Millet and Tanner. And some of us are not crazy about the spirituals, and yet will walk two miles to hear Dett's "Music in the Mine," if it is well done, and if it is not well done, don't feel that we are traitors to the race if we say so.

And some of us hate liars, be they white, black, brown or yellow, and feel that it is no evidence of lack of racial harmony if we comment on the fact that our neighbors have not yet memorized the Ninth Commandment.

But—when it comes to a great issue—like the Dyer Bill, for instance, or the Sweet case, and similar segregation cases, or the question of Negro presidents for Negro colleges, or the appointment of worthy men to high office, if they have qualified, or Jim Crow schools in Northern cities—well, if anyone believes that "your people do not agree," let him read the files of the Negro newspapers of the past two years—or, better still, ask Prof. Robert T. Kerlin, and see what the answer will be. After all, aren't Negroes human beings?

* * *

Come to think about it—the Ku Klux Klan does not agree, even with itself. It is all split into factions—as many as there are in the Protestant churches—and then some.

But then God never made two leaves similar, so why suppose that human beings can be cast in like moulds?

July 3, 1926

·   ·   ·   ·   ·

Just as we were getting used to Winold Reiss, and trying to smile blithely when his art is mentioned, and "chirp" "isn't it wonderful," with just the right sophistication of accent, and rolling eye of appreciation, and just as we were getting so that it didn't give us a pain every time we looked at the portraits of our friends done by his cubistic pencil, along comes Miguel Covarrubias, and we have to get adjusted all over. These "highly modernistic renderings of dance types, scenes and groups as they may be studied in the Negro cabarets in Harlem," which illustrate W. C. Handy's *Anthology of Blues* are modern, all right, but to quote Kipling in reverse, "It's interesting art, but is it pretty?"

But then, beauty is no longer to be expressed in art, and if poor Keats were alive, his "A thing of beauty is a joy forever," would be so completely out of date that he would have to suffer more shame than ever he felt at the *Edinburgh Review*.

That poor creature whose plaintive eyes inform you that "I'm gwine lay my head right on de railroad track" in Mr. Handy's book might find that the train will jump the track when it sees the obstruction ahead.

·   ·   ·   ·   ·

July 10, 1926

·   ·   ·   ·   ·

France has issued the *Golden Book of the Blacks*. In other words, the *History of the First Regiment of Senegalese Riflemen*, in an outburst of joy over her success in the Riff. Ten thousand black troops were sent into the Riff. Badly trained, inadequately instructed, and ignorant of the task before them.

Yet some exploits of valor by single heroes, or in groups, reads like a medieval romance of some epic hero. In all the costly war of a year and a half these Senegalese saved many a situation that might have spelled carnage and ruin.

France praises her black troops, and gives them full credit for their valor and heroism. America lynches hers, and tearing the uniforms from their crippled forms, bids them forget that they were once men. Then she allows her army officers to publish books, not only depreciating their services to their country, but insulting every Negro in the land.

July 17, 1926

The extent to which Negro news is more or less a closed book to the mass of white newspapers is evidenced by a recent editorial in the New York *Times*. It congratulated Bishop Gregg upon being elevated to the presidency of Howard University, and commended the school for its bold stand in placing a black man at the helm. The intent was fine, but the editorial appeared two weeks after Bishop Gregg had declined the presidency, and five days after Dr. Johnson had accepted. One or two smalltown Caucasian papers took the cue and still several more days later editorialized in the same vein and with the same lack of accurate information. Which bears out yet again the contention of this column—that we're not getting it across to the pale-faced brethren.

* * *

We were speaking of temperance, and the dear lady with the white ribbon bow was almost in tears over my hardheartedness on the subject. She commended to me the example of the late illustrious William J. Bryan. When I firmly told her that the dear gentleman died of one of the seven cardinal sins—gluttony, and that in the church calendar it ranks with murder and adultery, and that I would spank all the boys that I could reach black and blue if I dreamed they would follow in Bryan's footsteps and eat enormous twenty-pound meals five or six times a day every day in the year, and then call for more; that it would have been far better if he had indulged in a bit of home brew and curtailed his solid food to three per diem—she shook her head unconvinced. But that's the way with reformers. Intemperance means but one thing—liquor with alcoholic content. Greedy and gluttonous eating, covetousness, hypocrisy, cant, malice, envy, mendacity, concupiscence and fornication—all are pure white traits beside the blackened soul of the decent workman who drinks a glass of four and a half per cent beer in the bosom of his family.

* * *

Who was it who said that the mind of the American people has been caught up in some dreadful frenzy like that wrought in the Middle Ages by the superstition of witchcraft and heresy?

. . . . . .

July 24, 1926

. . . . . .

Down in Argentina they are shivering in the worst winter on record—eight below zero, and blizzards a-plenty. Up here we are sweltering at ninety-eight above zero—and still some people are never satisfied. Where else could one find such a delightful variety of climate, except on this earth? Page Sir Oliver Lodge and ask his opinion.

* * *

What with the President catching fish, developing freckles, having correspondents nearly drowned in canoes, sitting before log fires, and refusing to be drawn into political embroglios, it looks as if it is to be almost as busy a season for the newspaper men as if Congress were still in session. Now that "Al" and "Cal" have had lunch together, nothing could be more serene. That was a scintillating newspaper man, by the way, who gravely wrote that "there was no political significance" to the luncheon. Wonder if he had dreams of a coalition between the governor of New York and the President of the United States?

* * *

In the Chicago *Daily Tribune*, in the "Line o' Type or Two," appeared a "tribute" to Countee Cullen on July 6th. The poem is being copied and hailed as a compliment. It has a swing that the author vainly tried to make simulate the beat of tom-toms. But the covert patronizing of the poem to the discriminating taste must necessarily darken whatever radiance of appreciation is intended:

> It matters not if your skin is dark
> As the midnight jungle track,
> I thrill to the beat of the song you sing—

Now, what, to the real reader of poetry, has the color of a man's skin to do with the printed line? One reads a poem without looking at the portrait of the author. And those very first two lines reveal an ancient prejudice that trails a musty slime over the intended tribute.

In the third verse:

> Chance gave you the soul of a minstrel fair
> Housed in a blackamoor's frame,
> With your heart tuned high to the upper air,
> Though a scion of scorn and shame,

Refusing an outcast's usual lot
And turning it into fame!

* * *

According to "The Faun" as the author signs himself, only
fair folks are minstrels. Song, it would seem, to be the
inherent property of blondes. Why Mr. Cullen should be
branded as a "Scion of scorn and shame" is not evident.
Rather strong language to use of a gentleman, and carrying
a connotation that has made many a newly mounded grave
when spoken face to face. Nor is it evident from the information to be had of Mr. Cullen's private life that he is an
"outcast," and has succeeded in turning his terrible lot into
fame.

* * *

No, Mr. Faun, those verses won't do. You are a Southern
cracker, plus, and then some, and if you must write poetry,
write it about the dear Southern chivalry and such rot. And
if you must appreciate Mr. Cullen, forget your Southern
ancestry, and come on out in the open, and be a real critic,
judging things as they are, and not as you would have them.

* * *

Still, we have much for which to be thankful, after all. When
Judge Broomall, of Media, Pa., kissed his old nurse, Mrs.
Margaret Hilton, who had nursed him from infancy to
childhood, and who had come all the way from Cambridge,
Mass., to Media to see him take the oath of office, the
newspapers, with fine restraint, refrained from calling her
his "black mammy." At least the Pennsylvania newspapers
did. Haven't seen those from Georgia and elsewhere yet.

• • • • • •

Another "prince" gone wrong. Just as the pale faces are taken
in by pinchbeck Russian Grand Dukes, and counts from

Monaco, and princes from Bulgaria, so both races have been swindled by Prince Kovo Tovaleu Huenu of Dahomey. The prince had a grand and glorious time while it lasted. From the hectic night when his presence was objected to in a Montmartre cabaret by Americans, through his experiences in Chicago and New York the "prince" had no dull moments. And now he turns out to be the son of poor but honest parents in Dahomey, who gave him an excellent education. The counts and grand dukes and princes of the Riviera do not always qualify even that well. It is to be hoped that the prince enjoyed his excursion into the bright lights of two continents before he was clapped behind the unsympathetic bars of the Dahomey prison.

.   .   .   .   .   .

July 31, 1926

.   .   .   .   .   .

We hear that "Farina's" salary is $75 a week. But no one has risen to tell us what "Mickey" or "Mary" or any of the rest of the child actors in *Our Gang* get each week. Before we exclaim with bated breath about Farina's stipend we'd like more information. For without Farina *Our Gang* would be a tame bunch of naughty kids. With Farina, there is—well, to say the least, local color.

*   *   *

The Chicago *Evening Post*, commenting on the conference of the N.A.A.C.P., has, among other things, this to say: "But in point of fact, the Nordic, like everyone else, is what he does. Let him keep up the pace of recent years; let his poets produce work of the quality of Mr. Cullen's, and Mr. Hughes', and his business men build up cities—and the pseudoanthropologists can wear out their calipers measuring skulls, or wear out the matrices of those letters in the linotype printing the word 'Nordic,' and it will not make a particle of difference. Unless, indeed, some satirical Negro writes a 'Nordic Blues,' and they sing it in Harlem."

When the Ambitious Youth read those lines he at once set about producing "The Nordic Blues." And because he was too modest, or too frightened, or too sensible to send it to a paper himself, he gave it to me. And since the Chicago *Evening Post* calls for a "Nordic Blues," here they are, according to specifications.

Nordic Blues

Dat Nordic Blues, dat's what I've got,
Dat Nordic Blues, dat's what I've got;
     Want to be bleached white, wid golden locks,
     Want to have blue eyes, an' dem straighten' locks,
     Want to go where I want an' do as I please,
     Want to lynch some niggers an' hang 'em on trees.
Got de Nordic Blues, dat's what I've got.

Dat Nordic Blues, dat's what I've got,
Dat Nordic Blues, dat's what I've got,
     Want to vote all day an' shoot all night,
     Want to kick ol' black women ef dey don't talk right,
     Want to tote a mean gun an' spit in de eye
     Of a nigger down Souf ef he talks too high;
Got de Nordic Blues, dat's what I've got

Dat Nordic Blues, dat's what I've got;
Got de Nordic Blues, dat's what I've got.
     Want to burn niggers' houses ef dey move too nigh
     Ter my own lil' shack, er dey got too fly.
     Want to show nigger soldiers dat dey can't wear de coat
     O' de 'Merican ahmy, er dey'll git my goat.
Got de Nordic Blues, dat's what I've got.

Dat Nordic Blues, dat's what I've got,
Dat Nordic Blues, dat's what I've got;
> Want to wear white gowns an' bu'n de cross,
> Want to show I'M a hund'ed per center, an' ride a big hoss,
> Want to wave de big flag of de Stripes an' Stars,
> Give a rebel yell for de Southern stars an' bars;
Got de Nordic Blues, dat's what I've got.

August 7, 1926

. . . . . .

"The greatest migration that the Negro ever planned" is now under way according to the papers, and we see a recrudescence of the great wave of 1916 dashings its power against the sea wall of Northern industries.

Far from the North choking with indignation that crudity is pouring in to upset its comfort, let it reread what H. G. Wells has to say of migrations:

> Whenever civilization seems to be choking amidst its wealth of debt and servitude, when its faiths seem rotting in cynicism and its powers of further growth are hopelessly entangled in effete formulae, the nomad drives in like a plough to break up the festering stagnation, and release the world to new beginnings.

Who shall say that the crude power of the Negro overwhelming the North will not bring about a still stronger ebullition of power and might and wipe out the last vestige of pale-faced, sickly pseudo-superiority?

* * *

Dr. W. W. Faust, a prominent white Baptist pastor of Atlanta, Ga., avers that "White Christians of Georgia are not spending enough money to educate and evangelize Negroes."

No, and white Christians of Georgia are not spending enough money to educate and evangelize white men and women.

White Christians of Georgia could do nothing better than raise a huge fund to educate their own kind into learning the Golden Rule, and applying it, for instance, to:

The Georgia legislature;
The Georgia Ku Klux Klan;
The Georgia Stone Mountain Committee;
The Georgia white barbers;
The Georgia lynchers;
Georgia;

And the good white Christians headed by Dr. Faust would be kept so busy for the next million years or so that all Georgia would be a paradise.

. . . . . .

August 14, 1926

. . . . .

The Baltimore *Sun* has the best blurb of the month:

There is apparently no reason why the Negro should not register under these Southern laws (a resume of the primary laws of the Southern states) today just as easily and freely as the white man. And there would not be any discrimination against him either, *unless he tried too numerously to do so.*

The emphasis is our own.

. . . . . .

The Atlanta *Independent* is all hot under the collar about the way Georgia spends its educational funds: teachers' salaries, $17.93 for each white child; $2.58 for each colored child. School buildings, $58.72 for each white child; $10.02 for each colored child. Expenditures for new buildings, for each white child, $2.84; 27 cents for each colored child. Equipment per white child 40 cents; colored, three cents. The State appropriates for every child between the ages of 6 and 16, $4.45 per capita, but by the time the money is "equitably" distributed, each white child receives for education, $12.00 per capita, and each Negro child, $1.50.

Mr. Davis asks the Georgia white people, "White people, where is your conscience?"

Ben Davis always was an optimist.

* * *

Haven't a squeamish bone in my head. Can swallow all kinds of stuff on the stage. Not finicky about imitations of colored preachers, camp meetings, revivals, Bible beaters and the good sisters in prayer meetings; get only bored at Uncle Tom preaching with his chicken and watermelon stuff; can listen without writhing at some of the jokes on the sacrament of marriage, and have learned how not to walk out of a theatre when motherhood is made a joke.

But—that parody on the Lord's Prayer, that the very snappy young man in Ethel Waters' show, recites is just a bit—too—well, the Lord's Prayer is the Lord's Prayer. It is the most sublime expression that ever fell from the lips of man, and its summation of faith, hope, love and the eternal verities of life, have been the sustaining staff, the anchor of countless millions of human beings. Scoffers, sinners, murderers, thieves, atheists, skeptics, prostitutes and panderers. None so low, but that the simple recitation of the faith of their childhood would not evoke some stirring of conscience and glimmering memory of an earlier day of hope.

So—aside from any thought of the sacrilege of making a silly parody on these beautiful thoughts, there is manifest unfairness in setting up in the minds of hundreds of people an ugly image, where a beautiful one should remain untouched; incalculable harm done to children, who go to theatres, by making them feel that a prayer may be played with and made ridiculous. Not wrong, but unfair, unkind, cruel—and in wretched poor taste.

Ethel Waters has a good show; pretty girls, good dancing, snappy comedy, clean dialogue, artistic setting. If she will put that prayer in the waste basket—she will be doing a great service—not to religion, but to art, and the eternal fitness of things.

The best thing about it is—audiences don't applaud that parody.

Human nature is pretty much of a muchness everywhere. Commit murder, if you like, but don't meddle with their religion.

. . . . . .

August 28, 1926

. . . . . .

I rise in the name of the Negro school teachers of these United States to take serious issue with Mr. George S. Schuyler, who in a recent issue of this paper paid his respects to the profession. Mr. Schuyler usually knows what he is talking about—but I fear he has not looked enough into the subject of the teachers of colored youth, or rather colored school teachers, to be reasonably fair in his strictures.

"In the first place," he avers, "we have a disproportionate number of teachers."

Disproportionate to what? The census of 1920 says that there were 3,796,957 Negro children from 5 to 20 years of age. Now someone has to teach them. Most of them are in the South. In fact, in 1924 there were in the former sixteen slave States, Oklahoma and District of Columbia 3,141,869 children of school age. The number of Negro public school teachers in these States is 42,018. Over an average of 77 children to each teacher.

If we do not have colored teachers teaching these children in the South, white teachers must do it. And no person with a spark of humanity in his breast would want to see little colored boys and girls taught by Southern white teachers.

In the North teachers teach where they can get jobs. I don't suppose there is a man or woman anywhere trained professionally who would not rather teach in a system like New York, Chicago, or any other large system where there is no discrimination than in a "Jim Crow" system. But there is only one New York. Only one Chicago. Children must be taught. Jim Crow public school systems exist, even as Jim Crow churches, Jim Crow banks, Jim Crow fraternal organizations, Jim Crow theatres, Jim Crow newspapers, Jim Crow social systems, Jim Crow Pullman porter organizations. It would be a fearsome thing if every man or woman who has the urge to impart what he knows to the youth of the land would fold his or her hands, and refuse to teach unless he could teach in an unsegregated system. Where would be the youth of tomorrow?

"They swarm everywhere, and their whole interest is to draw their pay checks and not 'rock the boat.' "

As to "swarming"—the poor teachers, like ministers, newspaper men, porters, politicians, musicians, saxophone players and other human beings have to go to places. They can't sit at their desks or hide behind the blackboards. They must get out and know what is going on; must go to summer schools, theatres, lectures, concerts, social gatherings and labor meetings. If they did not, they would be sorry souls, and we would hear the complaint that they don't go anywhere to learn anything except schoolroom routine. As to the pay check, and their sole interest—that is a matter first of necessity, second of opinion. Many a teacher has elected to stay in a position which paid a smaller salary than one which made a flattering offer, simply because he thought he could be more useful in the smaller place.

"As a class the school teachers are contributing little or nothing toward solving the manifold problems facing the Negro masses."

Humph. And is not the moulding the opinions and lives of countless ten thousands of children a contribution towards the solution of the manifold problems?

Who has been responsible for the increased pride of race now noted in the present generation?

Who have hammered and hammered and hammered again at Negro history, taught the facts about the race, developed a racial consciousness in the young people?

Who have put across the nationwide observance of "Negro History Week," thereby not only teaching the Negro youth what makes him proud of himself, and proud of his race, but also the white communities, school boards, children, and adults about the contribution of the Negro to our civilization? What has done that? And if that is not a contribution and an aid to solution, what is? Who have taught and trained the youth of the race, and brought it to the point where it can criticize and find fault and be race leaders, if necessary?

You don't suppose it was the clergy, or the homes, or the newspapers, or the columnists, or the agitators, or the critics, do you?

Upon the overburdened and muchly depreciated shoulders of the teachers must we lay the praise of these achievements.

Again, "teachers are afraid to speak up or be put on record as favoring anything"—"their one care is not to 'rock the boat.' "

Well—there is much truth in that point. But once a man or woman has prepared for the teaching profession he is about as fit to change as if he had prepared to be a lawyer, a doctor, a minister, or a carpenter. That is his vocation, his job, his work. And that job must be work.

And school boards, communities, boards of trustees, superintendents, supervisors, parents, churches, and all don't want teachers who "speak up." The churches want them to come around and help out on Men's Day, Women's Day, Coal Rally Day with a "paper," or teach in the Sunday school.

But an outspoken opinion on a public matter meets with a very cold shoulder from the churches.

And the parents talk about the teacher who has opinions other than those on education, as being well—perhaps a trifle unsafe.

And principals, under the direction of boards and superintendents, mark them down, and their salaries get cut because of a "C" grade, where their work deserved an "A."

And superintendents and boards of education of city systems, and boards of trustees of institutions fire them if they get the reputation of being "radical." Being "radical," meaning that they believe in the inherent truths of the Declaration of Independence, and maybe don't always vote the straight Republican ticket.

And a teacher who is fired from one system is ever after a discredited man or woman. It makes no difference how the matter may have been afterwards adjusted, smoothed over, settled, or apologized for to the sufferer, or the lie nailed. That man or woman is marked, and can never more get a position worthy the name in any system or under any board. Neither years of service, finest preparation, splendid record nor valuable work count. He or she may as well forget the principles of education and go on and carry the hod or take in sewing. He is "unsafe."

Can you wonder, Mr. Schuyler, that the 50,000 or more teachers in colored schools are careful not to "rock the boat"? Lots would like to. But in the interest of their youthful charges, whose ideals of life do not need to be warped by unnecessary upheavals in our educational systems, many refrain.

And yet, while we do need a "militant upper class," there are many besides the teachers to do the militanting.

And then there were Booker Washington, Du Bois, James W. Johnson, Eugene Kinckle Jones, Mary B. Talbert, Dr. Carter Woodson, both of the Terrells, William Pickens, many of our newspaper editors, and Neval Thomas and scores of others who were teachers and militant at the same time.

September 4, 1926

The last two weeks in August! Sacred fortnight! Sacred to the working girl and working man everywhere, and sacrosanct to the Man and Brother and Woman and Sister. Time was— you remember when you were younger, in the dear Age of Innocence, when the dear girls saved all winter, and slaved at the sewing machine all summer making innumerable dresses with innumerable frills to wear "down at the shore." And when the middle of August came, such a packing and preparing and last stitches, and last minute shopping and getting ready, and finally a huge trunk packed to the brim with dresses and more dresses and still more dresses. Dresses befrilled, be-furbeloved, be-trained. Bows and sashes, and accessories and regalia. And petticoats! And unmentionables! And corsets! And shoes, high shoes, and oxfords, and dancing slippers, and evening gowns, and bathing suit—silk, if one was daring, with bloomers and skirts, and sashes, and everything! And then a suit case. And a paper hat box, with several hats, leghorn hats, and other kinds of straw hats, and hats with streamers. And lacy parasols, and silk sunshades, and a wild sport dress, plain, with only one ruffle on the bottom, and daringly showing the instep. And the real athletic girl had a pair of full, roomy, terribly ultra, fin de siecle bloomers in which to ride her bicycle.

And then the wonderful journey on the train down to the shore. And the stuffy little room hardly big enough for a kitten, where two were crowded in with two trunks and bags and hat boxes and shoes and parasols. And the dressing for breakfast. And dressing for luncheon. And another dressing for the bathing beach, where coy young things in bathing suits that almost showed the calves of their legs, flirted on the sands with daring young Apollos whose trunks were fearsomely short—almost to their knees! And dress again for dinner! And perhaps a dance that night, and another dressing.

And so on for two whole glorious never-to-be-forgotten weeks, of moonlight and romance, and all the rest. And then home by the first of September, tanned and happy and broke. Fifty weeks' work for two weeks' joy, and well paid for it at that.

*   *   *

We still have the last two weeks in August sacred. But where are the trunks! Nobody owns trunks any more, except teachers who have to go South for nine months in the year, travelling salesmen, brides, and very young men just out of college with their first job. When your friends invite you to drive down to the summer resort for a weekend or a short stay, they would elevate their eyebrows and give you a mean look if you came tripping out of your house with anything larger than a collapsible leather hat box. Gone are the petticoats with ruffles, and the horde of ruffled underthings. Your "scanties" take up about as much room as a pound box of candy—a whole half dozen of them, at that. And the dresses can roll up in a corner, underneath the sport hat. And the bathing suit is like the rabbit's tale in the Japanese schoolboy's essay. Anyhow, if you haven't what you need, there are plenty of shops everywhere, and better bargains perhaps than to be found at home.

And who dresses for every occasion nowadays? Only the poor little greenhorns, and clothes being pretty much of a muchness, anyhow, what difference does it make what anyone has on, so that the tout ensemble is good, and the skirt short enough, and the makeup skillfully applied?

Economical? Don't have to save fifty weeks for those last two hectic weeks in August, since there are so few clothes to buy?

Never delude yourself, Dear Heart. One spends just as much, infinitely more—and if one is a man, and the oxford bags, and rainbow sweaters and lifeguard bathing suits are all settled—why—

There were no cabarets back in the Age of Innocence. And with ginger ale at a dollar a bottle, and "cover charges," the High Cost of Enjoyment goes merrily on.

. . . .

September 11, 1926

Back home from the annual holiday, and find that politics are sizzling more or less. No one has said a word; no one needs to. One has only to look at the Man and Brother, and note his stride; his pompous look of mysterious knowledge; his knowing air of self-satisfaction to realize that there will be some kind of an election soon. For the Man and Brother takes his politics seriously. Oh, very much so.

* * *

Politics in this column is taboo. Absolutely. And I'm not going to say a word about politics. Orders is orders, notwithstanding and contrariwise. I'm Organization enough to know orders and obey them. But there was no injunction laid on comments on people in politics. And the gods on high Olympus—as has been noted before—must crack their sides whenever they look down upon the Negro of today, taking his civic duties seriously. For he has yet to learn that before he can even be said to have passed the outside door of the threshold into the kindergarten of politics he must learn the white man's lesson—that race is bigger than imaginary lines of political demarcation, and that the Negro is never going to be a factor until he puts his own race above the totem pole of the Caucasian's political self-interest.

* * *

For instance: In a certain one of the 48 States of these United States there lives a large and wealthy family. There are many branches: brothers, cousins, second cousins, et al. It is an old family, having been in this country for over 150 years, and always prolific, given to marrying outside of its own lines. So that there are many branches, many bloods, many ramifications. And, by the same token, many family feuds.

It so happened some twenty-odd years ago that one of the wealthiest of the older scions married. Then came the inevitable scandal. His wife divorced him. He re-married, this time to the lady with whom he had been indulging in a bit of romance on the side. Although the lady in question was one of the best socially and of impeccable birth and breeding, there was a scandalized feeling on the part of the family. A dinner was given; the bride was not bidden. A ball followed. One of the sisters-in-law passed by the newly wed couple without speaking. The bride of the divorced scion was to be cut socially, so went forth the edict.

Tears. A social war. The bride was wrathy. The husband vowed vengeance. He would show them all where they got off. Snub his bride, would they? Well, he'd see.

* * *

As the movie captions say, came a political campaign. One scion of the family aspired to public office. The bitter husband entered the lists against him. Not by running for office, but by building up an organization against him. Ensued then one of the bitterest, most disgraceful feuds in all the history of inside party factional feuds.

Now enters the Man and Brother. As far as I have been able to glean, he was not one of the dinner party, nor was any representative of the race invited to the ball, except as a waiter, or maybe a musician. But there was no relative of the snubbed lady's; no relative of the divorced wife's more bitter, more denunciatory, more violent in factional loyalty than the representatives of the Negro race. It is fairly safe to assert that not one in a thousand knew the origin of the feud. It was enough that there was a feud—which has waged for over 20 years now. He espoused one or the other of the factions firmly and noisily. He was either for Cousin Al, or for Uncle Henry, and he told the world, and was ready to fight himself into jail for his faction. Stand on the side lines and let the white folks settle it among themselves, he refused to do.

Of course, there is the consideration that in those halcyon days they used to back delivery wagons up to the polls, and unload peach baskets of mazuma, coin, greenbacks, dough, long-green, whatever you choose to call it, to help in the performance of civic duties. At least that is what I am told. It happened before my time.

* * *

But the Man and Brother was bitter beyond even that. And fell out with his friends or his family; and stopped speaking to everyone who did not espouse his own particular faction. He was bitter to extremes. And whenever there was an election and Cousin Al projected himself and his private bank into the picture, the Man and Brother grew more bitter.

* * *

Once upon a time many years ago—I've learned better than to proffer political advice now—I said, "It would seem to me since you colored men don't know what these people are fighting about, to go into the row, get all you can out of it, and keep friends with each other. They're all going to make up some day."

And they called me so many kinds of apostate, traitor, renegade, silly woman, low-souled nothing, and other vile names, that I was ashamed to look at myself in the glass for a week, and didn't know that my hair was parted crooked.

* * *

Time sped. The bride became a staid married lady. The tribe forgot their defection, and welcomed her back to society. The breach healed. The lady died. The husband grieved a bit, then married again. And forgot politics. Forgot his enmity. Forgot the peach baskets of money. Though the S.O.S. has been sent to him time and again for the past half dozen years, he heeds not the call, and keeps his peach baskets locked up in the vaults of his 14-story bank.

And the Man and Brother is still carrying about the old

feud, and has handed it on down to the next generation, and none of them know what it is all about.

* * *

And Cousin Al and Uncle Henry and all the whole Tribe have long since buried the hatchet, and closed ranks. And even at their bitterest, even when the peach baskets were going around, they never forgot to leave the Man and Brother OUT of the inner councils. He never gleaned anything out of the fight but the last half layer of the smallest peach basket, when all the rest of it had been handed out to the Nordic, and the Jew and the Polack, and the Lithuanian, and the Italian and the Roumanian, and the Scandinavian and the white janitors of the office buildings. And when he came up after election with his hat in his hand and asked for a crumb at the pie counter, such as a minor city office, or a few janitorships, they told him about that last half layer in the bottom of the peach basket.

* * *

And they played one Negro faction off against another Negro faction, and while the lieutenants of both factions met in secret conclave, and schemed how they could put out the appearance of venom before the public, as they mapped out a plan to split things wider—to insure more and large peach baskets coming forth from the coffers of the bank. They KNEW, these lieutenants did—but there were never any Negro lieutenants in on the know. The crumbs of information they got were less than infinitesimal.

* * *

This is a microcosmic picture of the Negro in American politics. Call Cousin Al one of the major political parties, and Uncle Henry the other—and you have the entire situation. When it comes to the Negro, they close ranks, and behind barred doors combine forces to keep him in ignorance, waging a silly factional fight, the origin and the end of which are alike unknown to him. And the peach baskets are the political plums.

And when it comes down to the great issues where there is a racial conflict, the lieutenants, and heads even, of both parties present a solid racial phalanx. Sometimes it is camouflaged, but so faintly that the student of men and affairs may easily pierce behind its flimsy covers.

* * *

Cousin Al forgot that Sister Betty stuck her nose up in the air at his new wife of long ago, and talks now about blood being thicker than water.

And North is forgetting that she once fought to preserve the integrity of the Union, and to prevent the doctrine of States Rights superseding the Federal Government.

Uncle Henry forgot the time that Cousin Al's peach basket kept him from the office he coveted, and maunders about people getting too old for quarrels, and one should let bygones be bygones.

And the South is spreading its insidious poison of prejudice from Washington on up to Maine, and the North is talking about how lovely it is for the old feuds to be healed.

And in all four cases the Man and Brother is getting so left out of the picture that he doesn't even remember when he stood before the camera.

For blood IS thicker than water, and abolition days are over. In every instance, where there is racial conflict or argument, the white man stands shoulder to shoulder, a solid white wall barring the black man's advance.

When is the Man and Brother going to stop fighting the

white man's petty quarrels, and close ranks politically for himself?

September 18, 1926

. . . . . .

There is one thing that Carl Van Vechten's *Nigger Heaven* has done, if it does nothing else. It has released the largest, most vivid, devastating, complete, powerful, biting, scathing, prolific, asbestos-lined, vituperative, picturesque flood of adjectival vehemence spread over the pages of the "Race" papers that has been turned loose since the *Birth of a Nation*.

And all I have to say is that any time I pick up a book and get so enthralled that I forget to eat, forget that the sun is shining on my unpowdered nose, forget that I have an engagement to collect money, and then when I get through don't pitch it out of the window—as I did *Martha*, for instance—well, a book that has such power over me has my endorsement.

A score or more years ago Dunbar's *Sport of the Gods* treated the same theme in what was then a bold, daring, frank exposition of the Negro in New York. Harlem was a white man's habitat then, and the night life centered around the "clubs" of the thirties and Sixth Avenue. If you want to see how far the Negro has advanced, read the two books together. *The Sport of the Gods* treats of the good old days of Williams and Walker, for which Adora sighs in *Nigger Heaven*. But the sybaritic elegance which Van Vechten describes was undreamed of even by the luxury-loving Ada Overton.

Mr. Van Vechten knows how to tell a story, and that is the main thing in narrative. It is a relief to find him describing a cultured woman, like Mary, without patronizing her. As far as I know, this is absolutely the first time such a thing has been done by a white man. No explanation, no supercilious sneer. Just a plain acceptance of a cultivated brown woman. He should be called blessed for that alone. And he knows values. Whether his local color is correct or overdrawn, not being a Harlem cabaret-hound, I cannot say, but it reads convincingly, and there have been no protests from those who know.

The younger generation would do well to take to heart the advice of the editor to Byron. The prophecy that some day some white author would mine in that Harlem gold and produce a worthwhile novel has already come true. Mr. Van Vechten has done it. Others will follow this lead. The Negro will find himself standing aside looking on, while his rich gold is minted and spent by alien hands. And that event, or rather situation, is so imminent that it is appallingly here.

More novels, please, young literati, and fewer propaganda pamphlets.

But Mr. Van Vechten does not leave much to the imagination, does he?

And does he know the "Race"? Through and through he does.

. . . . . .

It does seem unfortunate, does it not, that there is no little colored girl to do the part of Topsy in the forthcoming film of *Uncle Tom's Cabin?*

* * *

Some time ago a peculiar advertisement appeared in the Philadelphia *Ledger*. It was headed with the caption, "What Price Brains."

"I am a girl two years out of college," it went on to say, "and fully convinced that the world is not her oyster. I am looking for a position in which straight thinking and ingenuity will be most appreciated—where sincerity and ambition will be recognized, and where sterling character and finest references are an absolute necessity. Somewhere a business executive is seeking just such a secretary." Followed by a code address.

The pathos of this struck forcibly home. College training, sterling worth, absolute sincerity, finest references, ambition, youth and yet not inexperience, and no opening. A whole volume of discouragement and baffled ambition, heartache, thwarted purpose, temptation to lower the banner of self-respect, is couched in that strange advertisement found in the classified section. And does it not sound like the epitome of thousands of boys and girls, men and women of our own race? To bridge the apparently yawning chasm which lies between those who have something, and those who want that something, is ofttime a Herculean task. In the case of this girl who had failed to find the world her oyster, perhaps the arresting advertisement in the newspaper will suffice.

But who shall bridge the gap for the 1,300 young college graduates of color who received their degrees last June?

AS IN A LOOKING GLASS

February 17, 1928

Twenty plays of the contemporary Negro Theatre are gathered together in a volume, highly decorated by Aaron Douglass, edited by Alain Locke and Montgomery Gregory, with a chronology and bibliography of Negro drama, the whole published by Harper and Brothers. A fascinating volume.

Mr. Locke has written the introduction, which is just long enough to whet the appetite, and not long enough to bore one before you dip into the plays themselves. Mr. Locke has the spirit of the true artist, for he says "But it is not the primary function of drama to reform us." Now when the race as a whole gets that attitude of mind—that drama, poetry, fiction must not be blatant popaganda, but "free" and subtle in their preachments, we shall have advanced a far stage toward that pinnacle of artistry which is our present goal.

Eugene O'Neill, Ridgeley Torrence, Ernest Culbertson, and Paul Green are the Caucasian writers, whose plays have been selected to appear. Among our own, there are Willis Richardson, Frank H. Wilson, Eulalie Spence, Georgia Douglass Johnson, Jean Toomer, and Richard Bruce. *Abraham's Bosom* is here, and *Emperor Jones* and *The No Count Boy*, among the rest.

* * *

Folk plays. Plays of sordid Negro life. Plays of lynchings and fear and repressions. Plays of funerals and deaths and grim soul tragedies. Plays of raped Negro girlhood, and white men going scot free and honored. Plays that make your throat constrict with fear and pain, that leave your eyes hot with unshed tears, and your fists clenched with anger. If this is a carefree, merry light-hearted race, heaven help the sober ones. This drama of ours, or this drama by us and about us is sombre, gloomy, pitiful. Even the Dance Calinda is a tragedy. John Matheus *Cruiter* ends with a note of hope, but even that is on the heartbreak of Granny. And Eulalie Spence's comedy of Harlem life, *The Starter,* leaves a bad taste in the mouth for you know that out of the comedy, tragedy will eventuate.

* * *

Yet these plays are worthwhile, not only reading, but possessing to reread. For they are a faithful transcript of a phase of Negro life that is real poignant. After all, as Carlyle says, is not every life a tragedy? For it ends in a death bed. As Mr. Locke says, "Forced to laugh outwardly and weep inwardly, the Negro has until lately only been in the position of successful clowning. With better emotional compensation there will come the power to smile satirically and reflect with ironic composure."

* * *

You feel something of this change of viewpoint in the comparison, for instance of the play *Sugar Cane* by Frank Wilson in this volume, and the recent play of his now in New York, *Meek Mose.* Both plays satirize the "White folks nigger," but *Sugar Cane* is so nearly a tragedy that even at the end you can scarce feel relief. *Meek Mose* is almost a fairy tale of unbelievable wealth coming to the down and out. But the irony is so detached, that one is almost deceived into believing that the playwright believes in what his characters believe.

* * *

I sometimes wonder if we do not go about hunting for trouble, ofttimes where no trouble exists. That is most natural. We are so used to segregation, and snubs and the drawing aside of skirts at our approach, and the being shunted off into corners that we find it where it is least intended. The problem then is whether we shall develop pachydermatous hides, and never be insulted, or whether we shall like Scott's stag be ready with pricked ears and uplifted foot to flee at the whiff of a zephyr.

Recently a conference of girls and leaders in a nearby city was headed by the moving spirit—a whole-souled woman of the Caucasian persuasion—wholly free from the cant, hypocrisy and insidious prejudice which too often permeate the souls of such workers. Without the dangerous spoken word being used, it was evident that the whole spirit of the conference was to be absolutely devoid of prejudice, segregation, proscription, or anything that might be construed into an unfriendly act, or even thought. To the credit of the leader be it known that this occurred in a town of Southern sentiment and known prejudice. And the whole thing worked beautifully. For two days the actual spirit of Christian love and amity reigned. One would have to be jaundiced indeed to have seen anything in that gathering of two hundred or more girls and women, forty or fifty of whom were colored, that might have touched the most sensitive of us on our tenderest spot.

And yet, there were some who looked for trouble. Ached for trouble. Saw prejudice in every gesture. Found segregation in every action. Whispered poisoned suspicions into the ears of young and unsuspecting girls, and placed misconstructions upon the most friendly acts. Mistook the natural selection of congenial friends for drawings aside for racial reasons, and found fault with the natural adjustments of the ordinary intercourses of life.

Vigilance in defending our constitutional rights is necessary. But plain bad manners in social gatherings is quite another proposition. Do we want equality of opportunity? Or are we always looking for the best and highest place, the most attention, the greatest amount of concessions on account of our race? Let's be honest. Is it equality we want or superiority of consideration?

March 2, 1928

Sympathy is extended to poor Dr. Jerzabeck, leader of the Clerical Party in the Austrian National Parliament. He objects to Josephine Baker, not because of her color or nationality, but because she appeared before the public "dressed only in a postage stamp."

Josephine is getting good publicity. Any time a dancer can "stop the show" of a National Parliament by discussion of her appearance, she doesn't need a press agent. And poor Dr. Jerzabeck shouting about the scandalousness of paying 100,000 shillings to see nudity when a hundred thousand workmen are searching for employment and food is but an innocent party to Josephine's publicity stunts. Therefore we sympathize with the Austrian doctor. Nothing is more pitiful than to pull another's chestnuts from the fire.

. . . . . .

We are right back where we were fourteen years ago. The German army is goose-stepping again, and two dogs have been found who can talk. Fourteen years ago it was a German dachshund who could ask for cake. Again a machine has been found that can produce diamonds, and an American has produced a real Robot. Another fuelless motor has been invented, but this time it is in an airplane. The British birthrate has fallen again, Harry Thaw is figuring in another law suit, doctors are scoffing at pet superstitions of their patients. Chicago is beginning to oppose its mayor, and the League of Nations is at it harder than ever. Emil Ludwig lists the great women of the world, and they were all twenty years ago. Charlie Chaplin has a new play, and Ethel Barrymore has not. And so the world wags on through its everlasting cycle. Except for the new Ford car.

* * *

Down in Georgia they stole the body of a colored woman from the white cemetery and buried it in the colored one, in the dark of night, and with no known witnesses. When men are willing to rob graves for their prejudices, you cannot expect to talk them away by quoting Bible texts.

· · · · · ·

Out in Watts, California, the citizenry object to Negroes owning and driving busses. they may patronize them, but own them never. Therefore the franchise of the bus line is revoked. A fine incentive for the Negro to "acquire property, thrift, and a steady position in the community."

· · · · · ·

March 9, 1928

· · · · · ·

Elizabeth Madox Roberts, whose book *The Time of Man*, was adjudged one of the outstanding events of the past year, comes forth with one now that fearlessly touches the question of the impinging of the Negro's life upon that of his white neighbors. Seldom has a Southern writer been so frank in her confession of the lack of morality of the white man in his dealing with Negro women. How Theodosia discovers that her father is also the father of the half-witted Negro stable boy, Stiggins, and the two brown sisters, Lethe and Americy, and of still another mother than Stiggins—no better than they should be; how she tries to inject her life into theirs, to become part of them, and how her health and her reason are almost swept away in the final merging of her identity with the jealous Lethe, living over her own love disappointment in the insane jealousy of her half sister, is something not to be told, but to be read in all its bitter intensity. For one cannot tell the story of Elizabeth Madox Roberts' books, nor hardly read them. They are felt, experienced, sensed, lived, rather than read.

It is a healthy sign when Southern white women can look calmly at the curse of the South—mulattoes—and not blame black women for them.

.   .   .   .   .   .

Elijah Reynolds, Master-Sergeant, U.S. Army, retired, finds that "The Negro has been denied his full opportunity, according to his ratio in the country's population, to acquire his due measure and standing of military efficiency."

Putting it baldly, we still have the 24th and 25th Infantry, and the 9th and 10th Cavalry—which is what we had in the early 90's. No increase in the regular army in proportion to the increase of Negro population. 12,000,000 Negroes, constituting one-tenth of the population of the country are represented in the Regular Army by about 4,000 Negroes, of which number only about 3,000 are combat troops. In the National Guard there are fewer than 3,000 Negroes on the roster.

Getting still farther down to bed rock it would seem that this country does not wish to arm Negroes, does not want Negro soldiers, does not choose to use us as fighters.

Which is a very fine thing for the Negro. The burning zeal to lay down his life, and make widows and orphans of his women folk for the white man's money quarrels, which we are apt to evince in moments of national hysteria, should be considerably cooled by the conning of the above figures.

. . . . . .

The merry controversy between the horned toads of Texas and the talking dogs of New England, the wets and drys of the North and South, the lectures on companionate marriages, and the latest presidential candidates goes blithely on, and it is all equally unimportant. Meanwhile thousands of women and children starve, and atrocities are committed in the mining districts that would put Russia to blush. But you do not hear of those things in the daily papers.

March 16, 1928

Says the Associated Press of a recent date, "A perceptible move is under way by a number of members of the House Immigration Committee to strengthen existing immigration laws."

Which being translated into Americanese means that a bill be approved to exclude all races except those of white blood. This would bar the Mexican, the South American of mixed blood, while admitting the Canadian. The West Indian, the African, and so forth and so on, anything dark and anti-Nordic, it seems. Poor Nordics, they must be frightfully unhappy—always fearing, dread and preparing for the inevitable Gotterdamerung.

Meanwhile the Wahabi tribesmen in Arabia have launched their annual "holy war" against the infidel white man, who has so ruthlessly invaded their Transjordania desert. Whether or not this is mere newspaper talk, propaganda against the natives, or a bid for sympathy for the poor Britons who risk their lives in order that the sun may never set upon Great Britain is of little moment. It is merely a part of the great unrest, the constant warfare that is unceasingly being waged below the surface of Western consciousness, between the darker and lighter races. A smouldering fire of hate and distrust that if not checked will involve the world in a conflagration of destruction.

Mostly because so-called civilization wants oil, coal, rubber, iron. And so-called savagery does not see the necessity of being ruthlessly slaughtered to furnish said oil, coal, rubber, iron.

. . . . . .

Just suppose, for example, that every intelligent Negro, every man and woman of force and character, stayed out of the political broil, and urged others of the weaker calibre to do likewise, instead of hanging hungrily around for a stop here and there, and a chance to ease the itching of their palms? Just suppose they let the Bourbons and the Lily-White fight it out among themselves, and at the critical moment put a black ticket in the field, which the Negroes would support solidly—well, the political history of the United States would be a very different affair from what it has been, and is likely to be from present indications. It does seem ridiculous for Samson to go on grinding corn in Gaza when his mighty muscle can not only pull down temples, but build them anew.

. . . . . .

There seems to be a grim determination on the part of this country to go to war with somebody about something at some time. Just who we are going to fight now, is not quite clear. But apparently we must fight someone, other than the Nicaraguans—which is merely guerilla skirmishing. What we will fight about is also not apparent. But we can fix up a pretext, and all the advertising experts can begin to cudgel their brains for slogans for us to shout and wave flags about. When the war will begin has not yet been fixed. But give us time to straighten out Congress, pile up some more national debts for preparedness, and then the party may begin. You may have noted that the word, "preparedness," which had lapsed from our vocabularies for a few years, is springing up here and there and is on more lips and in more editorial columns of newspapers than at any time since 1918.

And now is about the time for the Negro to make his choice, whether he will join the ranks of the unthinking multitude who know not what they do, but will bring disaster upon the heads of their children—or of the true patriots, who will aim to keep the keel of the ship of state steady and true.

March 23, 1928

Now and then there appears a book which has nothing at all to do with the Negro, does not mention his name, and is not interested in him one way or the other, but which Negroes should read, for the good of their souls. Such a book is *Meat*, by Wilbur Daniel Steele, which has been so much talked about. I wish all Negro mothers with intelligence could read it. There is a message therein on the rearing of children which we need sorely as a race. It is not the obvious message of the book—which has so shocked and stirred the reading public: that of the sacrifice of the well and strong and normal to the unfit. That, of course, is powerful enough, but the one which seems to me to need emphasis to our women is the damage that can be done to the souls of children by the nasty suggestiveness which passes for moral teaching. No one will ever know the irreparable loss of virtue that has followed in the wake of so-called moral percepts, which were too often the inhibitions of sex-starved ascetics. The "Don't," with the suggestion of something unspeakably vile, arouses a curiosity, which is either going to be satisfied in dark and devious ways, or will suppress itself in hideous inhibitions, ruining a whole character and life. The teachings of children that their lovely little bodies are vile things to be thrust away from sight—

Well, there are still persons who think that legs are something horrible. Some are, maybe, but that is irrelevant. The lesson our women need to learn is the difference between morality and pruriency—and teach it to their children.

* * *

An interesting little book is *Baha'u'llah and the New Era*, by J. E. Esslemont, published by the Baha'i Publishing Committee, New York. Mr. Esslemont appears to be an Englishman, but he has thoroughly absorbed the teachings of Baha-'ists. His work is regarded by members of the Baha'i Movement as the most reliable and satisfactory introduction to the teachings and history of the Religion yet written.

The author, so the note says, submitted his manuscript to 'Abdu'l-Baha in the winter of 1919–1920 at Haifa, and in accordance with his suggestion amplified the text. Before its publication in England in 1922, the manuscript was read and cordially approved by Shoghi Effendi, administrative head of the movement since the death of 'Abdu'l-Baha in 1921.

The author takes up in detail, which is most readable and interesting, the principal episodes in the lives of the three great teachers of the Baha'i Religion, and the principles of the religion. He deals specifically with the relation of the Baha'i Faith to Christianity, Islam and other religions, which it claims to fulfill, and with the relations of science and religion in the experience of the Western world.

practical in its idealism. That is the appealing quality of the
whole volume—its intensely practical appeal to the Western
mind, while having at its root the idealism and mysticism of
the east. It is easy to see how Baha'ism has gained a hold on
the Western world. It satisfies the yearning for the spiritual,
while not offending one's need for the material.

.   .   .   .   .   .

The Republican sisters are raising a howl because the Republican brothers are making trouble about their accommodations
at Kansas City next June. Well, they're not the only ones
disgruntled. The Republican brothers, white, are about to
put the little dark delegates off in little dark corners, where
they won't be in the big hotels listening in at the deep
conferences, and knowing too much about the inner secrets.
There may be some more of those three a.m. sessions, where
in sheer fatigue a very dark horse is chosen to lead the
fortunes of the country for the next four years. And it wouldn't
do for the women to know too much. And it would certainly
never, never do for the Man and Brother to know anything
but the crumbs of information dropped from on high. Republican sisters, you're not alone in your wounded pride.

March 30, 1928

.   .   .   .   .   .

Edwin Alden Jewell, in the *Times Magazine* section, writes a
sympathetic appreciation of the exhibit of Archibald J. Motley, Jr., which is illustrated by reproduction of three of Mr.
Motley's remarkable paintings. Thank Heaven, Mr. Motley
is original enough to be modern without being cubistic,
futuristic or whatever "stic" it is that distorts things so that
it does not make any difference whether the picture is hung

upside down or not. He can deal in symbolism without expressing his soul in the form of ovoids, rhomboids or parabolas.

. . . . . .

April 8, 1928

Easter brings with it thoughts of spring, of service, of renunciation, of resurrection, of sacrifice, of hope, of peace, of the reawakening of the spark of belief that is in every heart.

All nature has been preparing for the festival of Easter, or of the Passover, or of the fete of Flora, or of the rites of Eostre, or of Isis, or of Ashtoroth, or of Persephone or of Balder, or what you will. For untold centuries mankind has celebrated the close of winter, and the advent of spring, the resurrection of the flowers, the beginning of new life, the resuscitation of a primitive and inherent belief in immortality. He has called this reaffirmation of his belief by various names, according to the country where he lives and the cosmogony to which he swore allegiance. But the story underlying it is the same, through thousands and thousands of years—death and rebirth. Winter killed by spring. Sorrow turned to rejoicing. Clouds dispelled by sunshine. Gloom supplanted by radiance. Despair succeeded by joy.

Therefore it is to be expected that at this season there will be something of the cheer and good will that characterizes Christmas. For if tenderness at the birth of a child fills the heart of humanity, how much more so should the memory of the supreme sacrifice stir us to deeds of kindness and love, of tenderness and mercy. The reawakening of nature, daffodils dancing in the sunshine, bird-song, shrilling of frogs and flutter of butterflies, should stir the souls of more than the poets and the suburban gardener. For is it not a constant attestation of immortality?

.   .   .   .   .   .

April 20, 1928

.   .   .   .   .   .

The Negro is very much a part of this modern trend against war. No one knows better than the Negro that war is not the kind of thing which will bring about understanding among races, and he must be deeply concerned with inter-racial amity. His fortunes are so inevitably interwoven with the fortunes of everyone else in the nation, that he must deplore all that is wasteful, immoral, subversive of the Ten Commandments, as war is, and welcome all practical methods to bring about international, inter-racial peace, and morality.

It is of interesting significance that the majority of the leaders of the Negroes in the United States are open advocates and champions of peace. That the younger generation has scrapped war with other useless and outworn traditions. There is no glorification of force in their writings, no paeans of praise for soldiery.

Most decidedly, the modern trend is against war, and toward peace.

.   .   .   .   .   .

April 27, 1928

.   .   .   .   .   .

It seems particularly fortunate that at the great crisis in the life of Fisk, her fortunes were entrusted to Dr. Thomas Elsa Jones. Long residence in Japan had removed him from any possible contamination of factionalism, and he is a man not afraid to say the right and manly thing at the right time. Added to this a wife with exquisite tact and graciousness, without gush. It was a superhuman task which confronted the new president—to mend the matters, adjust the broken relationships, heal differences, restore confidence, build the broken structure anew, gild as it were the spires of Jubilee Hall with the fresh gold of morning hope. These things he and Mrs. Jones have accomplished, changing the gravely critical glance with which both races watched, into enthusiastic and helpful acquiescence. For many of us felt that it would be years before Fisk could "come back."

* * *

As Dr. Jones phrased it so vividly to the teachers at Louisville, Fisk is the place where youth may learn the most difficult of the arts, the art of living; the right use of leisure, the knowledge and love of the arts and humanities. Let us rise and give thanks that there are still places where the youth of the race may be taught to be self-sufficient—to BE as well as to DO.

And may the towers of Jubilee Hall always dominate the city of Nashville!

May 11, 1928

. . . . . .

Now and then there comes a book which you lay down when you have finished reading it with a deep sigh of content and a sense of having envisaged something complete and eminently soul-satisfying. Such a book is W. E. B. Du Bois' *Dark Princess*, (Harcourt, Brace and Company). Dr. Du Bois has come a long way in the art of construction of a novel since the *Quest of the Silver Fleece* made us think that at last the great American novel had arrived. *Dark Princess* is close knit, marching steadily to a goal, pausing neither to the right for dissertations, nor to the left for extraneous incident. Matthew Towns is the hero. All other characters, clear-cut or vague though they may be, are subsidiary to him and his progress through the few years which comprise the action of the book. Even Kautilya, the "Dark Princess"—who vaguely reminds you of someone you have known for a long while—does not obtrude her personality to overshadow Matthew. As a matter of fact, Kautilya is less well drawn than Sara, the cold, hard, schemer. Kautilya seems an ideal, a vision, a dreamer of the author. Sara is a disagreeable personality who has rasped his sensibilities, tread on his toes, and disturbed his soul by her blatancy. He KNEW Sara; he envisioned Kautilya.

* * *

There are so many delicious bits of personal description in the book that you want to sit down and read it aloud to a sympathetic little group. What could be better than this:

> Corruthers was a cadaverous blond, red-head and freckled, a drunkard, a dope fiend, and a spell-binder, with brains and no self-control, thoroughly dishonest and extremely likable. He claimed to be a nephew of Frederick Douglass.

* * *

It seems almost uncanny, the prophecy of the death of a prominent member of Congress from the black district in Chicago, and the consequent nomination of a black man for his place. In fact, the whole analytic picture of Chicago politics, the dark thread weaving in and out of the action in and around the city, the plots and counterplots, the scheming politicians, the cheap intrigues, the cringing blacks and sneering whites, the graft, the petty politics, the double-crossing, the stalking of prey, all is told with such a sure grasp that one is amazed to remember that the author lives in New York and does not play the political game in Chicago. He picks up each specimen—who are rather thinly veiled public personalities—and holding it upon the cruel scalpel of his pen, dissects it for his delighted readers in a way that must make the originals of the portraits squirm—if they have read the book.

Much less convincing are the chapters which tell of Matthew's purification by his self-imposed descent into the depths of gruelling labor and physical discomfort. Even his letters to Kautilya hardly seem to clarify the situation. We have guessed from the beginning, when she fled to Matthew's mother in Virginia that the final chapter of the book will have to be written as it is. But that it would be just as it is hardly seemed possible. And to tell the story is to spoil the whole tale most effectively.

* * *

Dr. Du Bois is always somewhat bitter, even though the advancing years are tempering his acidity with some of the alkali of pity for the non-understanding, and he can more gracefully act the showman's part than he could some years ago. Albeit that showman is a bit given to a few asides of caustic cynicism. But he manages in *Dark Princess* to pay his respects to women politicians, the Ku Klux Klan, the Negro grafter, snobbery in Negro society, over-inflated Negro churches, which were once Jewish synagogues, English insolence in the face of royal Indian blood, the futility of porters' organizations, Chicago divorce courts, American universities in hands of Southern professors in the North, Strivers' Row, Negro ministers, Negro politicians, Marcus Garvey, Pan-Africanism, the inferiority complex of social climbers, reformers and Bolsheviks, Jim Crow cars, and Jim Crow souls. As Bert Williams used to say, "He spares nobody."

Dark Princess is artistic. The propaganda contained therein is so disguised that it is not obtrusive as it was in *The Quest of the Silver Fleece*. You know that in the back of the author's mind is a plea for a union of the darker races of the earth. But you know also that he recognizes the difficulty of achieving such a Utopia, indeed states all the objections himself. We must content ourselves with the implied vision in the union of the hero and heroine, and the feeling that together they will work out their plans, if not in this, then in some future incarnation. That the Maharajah of Bwodpur will be indeed, "Messenger and Messiah to all the Darker Worlds"! In these later chapters Dr. Du Bois grows apocalyptic—and rightly so. It is a big theme. A very big theme. Not to be lightly dismissed as a daydream, but to be embraced as a Heaven-sent vision.

The main thing after all in a work of fiction to be considered is the story. Once you pick up *Dark Princess* you will not want to lay it down. It is the sort of book that makes you leave the house-work undone while you dig into the pages to find out what happens next. That's the best tribute to pay a story. And when that tale is told in a faultless English, with due regard for structure, with the inevitable sex glorified into a thing of rare beauty—as it should be—instead of a thing of mud and putrescence, with all one's pet aversions properly allayed, with Truth and Art stamped upon the whole—you have, as we said at the outset—a soul-satisfying piece of creative writing.

June 8, 1928

. . . . . .

But of the actual facts in the history of Reconstruction in the South it is evident the editor of *Liberty*, in common with some millions of other white men North and South has never heard, would not believe if he did hear, does not want to hear, and would rather be shot at sunrise than be compelled to hear. The average American sixth grade moron has a primitive idea of history. He believes that Columbus set out to discover an already named continent called America. That Indians were waiting to scalp all white men, and were addicted to the use of whiskey. That the War of Independence was a unified rising of all the Colonists against the tyranny of King George. That the Civil War was fought to free the slaves. That the United States freed Cuba from the tyranny of Spain as an act of pure altruism. That great generals and heroes spend most of their time either leading a charge up a steep hill, sword in hand enunciating immortal epigrams, or else posing in difficult attitude at great national crises. He does not want to know any more. He would not understand it if he did.

.   .   .   .

June 22, 1928

The cynical, staccato, impersonality of the style of *Time*, the weekly newsmagazine was never employed more effectively than in the issue of June 11, when it commented upon the story of Ben Bess of Florence County, South Carolina. "After he had had the Collins woman some time Ben Bess went to jail for thirty years of hard labor. That was in 1915. That trash, Frank Collins, hadn't minded at all about Ben Bess and the woman, until Ben Bess decided not to rent his land any more. Then Frank Collins brought the charge that has lynched many a nigger. The Collins woman, old Maude, backed him up. They said Ben Bess had raped her."

You can almost hear the writer of the cynical story spit as he types, until he says, "Governor Richards agreed that South Carolina's debt to Ben Bess is irreparable."

.   .   .   .   .   .

Delaware is to have a Negro lawyer at last, and there is one more bit of campaign material gone. Delaware has been the only one of the forty-eight states that refused to allow a Negro to practice law within its bounds. There was no law against it, but the Negro applicants for admission to the bar simply did not pass the examination. And then came a law on the statutes that before anyone could be admitted he must serve in a practicing lawyer's office for a certain time. This debarred not only Negroes, who could find no white lawyers to take them in their office, but white applicants, who had no friends as well. Colored people have hammered on that "No Lawyers in Delaware" for a number of years, and various and sundry applicants have gone down to defeat. It became an issue that stuck out like a sore thumb about six years ago, and has been one of the best campaign slogans against the existing administration that could ever have been invented. The Anti-Lynching Crusaders used it, and the party in power squirmed. The anti-administration insurgents hammered at it, until the powers in charge turned green at the very thought of the word *lawyer*.

And now on the eve of one of the tightest presidential campaigns of the century, with Delaware a doubtful state, and the Negro the balance of power—and lo, it is discovered that a Negro lawyer can be admitted to the bar. Lewis L. Redding, a native son, graduate of Brown University, A.B., and Harvard Law School, LL.B., will not only pass the examination, but will enter the office of a prominent lawyer, a judge in the municipal court—one of the shrewdest and most astute politicians to be found anywhere in a month of Sundays. And that is cutting some of the ground from under the feet of the insurgents.

But it only shows what the Negro can get by persistent hammering. If the "No-Lawyers-in-Delaware" had not been taken up by the fighters some six years ago and made a political issue—young Mr. Redding would be compelled to hang out his shingle in Pennsylvania—as other Delaware lawyers have done.

July 20, 1928

Dr. Rudolph Fisher has come to the front with a novel, *The Walls of Jericho*, published by Alfred A. Knopf, New York. I must confess to having had a small qualm of misgiving when the jacket design of Aaron Douglass loomed at me, with the traditional square black individuals proclaiming this a "race book" of the "New Negro" type. But the misgivings faded with the opening sentence, disappeared with the second page, and were so completely obliterated as to be forgotten before the end of the first chapter.

For Dr. Fisher has achieved a clean story of Harlem, a story of the ordinary street Negro of Harlem, the black-jack playing, hard drinking, hard-hitting laborer living in Harlem, and his sweetheart, a maid, a slim little brown-skin girl, wholly sweet, and completely decent. Joshua Jones, the piano mover, was "so hard that his spit bounced," and Linda was just a K. M.—which the glossary tells, wholly unnecessary to the sophisticate—means a kitchen mechanic, a worker in white folks' kitchens. And these two in the atmosphere of Harlem, with all its gin-guzzling, crap-shooting, its argot and night life, have a clean romance, one of the kind which we feared had been forgotten. They meet, they love, they woo, they quarrel, they are reconciled, and they marry, cleanly, decently, sweetly. And you feel like saying, "Glory be!" when the last tender fade-out swims across the last page. And that last paragraph is a gem of lovely description— "Shine" and Linda, on the seat of "Bess" the truck, fading away into the sunrise, her head upon his shoulder, the roar of the truck a triumphant accompaniment to the thoughts of the amazed lawyer, Merritt.

Once you pick up *The Walls of Jericho* you do not put it down until you have finished it. For Dr. Fisher has told a good story, slight though it is. There is no attempt at fine writing, no delving into mud and slime, when he portrays the life of the poor parlor and the street corner. He simply tells his tale, with due regard for unity of action, central figures, contrast of characters, climacteric construction, opposing forces, and all the elements which, sneer at them if you will, mark the difference between the well constructed and loosely constructed narrative. There is no propaganda, no whining, no sneering, but there is a lot of quiet fun in the whole story. The author has written with his tongue in his cheek, and deep reminiscent chuckles. And he evokes from his delighted readers correspondingly appreciative chuckles. It has been a long while since I have enjoyed so many chuckles in one book.

There is much sly irony, some good-natured fun-poking. We have all known and met Miss Agatha Cramp, the perpetual reformer. Her colossal ignorance of Negroes, and her calm refusal to believe what she did not want to believe are unfortunately characteristic of too many reformers. And the crowd of "dickties," some of whom are quite recognizable, are amusing enough, but not nearly so amusing as the crowd down at Pat's Pool Parlor. Indeed, if the inimitable dialogues of Jinx and Bubber could be put into a vaudeville sketch, Moran and Mack would have to look to their laurels. And as for the ball of the G. I. A., which is a very thinly disguised appellation for another association, not Marcus Garvey's, it is so true to life that you actually yawned in sympathy for the bored "dickties."

There are many quotable passages, but space will not permit anything more than a general statement of their uniform delightfulness. *The Walls of Jericho* is not a great book, but it is an interesting and readable one. It will not "unscrew the unscrutable," but it has shown that one does not have to wallow in filth to write about the most interesting spot in the United States—Harlem. It has no fierce and withering propaganda to point a moral and adorn a tale, but it tells of decency in the lower middle strata of Negro life, which is only fair and just and right, for after all, there is more decency than there is dirt in ordinary life, and much more wholesome love than the modernists will admit.

You will enjoy reading *The Walls of Jericho*. It is a pleasant antidote for a lot of psychopathic slime masquerading under the name of novels.

* * *

The Rev. Thomas H. Whelpley, pastor of Chelsea Presbyterian Church, "The Skyscraper Church," at 214 West 23rd Street, New York, has been delighting the readers of the New York *World* with the story of his experiences of the flaming life of Manhattan from the driver's seat of a night-hawk taxi-cab. The third of the articles tells how he overheard the conversation of two well-dressed girls whom he thought were white, but who passed by a hotel and picked up a dusky friend, who was apparently a hat-check girl. The reverend taxi-driver learns that these girls have been "passing" down-town and that 8,000 right in New York daily pass for white. He gets his first glimpse of the night life of Harlem, and is thrilled, frightened, edified. But in the end he takes the advice of his fellow cabbies and "hurries home from Harlem."

* * *

That sheriff's convention which met in Erie, Pa., and had so much wet goods with them, that they had to move to Canada to finish the sessions, because of the raid upon their quarters by the local exponents of law and order, is a fine example of the sort of thing that goes on among the officials who are supposed to be sworn to enforce the law and uphold the Constitution of the United States.

. . . . . .

July 27, 1928

. . . . .

Newport, Rhode Island, is a town of quaintness and charm immeasurable. The loud and blatant Newport of the marble palaces and Bailey's Beach and gorgeous homes is all very well, but the real Newport of the crooked lanes that call themselves streets, the quaint old houses leaning confidentially over the streets, the funny little shops and the sidewalks all on one side of the streets, because there isn't room on the other side is another and more charming matter. It makes you think of St. Augustine, Florida, water, fortresses, mid-shipmen, and all. You feel that it must have been settled in cold weather, and that the pioneers put the houses close together for warmth, and made the streets narrow and wind-ing, so the winds could not whistle too keenly down their crooked length. It was winter when Roger Williams was driven from the Massachusetts colony, was it not?

It was in Newport that the Northeastern Federation of Womens' Clubs met last week. Newport did itself proud. It entertained the delegates, and the mayor and other public officials came out and welcomed everybody in the most delightful fashion. And there wasn't anything in the town too good for the visitors, who were bent, however, upon the business of the week—attending strictly to convention affairs.

"No segregation in Newport, no race prejudice, no Ku Klux Klan," said Mayor Sullivan to the visitors. Hurrah for Newport!

August 3, 1928

To talk about anything else this week but the convention of the National Federation of Colored Women now in session in Washington would be a sheer waste of time and energy so far as colored women are concerned. It is "The one great divine event, toward which the whole creation moves." Or to paraphrase it, the one great event in the life of the club women of our race, toward which their energies are bent for the two years intervening between conventions.

Sidelights and highlights are plenty. Everyone who has a program to put over, an axe to grind, a bit publicity to be gained, a resolution to be endorsed, advertising to put forth, a friend to meet, a date to make, someone to find, old friendships to renew, old acquaintances to seek, new contacts to be made, propaganda to spread, subscriptions to take to publications, articles for which to take orders, pamphlets to handout, cards to distribute, pictures to take, pictures to sell, gossip to disseminate, joy to spread or gloom to distribute—all such persons, and their name is legion, are to be found around the halls, in the lobbies, in the auditorium, on the platforms, in the committee rooms, in the yard of the Armstrong Technical School and at night buzzing up and down the stairs and in the lobby of the Metropolitan A. M. E. Church. For you will come pretty nearly running across every colored woman in this country who is in public life, or who hopes to be in public life, or who has been in the public eye.

The presiding of Mrs. Mary McLeod Bethume is a joy to behold. Absolutely fair and impartial, judicious, pleasant, cheerful, unruffled in the face of upheavals, giving everyone a chance, without crowding out anyone, compelling obedience without arousing antagonism, refusing to allow the association to commit itself to anything of which it might afterwards be ashamed, maintaining an attitude of strict impartiality and neutrality in the face of all efforts to swing her to one side or the other—she is a marvel to behold. You wonder how her physical being stands the fearful strain of wielding the gavel all day from nine to five, of attending executive board sessions every morning from eight to nine or ten, of presiding over long evening sessions from eight to eleven and eleven thirty, dedicating and opening various buildings, cottages and association activities, socializing with the friends who must have her time—and then appearing every morning on time, fresh, smiling, happy, firm, physically fit. You marvel at her every day and wonder at nature in putting so much that is splendidly worthwhile in one body and mind.

The weather man was kind and gave a few cool days at the beginning of the long week before the inevitble August days set in. But crowded buildings are hot, even in autumn. Washington does not care. It goes night after night to the Metropolitan Church and sits patiently through programs that last until nearly midnight. Sits, and listens, and applauds, and fans, and then comes out during the day down at Armstrong outside the new National headquarters Tech. Washington stood out in the sun and stands in the lobby of the church with whom it has not shaken hands and shakes hands with all the people at Twelfth and O streets N. W., on Tuesday afternoon while the building was dedicated, presented, accepted and consecrated to the services of the Negro women of the country. It was an impressive sight. It was an impressive occasion. The Negro women of the country making for themselves a permanent home in the capitol of the nation.

One of the most interesting characters at the convention is that of Mrs. Maggie Walker. She is a dominant figure wherever she appears, and she appears everywhere, enthroned in her chair wielding her sceptre of love. when she speaks, there is a reverent hush over the throng, be it at night or by day, out of doors, or within halls. She has caught and fired the imagination of the woman with the magic flame of her personality.

There is a Gibraltar-like calm and strength about Sallie Stewart—the unopposed candidate for the presidency for 1928–1930. You feel somehow in looking at her that the National Association of Colored Women will be in strong, firm hands, and that it will maintain its high standard of integrity and accomplishment.

The two big jobs that were put over in the closing administration—the purchase and furnishing of the National headquarters, with the proposed opening of a clearing house for the activities of all the colored women of the country; and the building and opening of the caretaker's cottage of the Douglass Home and Shrine at Anacostia, mark it as one of the most successful and business-like administrations of the thirty-two years of the association.

The middleaged flappers of the convention have had a hard

time this week. Short skirts, pretty hats, fluffy frocks, chiffon hose, spike heeled sandals, lip-sticks, shingle bobs and permanent waves have transformed them into pretty excellent imitations of their daughters and nieces. But alas, good memories are frequent, omnipresent and irrepressible. "Do you remember when?" is on too many lips. Dates, such as 1895 and 1896 are too frequently referred to, and "First this, and that and the other" and referred to loudly from platform and seat. And most everyone can add and total years and dates. And it takes no stretch of imagination nor of arithmetic to count the disciples of Edna Wallace Hooper in the convention.

. . . . . .

August 24, 1928

The sessions of the Business League are always interesting for one reason or another. You manage to get a lot of viewpoints, if nothing else—and there is generally a lot of "something else."

But one section of Dr. R. R. Moton's annual address at the Business League in New York last week was particularly notable, because it strikes a responsive chord in the hearts and minds and souls of most of us who through race pride and race loyalty earnestly try to support Negro business enterprises. He noted how often when making a bid for business the Negro does not feel it necessary to give real service, to treat his patrons with courtesy, to appreciate their custom, or to make an effort to keep their friendship. And, Dr. Moton added, Negro business is not going to be able to compete with the business of the white man, until the Negro realizes that the business of the business man is to SERVE.

* * *

Dr. Moton told a number of interesting personal experiences illustrating his point. Probably everyone in that audience of 1500 or more could have multiplied his experiences by five or ten. Few and far between are the places managed by Negroes where courteous and willing service seems to be second nature.

A group of loyal race men and women discussing Dr. Moton's remarks swapped experiences, covering twenty-five years or more, and extending over forty-five states. Here, in brief, is the tabulated aggregated experience of about seventy-five or eighty per cent of Negro enterprises.

Restaurants—Rarely do the waiters or waitresses bring a glass of fresh ice water immediately when the patron seats himself at the table.

The patron usually has to ask to have his glass refilled.

Menus are apt to be soiled and fly-specked. One usually has to ask for a fresh table cloth, if the cloth has been soiled by the last patron.

The value of attractive china, glassware and linen is apt to be discounted. And time means nothing! It takes three times as long to get an order as in other restaurants.

Beauty Parlors—The girls in beauty parlors seem to be laboring under the delusion that they are doing a rare favor by serving a customer. Pert, curt, and often almost insulting to the poor woman unfortunate enough to have just reached the city, and not having made an appointment.

Women in business enterprises drag their social ambitions into their commercial life. A woman or girl from a class which they feel is superior socially to their own gets short shrift, poor service, and insulting discrimination.

Men and women fastidious in their personal habits have to contend vainly for clean towels, sanitary appliances, immaculate settings in barber shops, restaurants, beauty parlors, boarding houses, offices.

Some of our so-called "best" places are on a level with those kept by the "dirty Greeks" whom we all are agreed to despise.

* * *

This arraignment could go farther, but it is sufficient. We spoke of grocery stores who are out of a wanted article, and make no attempt to get it for the customer, and continue to be out of it for weeks. Of drug stores, whose prices are as high as the most exclusive firms, and whose service and quality are far below the worst cut-rate places. Negro business enterprises cannot thrive without Negro patronage, and Negro patronage cannot afford to pay the prices and get the lower quality of goods and service which they offer. And there is the vicious circle.

Now this is not true of all of our business places. There is a good twenty-five per cent which is offering excellent material, service, setting and all. But unfortunately, the majority of these are in the large urban centers. The small communities and the small places are reprehensible, and we are judged by the other race very often by just such enterprises.

. . . .

September 21, 1928

That was a fine tribute paid to Charles S. Johnson, retiring editor of *Opportunity*, by his many friends last Friday night at the Cafe Boulevard in New York. A spontaneous movement was inaugurated some short time ago to honor Mr. Johnson with a testimonial banquet on the eve of his leaving

New York, and soon there was a chairman, in the person of Arthur A. Schomburg, and a secretary in charge, James Hubert, of the uptown Urban League office. It was difficult to keep the list of guests within a limited number. Everyone wanted to pay tribute to Mr. Johnson; to voice in some way what he has meant to New York in the past five years. Not only New York, but sections of New England, of Pennsylvania, of Delaware, of Washington, of Baltimore, flocked eagerly as soon as it was whispered that Mr. Johnson was to be banqueted.

*   *   *

The Cafe Boulevard, if you remember, is a picturesque place, admirably lending itself to such an occasion. About a hundred were seated around the small tables, and at the larger table of the guest of honor. Everyone that you know was there, and those who were not, sent letters and telegrams and messages and congratulations and God-speed, and "What will New York do now?" expressions. The ministry was represented on the program by the Rev. William Lloyd Imes, the N.A.A.C.P. and the *Crisis* by Miss Ovington and William Pickens; contemporary journals by Walter Frey of *Forbes Magazine;* sociological research by Dr. Donald Young, of the Department of Sociology of the University of Pennsylvania; the younger writers, those who are largely indebted to Mr. Johnson for the opportunity for self-expression, by Brenda Morwyck; schools were represented by Dr. John Hope. Alice Dunbar-Nelson voiced the gratitude of the teacher of English who saw her promising pupils given the chance to publish, otherwise denied them. Lloyd Garrison, 3rd, spoke and Eugene Kinckle Jones paid the tribute of the co-worker and senior officer, and Charlotte Wallace Murray sang divinely as usual. Mr. Schomburg was the toast-master, and the Rev. Charles Martin opened with an invocation, so that all was regular and in good shape.

* * *

After Mr. Johnson had modestly disclaimed all the wonderful things attributed to him, and looked modest at the sheafs of letters and telegrams from most of the famous folks in the country, a portrait of him, painted by Ira Reid was presented to Mrs. Johnson, in order that she might remember him as he looked in New York, before Fisk University shall have put its stamp upon him. Not the least delightful feature of the evening was Mrs. Johnson's spirited acceptance of the gift and appreciation of the tributes paid her husband.

* * *

So *Opportunity* has lost and Fisk University has gained. Elmer Carter, the new editor, must have felt some dismay as he listened to the encomiums on his predecessor and realized the standard which he must maintain. But in a rather original speech he promised to carry on the work as it has been begun, and to make glad the hearts of both editor and readers. Eugene Kinckle Jones announced that Mr. Johnson would not altogether sever his connections with *Opportunity*, but will still be a contributing editor. The applause which greeted this statement was thunderous.

And so Mr. and Mrs. Charles S. Johnson say Vale New York, Ave Fisk University and Nashville.

. . . .

September 28, 1928

That was an interesting group of women who met at Eaglesmere, Pa., last week to discuss the church and its relation to the inter-racial question. In brief it was the second biennial session of the Inter-Racial Conference of Church Women, initiated by the women of the Commission on the Church and Race Relations of the Federal Council of Churches, in cooperation with the Council of Women for Home Missions, and the National Board of the Young Women's Christian Association. The group was biracial in almost equal proportions of colored and white. There were about seventy delegates in round numbers, and a more representative body of women of both races would be hard to find. And for two days, Tuesday and Wednesday, the 18th and 19th, they carried out a most crowded program, of a breathtaking scope. There was of necessity little enough time for discussion, and you rather felt breathless from rushing so fast and so far into the realm of applied religion and social science and the race question and reports of what has been done and what can be done, and what yet remains to be done.

* * *

Eaglesmere is delightfully inaccessible. When you leave the train at Muncy, Pa., the sign post tells you that you are a bit over 600 feet above sea level. There a bus awaits you. For two hours your vehicle is crawling up the mountain side, twenty-four miles, and 1600 feet more, until you are about 2200 feet above sea level. Going up in the daytime is delightful. Coming down on a stormy night—such as was last Thursday, when we got the tail-end, and a very business-like tail-end, of the West Indian hurricane, is another story But there had been so much emphasis upon faith and courage in the conference that the grinding of the brakes, the roar of second gear, the blinding rain and the slippery down-grade were unnoticed.

The Forest Inn has a lovely living room, and here in

pleasant easy chairs, around a wide fireplace where a comforting log fire crackled, the religious status of inter-racial relations was settled.

* * *

Mrs. Richard Westbrook of New York, is chairman of the Committee. Dr. George Haynes, by virtue of his position in the Federal Council of Churches, was efficiently handling the business end of the conference. Among our own women every possible walk of life and work was represented, and ably so. It was the colored women, by the way, who kept the discussions on a frank and open plane; who struggled hardest to prevent the conference from degenerating into a sentimental mutual admiration society, and who insisted that all is not right and perfect in this country of ours, and that there is a deal to be done by the right thinking church women of both races.

* * *

It is easy for inter-racial gatherings to deliquesce into sentimental experience meetings or love feasts. It takes real courage on the part of both groups to stick to cold, hard, unsentimental facts, and to pay homage to the God-of-Things-As-They-Are. The easiest path is the path on which you close your eyes and play, "Let's pretend" that things are all lovely. That is why so much inter-racial work loses the respect of the discerning, provokes the amusement of the critical, and incurs the wrath of the lovers of justice. But to the present-day workers in this field, much that has been sentimental bosh is being thrown out of doors, and the real facts are being faced in a manner that is heartening to the well-wishers of both races. So if a conference such as that at Eaglesmere does no more than clarify the wisdom of those present, it has justified itself. Mountain-peaks of religious experience are wonderful in personal retrospect, but far better in a searching after actual facts and conditions in various communities, and definite discussions of ways and means to better those conditions.

.   .   .   .   .   .

October 5, 1928

.   .   .   .   .   .

The usual news comes out of Florida, anent the recent hurricane. A repetition of the crimes against Negro refugees which featured the Red Cross activities in the Mississippi flood. Negroes forced to do relief work at the point of the bayonet, whether they are physically able or not, and regardless of the needs of their own families. To be expected, and therefore not extraordinary when it happens.

.   .   .   .   .   .

October 12, 1928

From Paris comes an interesting item, as reported in the foreign bureau of the New York *World*. It bears repetition:

The dream of Marcus Garvey, "Moses of the Black Race," who has for years endeavored to lead the Negroes of the world back to Africa, collapsed finally today. Pleading passionately in the Club du Fauborg for the founding of an African empire, he faced a number of French Negro intellectuals who frequently interrupted him with pointed questions.

Five hundred filled the hall to hear the man widely billed as the "Mark Antony of the Negroes." The boulevards of Paris had been placarded for weeks with high-sounding phrases. In bold black type was the title Garvey had conferred upon himself, "His Highness the Potentate of the Universal Negro Improvement Association and Provisional President of Africa."

He had not gone far in his portrayal of a fabulous paradise

for the Negroes alone on the massive continent below the Equator, when hecklers arose. They expressed doubt that American Negroes would leave the country where the arts are open to their gifts. They recalled what "terrible injustice" Negro slave traders inflicted upon members of their own race, and asked upon what practical grounds Garvey could convince them of the wisdom of his plan.

. . . . . .

October 19, 1928

Now this is a true story that happened within the month, in a city which is large enough to be one of the foremost in the world, where the Negro population is sufficient to make a metropolis in itself, and where education, art, culture, old families, and all that go to make up a cultural background are supposed to be pre-eminent.

The occasion was the first concert given by an artist of the race after a year's study abroad, and after that artist had been before the public for several years in the capacity of a great concert singer. Winner of prizes, soloist under symphony orchestras, and all that sort of thing.

The concert was scheduled to begin at 8:30. It was in the leading opera house of the city. An opera house old in tradition; beautiful in appointment, lovely in memories. To sing in this building alone is an inspiration. There is not a great artist in the world who has not delighted audiences from that classic stage. At eight o'clock our party was in its seat, and we cast a despairing eye over the house. Just a few stragglers here and there. It looked as if the home-coming would be a frost, and our hearts sunk. And yet, infallible sign of a sold out house—the stage was set with about four hundred seats—a few of which were occupied.

By and by the audience began to straggle in, then come in a bit faster. There were approximately one or two ushers to a balcony or circle. They did not seem familiar with the location of seats. People left to find their own way blundered hopelessly, and in desperation took the first seats vacant. By twenty-nine minutes past eight, there was a constant stream of spectators. From six doors in each circle people streamed in, and the ushers, swamped by the crowd threw up their hands in despair.

At eight-thirty to the minute the artist and the accompanist appeared on the stage. The crowd continued to stream in; the few ushers darting wildly here and there to adjust difficulties. Few noticed that the artist had appeared. There was a patter of perfunctory applause, but the main interest seemed to be to get into seats. The buzz and hum resembled the roar of a sea, or worse still, the whir of airplanes. The artist stood, waiting for silence, or at least cessation from the restless activity. The ushers were intent on seating people, at least those whom they could reach. The artist stood. Three minutes. Five minutes. Six minutes. And still the people streamed in. Still the large dame with the heavy coat and the raucous voice complained because someone was in her seat, and she must have THAT seat immediately, and a whole row of people must get up and satisfy her, or else her escort truculently called the usher and threatened the manager. And that large dame was everywhere.

Seven minutes. Still there was confusion. The artist, so cheerful at first, visibly drooped. The joyous little usher on the stage brought people in with a flourish and a bank and seated them with much scraping of chairs behind the artist.

Eight minutes. Someone must have slain one of the ushers on the first floor for there was a cessation of bustle there. The artist began and sang one of the first group of songs. Oh, so lovely that you wondered how anyone could have the heart to do it after that dreadful wait.

Applause. And like a hungry animal deprived of food, the noise began again. More streams of people. More contentions about wrong seats. More irate dames. More frightened ushers. The accompanist struck a chord. The artist shook a despairing head. And waited. Two minutes. Three minutes. Four minutes. Five minutes. A nod. The second song.

A few bars, and a wave of disturbance beat upon our senses. The artist stopped. And for the first time there was absolute silence. Like a whipped child, the audience sat still, chastened. And the song went on, in lovely peace, but not for long. For the heaving dame in the family circle developed a nervous cough—and well, any music lover knows what happens when one individual loses control and coughs. Stokowski knows and so does Kreisler. And they forestall the calamity.

That song being finished, riot broke out again, and again and again the artist had to stand patiently until the audience settled into some semblance of decency and order. By the time the first group was finished the friends of the artist and the lovers of music felt as if their nerves had been peeled with rusty knives.

* * *

To make a long story short, that audience kept coming in until the last group of songs was sung—which was nearly ten o'clock. The stage filled its seats, just before the last group. Arguments between the holders of wrong seats and the holders of the coupons to those seats went on throughout the entire concert. A music lover in the audience went to the manager of the opera house and complained. The manager put in more ushers, some of whom made more confusion than before.

The manager was asked why the ushers had to seat late comers right in the midst of numbers. He said he had no instructions to the contrary. Perhaps he did not. Perhaps the managers of the artist had forgotten that detail.

But the burden of the trouble comes back on the colored audience, or shall I say the audience composed of colored people. And since it is the fashion to draw up indictments, I am going to draw one against our "Race" people.

1. We are perennially, consistently, unnecessarily and determinedly late. Eighty-thirty means nine, ten, nine-thirty, anything BUT eight thirty. It is a habit. And yet we get to theatre on time. We know if we go to threatre late, we are going to miss the first act, and we get there. And we get to trains on time, even if we break our necks and speed laws to do it. We know if we are late to the trains, we will lose our reservation, or engagement, or what not. And we get to meetings or occasions that are to be presided over by the other race on time. Indeed, who has not heard the expression—"Oh, those Caucasians giving that; they'll begin on time"?

2. We have no regard for the other fellow's feelings. Music too oft is a cloak for conversation, so we cannot understand why someone might want to listen to the music, nor why he should object if we tread on his toes, or knock his program out of his hand, as we crash into our seat over his prostrate form.

3. We go too often to places to be seen and heard, not to see and hear. When we go to a public performance, we want everyone to know we are there, therefore we insist upon being seated during a number, walk all over half a row of people, stand up to take off our coat, take our time about taking off our hat, and as such late comers are usually fat and wheezy,

heave prodigious sighs of relief at the rest which the creaking seat affords.

Now this sounds like a burst of pentup irritation. It is. And I feel safe in saying that there are at this present time in these United States some several hundred thousand of our race who will agree with me.

And here ends the true story of the home-coming of a great artist. A heart-breakingly lovely performance spoiled by the pure selfishness and bad manners of a great crowd, which ought to know better, and does know better. Let us pray that the patron saint of the race, whoever he be, will teach us good manners, musical consideration, and regard for the other fellow.

November 2, 1928

. . . . . .

And here again we have the spectacle of the domination of the United States by the Negro. He is the greatest factor in the life of the nation, and here in the most interesting, hardest fought, bitterest, and most unconventional campaign for the presidency that has been waged since the Civil War, we have the injection of the Negro, overruling and overtopping many of the real issues of the campaign. In effect, the United States is being told: "Vote for Al Smith, and you will have Negroes taking an active part in the government, and social equality all over the land." Or, "Vote for Hoover, and you'll have parties of white men and colored women all over the nation."

Meanwhile, the Republican party, like the fair colored person who "passes for white," and is most bitter in his denunciation and renunciation of his erstwhile colored friends—

the G.O.P. is hurrying to disclaim the Negro lest it seem to be too nearly interested and therefore will not be invited to the All-White parties of the South.

November 30, 1928

. . . . . .

As the usual time for giving thanks has past, instead of counting our blessings one by one, we are going to be pessimistic and enumerate the things for which we OUGHT NOT TO GIVE THANKS. This will fit in more with the after mood of too much turkey, and too much social whirligigs. The morning after feeling.

The Negro ought NOT to be thankful that the recent election was such a landslide. Far better for the Brother would it have been could the vote have been more close, and the results have shown, particularly in the border and doubtful states, that the margin was won by the black vote. The overwhelming victory, far from making the Negro a power has practically shorn him of his claim upon the party. Therefore he should not feel thankful for the result of the election.

The Negro should not feel thankful for the growing wealth of the race built up in many communities by a subtle and polite form of gambling. We do need the money—but we need some of the grace of God too.

The Negro should NOT feel thankful for the growing discrimination and segregation in cities in the North. Particularly in the economic world. There is a field, whose scope is practically limitless, for endeavor in the adjusting of economic relations of the races, so that the Negro will not always be caught between the upper and nether millstones.

And he should NOT feel thankful for his life on this continent until the whole race has put its shoulder to the wheel to help adjust some pitiful inequalities.

The Negro should NOT feel thankful for any crumbs or sops thrown to him from the dominant group. There are certain inalienable things which are due every American, and the Negro should NOT feel thankful for less. Those rights which are considered inalienable for whites, radical for Negroes.

The Negro should NOT feel thankful for any lowering of his standard—and if he is not careful in this welter of weak gratitude in which he indulges now and then, he will be like Lily Dale—always regaining his foothold, but always gaining it on a lower plane.

And now, having gotten the dark brown taste out of our mouth, we can turn our attention to Christmas.

December 28, 1928

.   .   .   .   .   .

It was just after five o'clock when every street car was packed to the transom, and strong men were hanging on by their eye-brows. And it happened in a big city of two and a half million inhabitants. A large colored gentleman clambered aboard a trolley, with a paper bag in his hand, and leaned against the nearest projection. Some passengers debarked, and he succeeded in getting one arm free. He put the hand of that arm into the paper bag, eyeing the contents with a purposeful expression. But just then more passengers embarked, and his arm was again pinioned to his side. But every now and then he looked wistfully in his bag. Downtown the car lurched, and after some twenty or thirty blocks, there was

enough thinning out for the large colored gentleman to get a
seat on the very edge of the bench, his feet out on the
platform. This time he attacked the bag avidly. From its
dark brown depths he drew forth a part of a pig's foot. Short
work was made of it, and he threw the bone on the floor.
The conductor stared. White passengers smiled knowingly;
colored ones looked disgustedly away. Another piece of pig's
foot; another bone, and another and another, until the contents
of the brown paper bag were all distributed—the meat within
the capacious maw of the large colored gentleman; the bones
upon the floor of the platform. That done, he wiped his
mouth on the back of his hand, and his hands on the brown
paper bag, which followed the bones on the floor of the car,
and sat back with a look of supreme satisfaction on his face.
Then, and only then did he recognize a friend on the other
side of the car, and greeted him with a broad smile and a
mellow, "Merry Christmas, Bo!"

.   .   .   .   .   .

January 4, 1929

.   .   .   .   .   .

This seems to be the open season for baiting the race in one
way or another. Allison Davis, of Williams and Harvard,
Phi Beta Kappa, and teacher of English at Hampton, has
risen and flung stones at the "Race" before, notably in a
group of bitter verses in the *Crisis*. But this time he is not
playing with tropes. He girds his loins, and taking a basketful
of large and jagged rocks on his left arm, flings them one by
one with his strong young right hand, and grins sardonically
as they approximate their aim. In *Plain Talk* for January, he
writes an article, "The Negro Deserts His People." Lest
there be no misconstruction as to what he means to say, he
begins pleasantly: "The Negro has been a race damned in its

leaders since the days when the overseer demoralized any group loyalty by giving his favor to the treacherous."

When you have read this sentence you know there is to be no quarter shown to the so-called race leaders. And there is none. Mr. Davis goes after them with a vengeance. Someone called his article "sophomoric." And George Schuyler, in the Pittsburgh *Courier,* says that he "reveals a surprising degree of naivetté." We would hardly go so far as to make either of these statements alone, but if you care to mix them together, multiply them by one hundred, you will have a fair idea of the amount of damage that little David does to the Goliath of race leadership.

Mr. Davis is still young and unsophisticated, or he would have learned by this time that there is nothing in the world absolute—that all history, either ancient, medieval or modern can only be understood or interpreted by comparison. To say of the Negroes in America that they are this, or that or the other is to stultify one's own sense of proportion. But to say of the Negroes of America, this, that or the other *in comparison with* similar groups in America, similarly placed economically is sane and sensible. Mr. Davis has looked so long and hard at his object that he has not considered it in relation to its surroundings. All that he bitterly says of the upper group of Negroes is well within the circle of truth, except that not all are mulattoes, nor that all do all of the things of which he accuses them. But the same is likewise true of the advanced—economically and educationally—section of any race or group. All peoples rise on the backs of the masses, and kick those masses in the face after they get up. It is only the few philanthropists who have regard for the proletariat. This is true of Negroes, Jews, Hindus, Russians, English and what not. The Negro is running true to human form.

Mr. Davis writes so well, that we shall await with eagerness the day when he settles into his stride and stops trying to reform the so-called upper class Negro by throwing jagged verbal rocks at his defenceless head.

.   .   .   .   .   .

January 11, 1929

Georgia Douglas Johnson calls her new book *An Autumn Love Cycle.* (Published by Harold Vinal, Ltd., New York.) And a love cycle it is, telling a very definite story, delicately etched against a mist of memory. But I wish she had called it a "Love Chaplet." For these exquisite poems are like jewels, "literally diamonds and rubies and pearls," Zona Gale calls them. Each one finished, polished to perfection, admitting of no change of syllable or inflection. And since, in spite of the love tragedy suggested in the first part—"The Cycle," there is a perfect round, and the end completes the beginning and the beginning foreshadows and sustains the end, the book is indeed a jewelled chaplet of sorrow.

Georgia Douglas Johnson is one woman writer whose criticism of her own work is ruthless. She does not fear to prune, to cull, to throw away, to strike out, to reduce in quantity her own work. When she has admitted a poem into one of her books, or when she has allowed one of her poems to be printed, we know that it is perfection. There are no half measures; no allowing faulty workmanship to come before the public. This is a rare quality for any writer to have, and especially in this day of over production; of wild rushing into print; of accepting every ephemeral mood limned in limping language as worthwhile poetry—this quality is to be commended, applauded.

This is Mrs. Johnson's third book of verse, and fifth volume. The two previous volumes of verse, *The Heart of a Woman,* and *Bronze* have been worthy precursors of this latest, and most felicitous outpouring of her heart through her pen.

Alain Locke has an interesting foreword to the little volume—which by the way is appropriately bound in subdued tones of gold and green and red and brown, with a conventional autumn leaf design. Says Mr. Locke happily, "Fortunately to the gift of a lyric style, delicate in touch, rhapsodic in tone, authentic in timbre, there has been added a tempermental endowment of ardent sincerity of emotion, ingenuous candor of expression, and happiest of all for the particular task, a naive and unsophisticated spirit."

All of which is true, and better than that, it is good to find that Mrs. Johnson is an artist. Carving her exquisite word-images; painting her perfect vignettes; hinting at a world-old universal human experience; suggesting a tragedy of the heart—all with the great universal touch, and with no hint, no suggestion, no thought of an ulterior motive, no racial touch of self-pity, or clamor for interpretation in terms of particularities. Therefore Mrs. Johnson is an artist.

May *An Autumn Love Cycle* be followed by other books of poetry—not too many, quantity creates satiety—but just enough to keep the expectant interest in her gems pulsing and alive.

.   .   .   .   .   .

If it is true that the Socialist party has organized a "Jim Crow" division, as we are told by the recent news dispatches, it is indeed another example of a good party gone wrong. If Socialism ever did stand for anything, it meant no division on the line of race, sex, creed or color. If it is to be cross-sectioned, its initial appeal to the Negro must be lost,—unless of course, the division is made for purposes of educational appeal.

. . . . . .

The Children's Bureau of Philadelphia, Pa., is all het up because the animal report shows that delinquency is greater among adolescent girls than among adolescent boys. That while boys constitute only seven per cent of total delinquency cases, girls constitute 27 per cent. Whereupon we may prepare for a flood of denunciation of feminism, birth control, woman suffrage, short skirts, movies, lip-sticks, plucked eyebrows, modern literature, cigarette smoking, or Woolworth jewelry on the part of old ladies, reformers, and the clergy. Regardless of the fact that what in a girl is inexcusable delinquency, in a boy is often mere "high spirits," "boys will be boys," and "chip off the old block stuff." What is needed is not so much reformation of girls and women as the application of the single standard of conduct to boys and men.

January 18, 1929

. . . . . .

Speaking of antebellum situations, O.O. McIntyre reports that at a certain hunting lodge in the far South, much frequented by wealthy Northerners, and consisting of vast acreage, upon the arrival of the Northern guest, he is met by a colored lad, who takes his bag, and with an ingratiating grin, announces, "I's yi' black boy w'ile you's hyeah, suh!" And does the Northern guest protest? Never. He loves it. It satisfies all of his thwarted ideas of feudal grandeur, of baronial magnificence with slaves and vassals and what not.

For it was ever thus with human nature; it must feel itself superior to something, and the lowest beggar wants a dog to kick around and have it fawn upon him.

· · · · · ·

January 25, 1929

· · · · · ·

Meet Araminta. I came across her in a junior high school in Leipsic. Of course, her name is not Araminta, and the Junior High School is not in Leipsic. It is a mixed school, where about twenty-five per cent of the 1800 adolescents are colored. The principal said to me one morning, when I dropped into the school that she wanted me to meet one of the most interesting girls in the building. And so I shook hands with Araminta. She is about thirteen, well-built, pleasant, well-dressed, sweet-faced low-voiced, well-poised. She had recited before the school assembly, and had been applauded again and again. I learned that she had taken one of the leading characters in an operetta which the school had given, and where parts were assigned for scholarship and popularity. The principal had told me something of her history, but I wanted to learn it from Araminta herself, with no witnesses to prompt. She is from Liberia, the Basu tribe in the interior. Her father was in debt, or rather her foster father, and Araminta being a likely girl of nine or thereabouts, he decided to sell her into slavery for his debt. He was asking fifteen dollars for her, but as interest developed he went up to twenty. The American missionary saw the transaction and tried to stop it. The selling of children for debt is contraband in Liberia, but boot-legging in child slavery is common. There being no other way to stop the transaction, the missionary paid the required twenty dollars and brought Araminta to this country. Araminta was adopted by a colored

Baptist Sunday School in the city where the missionary brought her, and this Sunday School boards her in the home of a motherly Christian woman, connected with the church. She is being educated in the public schools, and Araminta hopes when she has gone through high school, and a school of social work to go back to Basu-land and try to keep other little girls from being sold into slavery. She was fortunate, she told me, but with a wise little shake of her thirteen year old head— "Lots of little girls are not so lucky."

. . . .

February 1, 1929

Vera Caspary in *The White Girl*, (J. H. Sears Company, New York) has probed closer to the heart of the almost white Negro than any writer who has thus far attempted to portray the girl who steps over—"passes" in short. She has not allowed herself to be swept into conventional mental attitudes, nor silly sentimentality. There is a delightful absence of "primitive passion," "back to Africa," "call of the blood," "Racial consciousness," "urge for service," "natural inferiority," "primitive fear." None of the popular shibboleths with which the white writer bolsters up his assumption of superiority, and lulls his sense of fairness and truth to sleep. Miss Caspary has visualized a fair colored girl, such as may be found among Negroes by the tens of thousands, with no especial race pride, no desire to be anything but just a girl among girls, with ambition, but little bitterness, and an average girl's lack of foresight.

"She was not indignant at the thought that white people's prejudice prevented her from earning a living from the work for which she was fitted. She did not once consider the

injustices suffered by her race. She did not care what happened
to other colored girls. She did not like Negroes. She considered them a shiftless people who deserved their lot. She
resented her Negro blood as one might hate a deformity,
because it stamped her an inferior."

* * *

Just how Miss Caspary came by this information it would be
interesting to know. For it is exactly the attitude of a great
many girls, fair of skin, who have to make their way in the
world. It is not given to all Negroes any more than it is to
all white people or all Jews or what not to be in a high strung
tension about the Future of the Race. The majority of them
are concerned about the mere business of getting on the best
they can—about food, shelter, clothes, work, social advancement, pleasure, love, homes, money, personal advancement.
It is the way of the world. Refreshing to have it brought out
so strikingly in a novel of the "race."

And as to the problem of "passing," and the lack of race
pride usually advanced as criticism, the author deals with it,
also from a purely practical standpoint, the standpoint which
is the real reason why the so-called 20,000 who "pass" each
year would tell you, if they dared be vocal. "It was more
comfortable to live as a white woman, to receive the homage
paid a handsome white woman. . . . She was guarding her
secret, not to protect her silly pride, but for quite practical
reasons. She could live more comfortably as a white woman,
she could go where she chose, she could earn more money."

* * *

There are several touches in the novel which show an almost
uncanny knowledge of racial life, even when lived at the level
of the "in betweens." One, the immediate recognition of one
of us, no matter how fair, nor how well racially disguised,

by another one of us. Solaria is hounded by the knowing glances of West Indian elevator boys, whose expressive eyes tell her that her secret is not safe with them. She is even driven to paying a silent blackmail. Though eventually she is forced to give this up, and flee from the dreaded influence of the basilisk-eyed West Indian, who invites her to Harlem parties.

* * *

There is but one way out of the situation in which Solaria Cox, by a series of fatal mistakes, and misunderstandings finds herself. There is no attempt on the part of the author— thank God—to point a moral of the weaving of tangled webs of deception, or the fatal consequences of turning the back on the race, or any of the rest of the hokum which we find in stories of this ilk. But the Gordian knot must be cut, and fate cuts it in a logical way. A weaker author, and one whose eye was more on the sales profits, or box office receipts, might have sent Solaria "back to her people" to do missionary work or marry some man like Eggers. But Miss Caspary is too logical a writer to commit any such literary faux pas. Solaria was a clear headed girl, ruthless, if you will, and hard, as life in Chicago and New York had taught her to be; as inheritance from Francia, the slatternly mother made her. She could see, blinded though she might be by her great love for David, just what the end of her career would be. She is a true modern, without so-called racial superstition, with no backward glance at her origin. Her end is as logical an outcome of her life as the end of a Greek tragedy is the outcome of the beginning.

* * *

The White Girl is not a great novel, but it is far above most of the ephermeral stuff put forth, and superior to any white person's interpretation of racial life. It is well written, close knit, carefully constructed. Every character is accounted for somewhere before the end. There are no loose threads dangling. No episodes that seem dragged in just for local color—though there are plenty of them. But each story, each incident, each character is a contribution to the whole. There are no unanswered questions at the end, except the great big one—Why does American life make such a tragedy possible? And above all, it is such a completely absorbing book, that you cannot put it down, once you have started it, and wish that the end might have been delayed.

* * *

Speaking of "Race." The article in the January *American Magazine* by Lewis Browne, called "Why Are Jews Like That?" is one which all of us should read. The question asked with disgust by the writer's Gentile friend, and re-echoed by Gentiles everywhere with snobbish inflection, is answered by the writer, "Because we can't help it." And the reason why the Jew can't help being like that is because the Gentiles everywhere all over the world have made him what he is—sensitive, clannish, aggressive, commercially minded, radical, if necessary. The sentence, "We attack life with a rush and fury, for we realize that a Jew must push twice as hard to get half as far as a non-Jew," sounds as if it had been written by a Negro about Negroes. We are fond of saying how much harder a Negro must work to get anywhere than a Nordic, for instance.

We need to read more about Jews, and the prejudices against them, about Japanese, Chinese, Greeks, Armenians, submerged groups everywhere in this country. Someday we will realize that we have not the monopoly on persecution, discrimination, unfairness. That such a statement as Mr.

Browne makes when he says "Non-Jews contribute much toward preserving us as a separate folk by discriminating against us," is spoken of a wealthy class of white-faced people in America, not of Negroes.

February 15, 1929

. . . . .

The Turks have turned against the old Koranic prohibition against wine. The United States is talking of enforcing prohibition in terms of billions, and the Kemalist government, which has made alcohol one of the sixteen state monopolies, has sent the director of the monopoly to Europe to study wine-making. The rich Anatolian grape region has already been selected as the location for Turkey's future wine industry.

This is direct defiance of the Koran. If we all do not hurry and make that Oriental trip there will be nothing to see— veils, harems, sheiks, bulbuls, nightingales, deserts, camels, caravans, oases, desert riders, all are giving way to electric lights, tram cars, modern plumbing and short skirts. Too much standardization, entirely too much. Picturesqueness is a lost art. We may expect at any time to hear that a collar ad is blazing its electric lights atop of the largest pyramid.

. . . . .

Speaking of the strange advances in this world of prejudice, I could not help but think at the Jules Bledsoe concert in New York last Sunday how marvelously the Negro has advanced artistically. It was not fifteen years ago when Bert Williams dared do nothing but black face comedy. There simply was not room for anything else for the Negro in the theatrical world. And when he was a star in the Ziegfeld

Follies he was never allowed to come on the stage when the white chorus girls were on. Perish the thought that a Negro should appear on the same stage with a white woman! It would have ruined Ziegfield. So Bert Williams' scenes were always solo ones, or else with some man. And when the Shakespearean travesties were staged, Bert's Othello was played to the Desdemona of Leon Erroll.

But last Sunday night Jules Bledsoe sang *Amonasro* in a scene from Aida with Lisa Roma from the Metropolitan Opera Company as Aida, and a section of the New York Philharmonic Orchestra accompanying. And all the preceding and following songs on the program faded into insignificance before this one scene—a Negro singing in grand opera opposite a white woman, acting the part with all its gusty passion and bitter cruelty. And no one especially excited about it in the crowded Gallo theatre. The colored people not especially elated or triumphant; the white ones not especially surprised, indignant or upset over it.

And if that is not a triumph of the Negro in art, then we do not know how to spell triumph.

* * *

Only a triumph in art, mind you. Let us keep a level head and a clear sane, well balanced attitude to the whole situation. There is yet too much to do to stop to congratulate ourselves. We had best learn to shift the load and do the backpatting while we step.

February 22, 1929

. . . . . .

For years the Negro has complained that the novels written about us have not stressed the cultured, refined, educated

Negro, he who has been through college, rides in automobiles, paints pictures, writes books, sings classic songs, lives in beautiful homes, attends cultured churches of his own, does not go to cabarets, and is not a decadent replica of the white man's worst. For years we have deplored that we are constantly being shown in cross sections that do us no credit. And yet too often when we ourselves write of our so-called best society, we are so anxious to exhibit that best that we "point with pride" in a manner uncomfortably like a child showing off its doll-house to a skeptical grownup. And when, sometimes our friends on the other side have attempted the same kind of description, their attitude is patronizing, superior, as if one were admiring that same child because it knows how to pour tea at a doll's tea party.

DuBose Heyward now solves the Gordian knot of this strange puzzle—how to treat the best of the Negro without showing off or patronizing. He does it by the very simple expedient of telling the story, describing the scenes in an easy, natural manner. We see the church service in the fashionable Episcopal colored church in Charleston; we attend a musical at the home of one of the leaders of the "blue vein" group; we go in the automobile of the wealthy banker; we discuss Negro artists at the club meeting. All quite natural—and yet Lissa, the climber, the third generation striving to Be, sums it all up wearily when she tells Mamba of her first social evening—"They seem to spend all their time saying how glad they are to be Negroes, and all the time they're trying their damndest to be white."

Has not the author put his finger unerringly on the sore spot in the social fabric of the Negro?

.   .   .   .   .   .

March 1, 1929

. . . . . .

If there are any lingering doubts in the minds of anyone as
to unemployment, let him take a ride down Sixth Avenue in
New York. You may begin somewhere in the Fifties, and go
on down to Greenwich Village. Employment offices, if you
remember, line one side of the street, on an average of three
to a square. And in front of each of them a seemingly never-
ending queue of patient men and some women, looking,
reading, whispering, craning their necks, for each new item
on the bulletin board. Hundreds of them; well-dressed,
ragged, white, black, all nationalities, down-and-outers, those
newly arrived at indigence, frayed or patched. Forty city
squares in one great city of the unemployed, pushing the
slush from under their feet as they hopefully or hopelessly
watch for another bulletin. And this is but one section of the
city, and but one city of the thousands in the country. As
Mayor Mackey of Philadelphia, said in a public speech the
other day, "We talked a lot about prosperity during the
campaign, but even while we talked, we knew better, and
now that the campaign is over, we can tell the truth because
we've got to face the truth."

. . . . . .

March 15, 1929

. . . . . .

Scribner's Magazine for March carries the opening installment
of a serial which promises to be intensely interesting as it
goes on. It is "An African Savage's Own Story" by Bata
Kindai Ibn LoBagola; the story of a boy belonging to a race
known as "Black Jews" from the practically unexplored "Bush
Region" of Western Africa. In this installment, the boy tells
how he was accidentally kidnapped and taken to Scotland.

Up to the time when he was kidnapped, he had never seen a white man. In future installments, he will tell of the impressions these strange beings made upon him.

It ought to be pretty racy reading as it progresses. This first bit is good.

* * *

The horrors of the Mexican War are being brought home to us by the expected shortage of early peas and tomatoes as the result of the revolution.

* * *

It is refreshing to find *Time* commenting upon the new cinema, *Hearts in Dixie* in this wise: "The voodoo doings, the cotton pickings, and Bible-shouting are just what a certain class of people, educated to consider Negro life 'colorful' and 'primitive,' expect of the race, just as people of another class expect vaudeville patter and tap-dancing." "A kind of Bostonian black-bottom." Comments of this kind are heartening. Perhaps, after all, Caucasian neighbors are beginning to learn something about discrimination.

. . . . . .

March 22, 1929

Of course, to those who love the stage, the most interesting thing about the recent twentieth anniversary dance of the N.A.A.C.P. in New York on last Friday, was the very excellent midnight program, with "Bojangles" the inimitable, as master of ceremonies. This meant that he not only introduced the stars, made witty remarks concerning them, but joined in the dances, inventing new steps—as for instance with "Peg Leg"—singing a snappy accompaniment to women and men alike, and enlivening the brief waits between acts with wise cracks, and side-splitting stories. There were scores of interesting people of both races to meet and talk with; plenty of refreshments—if you wanted refreshments—a floor to dance on and music to dance by. But the cream of the coffee was the midnight show with the acts from *Show Boat*, *Blackbirds*, Connies' Inn, Small's, and other lesser lights. "Snake Hips" had to do an encore, against the rules. "Exotic!" "Beautiful!" "Original!" murmured W. B. Seabrook, of *Magic Island* fame. At least one could not complain that you had not your money's worth.

* * *

And speaking of shows—"Race" shows: As one tramps from the Howard in Washington, the Alhambra, Lafayette, Renaissance in New York, to the smaller theatres in smaller towns, one cannot but be struck with the thought that in this golden harvest which the Negro is reaping on the stage, he will be improvident indeed if he does not make hay while this auriferous sun is shining. Racial fads on the stage are intense while they last, but all too short-lived. And once dead it is many a lean year before they revive.

Some of us remember the days of the Irish fad. When Chauncey Olcott was the matinee idol, and James K. Hackett was considered a perfect actor, because he was Irish. When Irish songs held the boards, and Irish stories and Irish poems always brought down the house. It was a fad that lasted several years, almost two decades. It was the easiest thing in the world to make a hit then. Talk a little brogue, sing about the "ould mither," and you went over big.

* * *

Then, do you remember the Hawaiian fad? When everyone was wearing grass skirts and dislocating their hips trying to do the hula-hula? When the home that did not have at least three ukeleles was felt to be on the verge of bankruptcy, and we were all wearing our fingers to the bone trying to play the steel guitar? Those were the days of "Bird of Paradise" and all its imitations, and we had almost forgotten how to talk English. No vaudeville house was without at least one Hawaiian act, for months, and we consigned our enemies to Molokai, instead of a more hectic climate, and called the children in to "Poi" instead of dinner. And now when the inevitable beach-comber strolls in, and the quartette off stage begins to wail about Oloha, we yawn and climb over the feet of our next neighbor in a wild effort to get out of the theatre.

* * *

And now it is the Negro. First *Emperor Jones*, and then a wild, mad rush that leaped the stages between minstrelsy and drama, with mad dancing in between. *Abraham's Bosom*, and *Porgy* and all the rest, and the musical shows. One succeeding another in wild confusion of hectic gyrations. Then the movies, and now the talkies. If you are not a Negro you just don't belong. For the most sought after powder, talcum and complexion, and the most advertised cold cream is "Sun-tan." You must make up brown if you would be thought ultra.

It is not fair to spoil the good time which is being enjoyed by all at this time, with grandmotherly admonitions. But I cannot but wonder what the hundreds of young men and women who are high in the public favor are doing now to improve themselves and make the passing fad something more than a brief candle-like existence soon snuffed out and forgotten. Do the colored girls who are enjoying adulation study new steps? Are the chorus of steppers trying honestly to make themselves perfect in their art, and thus delay by some years the inevitable revulsion? Wild abandon and un-synchronized gyrations were interesting, exotic, when they first appeared a dozen years ago, but are we not beginning to look for something different now, and frankly to yawn outright when we go from theatre to theatre, cabaret to cabaret and see exactly the same steps, the same undisciplined movements, the same lack of make-up on the legs and knees, the same umbilical appeal, backing itself up with nothing solidly artistic?

* * *

Two new things have come forth in the past decade—"Bojangles" tap dance on the steps, "Snake-Hips" undulations, both in *Blackbirds*. And yet the latter has not shown imagination to clothe that sinuous body of his properly in smooth material suggesting the reptile he imitates. He gets himself up in a flowing blouse and red sash, like a Hawaiian—and has not a single Hawaiian movement.

* * *

The way for theatrical folk to make hay while the sun shines is so to perfect themselves in their art, to devise constantly new approaches, to come as near being indispensable as possible. In that way alone can they stave off the inevitable. The Irish fad lasted long because it was constantly making new appeals. The Hawaiian fad was short-lived because it had nothing new to offer. It dumped its whole bag of tricks on the table at once. Will the Negro fad be like the former or the latter? It is up to the Negro actors to decide. From the biggest ones of the lot, the Robesons, the McClendons, the Millers and the Lyles and the rest, down to the smallest little brown skin cabaret dancer, wearing not much more than a few postage stamps and a winning smile, the issue is a grave one, fraught with possibilities of a long day of favor, or a brief snuffing out of the present prosperity. And the fate of the issue lies in that drab word—"STUDY."

* * *

I sat in a Philadelphia theatre watching *Hearts in Dixie* on the screen. All around me proud Nordics wept openly, and men blew their noses almost as vigorously as they did when Al Jolson sang "Sonny Boy" to his last sleep. For *Hearts in Dixie* is so full of pure hokum that it runs out all over and slops into the orchestra. As was said by *Time*, it is full of the things that the white man likes to associate with the Negro—plantation songs, cotton fields, superstition, ignorance, faithfulness, etc., etc. But there are many good things to remember about it. Though the Negro peasant is faithfully depicted in his native habitat, never once do we hear the words "darky" and "nigger" used, even in their most care-free moment. (Of course we know they were saying it in reality.) The acting of Clarence Muse as Nappus could hardly be better done, nor the inimitable Step-in Fetchit, as the lazy son. The child actors were good, more free and less self-conscious than white child actors are apt to be. Of course, the music was too much harmonized to be natural, though it was beautiful, appealingly lovely, but no plantation Negroes ever sang like that.

As we have noticed before, the "talkies" are showing the possibilities of the Negro speaking voice. It never rasps, never burrs, never croaks, as do the voices of white actors.

Hearts in Dixie has so slight a plot that you soon abandon trying to find it. It is just a series of lovely pictures, beautiful music, Uncle-Tom stuff, with plenty of hokum, designed for quick box-office returns. And if our folk are reaping good pay envelopes out in Hollywood thereby, more power to Negro hokum say I.

April 19, 1929

.   .   .   .   .

Jessie Fauset's *Plum Bun* deserves better at the hands of the critics than it has received. And this is entirely the fault of the critics, who in their sentimental rush to hail every book written by a Negro as one more perfect specimen of Exhibit A, stumble over themselves with injudicious laudation, which is just faint praise disguised in subtle regalia. Now *Plum Bun* is not a great novel, nor is it masterly. But it is a good story, well told and skillfully woven, so that the long arm of coincidence which gives it the desired happy ending is not too great a strain upon our credulity. It is a distinct advance over Miss Fauset's earlier novel, *There is Confusion*. She has made her story march to a definite conclusion, and her massing of scenic events, and handling of her climax show much thought and study since her earlier effort.

*   *   *

Some may choose to think the charm of the story lies in the study of the near-white girl who wishes to pass for white and does so with some modicum of success. Critics of the other race naturally hail the book as a searching study of that phase of American life. But to me the charm of the book lies in its poignant analysis of the casualness of human relations. Only one who has lived in big cities; made friends and lost them; drifted into relations and out of them; touched lives at queer angles, and forgotten them; suffered loneliness and heartache at the emptiness of life and the non-understanding of others could paint so clear and true a picture of a lonely girl. The tragedy in Angela's life was not race, but her own ultimate shallowness which never let her get to realities. It just was not there; she was as incapable of real living as an undeveloped child. It is in the study of this shallow soul, and the effect of the life which brushed her by that the real artistry of *Plum Bun* lies.

*   *   *

The title is interesting. "To Market, to Market, to buy a Plum Bun; Home again Home again; Market is done." And

so Angela goes to market, buys the plum bun, and goes home
again when the market is done, and she finds that the bun,
after all, was not worth going after.

* * *

It is rather interesting to select the fictional characters in the
book and fit well known names to their thinly disguised
personalities. Some might question the taste of this, but
perhaps it is the thing to do. Some individuals might squirm
at being likened to a bronze god or an East Indian idol,
especially when everyone can tack the right name on to the
person so described.

It is to be hoped that Miss Fauset will write other books.
She has yet to learn something of the technique which controls
final situations. This was the greatest weakness of *There is
Confusion*. But *Plum Bun* is such a distinct and definite advance
over its predecessor that already we are looking forward to
her next novel.

. . . . . .

May 3, 1929

. . . . . .

Nella Larsen delights again with her new novel, *Passing*,
Alfred A. Knopf ($2.00), New York. It is apparently slighter
in structure than the previous one, *Quicksand,* and you are
apt to think as you are reading it, that it is of comparative
unimportance. What could be more commonplace than the
story of a fair girl, a waif almost, who finds that life is easily
switched from one key to another, and takes the dominant
key? Clare succeeds, marries, and is apparently happy. She
has a strange urge to return to her own people, and therein
lies danger, disaster, tragedy. Slight the story, you feel as
you read it, slight, if absorbing.

Then the denouement comes. It is so surprising, so unexpected, so startling, so provocative of a whole flood of

possibilities, so fraught with mystery, of a "Lady or Tiger"
problem, that you are suddenly aware that you have been
reading a masterpiece all along, and that the subtle artistry
of the story lies in just this—its apparent inocuousness, with
its universality of appeal. You feel as you lay the book down
that the real tale begins at the end; that there has been only a
preface in the printed pages, and the novel goes on in the
mind of the reader, speculation, piecing together of fragments
to make a whole, ending of a situation, completion of a life,
following up of the emotional life of Irene and Brian.

* * *

The real situation is not that Clare "passed." It is that she
came back into the life of Irene and that she loved Brian.
She did not have to be a near-white woman to do this, nor
did the others have to be colored. It is a situation that is so
universal that race, color, country, time, place have nothing
to do with it. Of course, the author was wise in hanging the
situation onto a color complex: the public must have that
now. But the book would have been just as intriguing, just
as provocative, just as interesting if no mention had been
made of color or race. Clare might have been any woman
hungry for childhood friends; Irene and her brown skinned
friends any group out of the class of the socially elite.

* * *

Nella Larsen has written a book that will linger in your
memory longer than some more pretentious volumes. It is
compact and terse; stripped of non-essentials of language or
incident or description. It is hardly more than a bare outline.
But it etches itself on your memory, like stark trees against a
wintry sunset. The language is lucid, fluid; the descriptions,
when there are any, done with a sweeping stroke of the brush
that simulates the Japanese method.

Clare is an adventuress; Irene, the ordinary woman, afraid of life, wrapped in home, child, husband, gone Berserker when these latter are threatened—but why anticipate? The best way to enjoy *Passing* is to read it, and then discuss it, and ask about ten of your friends for their version of the ending, and get the ten different versions you are bound to get. But at all events, read it.

May 17, 1929

Significant enough is the list of Pulitzer awards. Significant to us, I mean. The way the Negro permeates the life of the nation must be interesting to the student of the philosophy of history; gratifying to the "race" lovers; appalling to the 100 per cent Nordics.

Note the awards:

Best editorial. Louis Isaac Jaffe in the Virginian *Pilot*. Subject: Anti-Lynching.

Best Novel. *Scarlet Sister Mary*, by Julia Peterkin. Subject: A Negro woman. (Secretly, if the subject had to be the Negro, I would have preferred *Mamba's Daughters*.)

Best volume of verse: *John Brown's Body*, by Stephen Vincent Barret. Subject: An abolitionist; the Civil War; the Negro's effect upon the nation.

Is not this the justice of the gods?

.   .   .   .

It is indeed gratifying to note that the Governor of Ohio has recognized the worth and services of Miss Hallie Queen Brown of Wilberforce. She has recently been appointed a member of the State Board of Moving Picture Censors at a salary of $2400 a year. Not a significant sum, but the position carries with it a dignity and responsibility that are in keeping with the years of service and worth which have accrued unto "Miss Hallie" during her useful and colorful career. At least there will be one member of the Ohio State Board of Censors who will have intelligence.

* * *

This is the season of the year when the Greek letter fraternities and sororities—whose name is anathema to the non-collegiates— justify their existence by their splendid drives among young people for increased interest in education. "Guide right," "Go to high school, go to college." "Educational Week" and other drives of like import take up the energies of the young Greeks during the months of April and May. The objective is the same: to induce Negro boys and girls to get education, and more education, no matter what the sacrifice. And in this day and time when a laborer must almost have a master's degree in order to hold his job, too much stress cannot be laid upon preparing Negro youth for the keen competition of life.

I have seen numbers of these educational programs this year; in Philadelphia, in Wilmington, in Washington, at Wilberforce University, and I have been struck by the fine spirit of self-sacrifice which these young collegians express in putting on their programs. Essay contests; oratorical contests; public educational meetings with nationally known speakers, whose expenses must be met; educational films and what not cost money, and there is no place for this money to come from save from the pockets and by the efforts of the young sponsors of education. Often a public meeting, a drive, a contest means a real and painful sacrifice. Yet there is rarely a word of complaint. Their watchword is Service to the Youth of the Race.

So let us pause and pay a deserved tribute to the Greek

letter fraternities and sororities—who are too often abused because they are young and sometimes would fain dance to the playing of the piper.

At least they pay the piper when they essay to lead their younger brothers and sisters to drink at the Pierian Spring.

May 24, 1929

Well, I have read the muchly talked about *Banjo* by Claude McKay. And in the language of the prophet Elijah, the less said about it, the better.

. . . . . .

Concerning the furore roused by the re-opening of the Senate restaurant to colored people since Congressman De Priest entertained some of his constituents therein, it might be interesting to recall that a few years ago all the restaurants connected with the United States government, including the one in the Library of Congress, were open to all people, white and black. It is only within the past two decades that discrimination set in. And the spectacle of black and white eating side by side in various government restaurants did not then incite the Southern solons to battle, murder and sudden death. A lot of this prejudice which seems so ingrained, has come about in comparatively recent times, as many of us oldsters can testify. Good thing to have the pendulum swing around the circle again.

. . . . . .

The meanest man in the world has been found. He is a Southern white man, and his specialty seems to be robbing the clotheslines of colored washerwomen, and the hen roosts of orphanages. He is in jail for thirty days, and will pay a fine of twenty-dollars. He should qualify as an exhibit in a circus.

* * *

Nannie Burrough's pageant, *When Truth Gets a Hearing* played to a record house at the Dunbar Theatre in Philadelphia on last Thursday night. It was mighty well done. The girls spoke clearly and delightfully. No mealy-mouth mumbling, but enunciation and articulation that was a delight to the ear. The acting was natural and graceful, and some quite dramatic. And the singing was excellent. We could have wished that the audience were less enthusiastic, for often they voiced their approval so vigorously and whole-heartedly that some of the lines were lost, especially in the very well done "Labor Chorus" when it gave Dett's "Music in the Mines." The story of the progress of the race, and all the good "Race Hokum" was so well presented that even the most saturated ones of it forgot to be bored, and applauded vigorously the fresh viewpoint of the young women of Miss Burroughs' school.

Needless to say the audience refused to go home until it had called Miss Burroughs before the curtain.

* * *

A new slant on the labor question came to light the other day. A story is going the rounds concerning the dismissal of colored girl elevator operators by a large department store—presumably in a Southern city. The management found itself deluged with complaints from their dainty Nordic patronesses concerning the said operators. Not that they objected to riding in elevators run by colored girls, but if such lines of employment were kept open for the girls, there would be a dearth of domestics for the Nordic ladies. In other words, the economic pressure must be brought upon colored women to force and keep them in domestic service.

Quite a new idea.

. . . . . .

June 7, 1929

. . . . . .

World War stories are going the rounds again. The funniest ones, of course, are about the Negro. And the humor in them always centers around his abject fear; his running away from danger; his terror at the sound of a shell, and his fleetness of foot in time of crisis. In view of the fact that the Negro must always be regarded as a coward, it might not be amiss, should the United States get into trouble again, for us to remind the government that a race of cowards would be more of a hindrance than a help in a war, and that the brave Caucasians had best fight out their own destinies, unhampered by shivering, eye-rolling blacks.

. . . . . .

June 14, 1929

"Negro Authors Must Eat!" announces George W. Jacobs in the current issue of *The Nation*. One feels that here will be the explanation of some of the current vaporings by and about the Negro which has been hailed as literature. So it is, but not an extenuation, thank goodness. Mr. Jacobs is convinced that the Negro author is not justified in "burdening his interpretation of nature with the servilities of a steward." If authors must eat, far better that they eat from the earnings of other than their pen, than prostitute that pen to pandering. "Aeschulus was a soldier and a public official. Sophocles was a general and the commander of a fleet. Cervantes was a naval commissary and tax collector. Art to them was more than a mere purveyor of groceries."

Mr. Jacobs calls attention to the "passion for a candid and comprehensive delineation of every phase of Negro life" which arose ten years ago. Promptly the Negro writers, "plunged beneath the surface of their environment hoisted the sewer system to one's very nose, and, amid the jingling of many shekels, insisted that his was all that there was of black Harlem."

Good words, those. It is time that someone protested against the "sewer literature" which has offended the nostrils of those to whom literature is a beautiful dignified mistress and not a strident, dishevelled gutter-snipe.

. . . . . .

June 21, 1929

. . . . . .

And now, having injected the political virus into this hot weather, let us discourse upon the world's worst movie.

Some time ago when I saw *Joan of Arc*, the perfect film, the ultimate in screen perfection, I vowed I would not go to see another picture as long as I lived. I wanted to keep the taste of this perfection always with me as a lovely memory.

But I fell from grace, and after several such falls, in a moment of temporary mental aberration, allowed myself to be cajoled into seeing *Noah's Ark*.

Therefore I rise and unhesitatingly name it the world's worst.

* * *

Your credulity is strained when you read that four historians worked to see that the picture was historically correct. If they did, they have access to tomes denied most libraries. Apart from the fact that a little thing like a hiatus of three years,

from 1914 to 1917 during the World War, is passed peacefully by two Americans, and one German girl in Paris—
without a passport, by the way—. That when the hero gets
ready to enlist in the American army, he just doffs his hat
and coat, and marches off with the uniformed unit. That the
heroine, the said German girl, goes blithely about her way
in various stages of life, until a scorned Russian suitor reports
her as a spy, and then when she is to be executed, the firing
squad contains her own husband, who halts proceedings until
a shell buries them all alive, where they remain buried until
the Armistice is signed, and they are all dug out, while the
flood obligingly is re-created for the buried ones.

* * *

All this is bad enough, but it is when the cut back to the
flood and its millions of tons of water appears that our
credulity cracks. The city which flaunts its sinful pride is Ur
of the Chaldees, which according to C[?] is Abraham's home
town not Noah's. Noah gets the sign from Heaven via the
burning bush—which any second grade Sunday school pupil
will tell you was Moses' own prerogative. Also, Noah goes
up on some high plain to receive the message from God
concerning the ark, quite after the fashion of Moses going
up on Mount Sinai to get the law. Also, this message comes,
after much thunderings and lightnings, in a huge stone book,
set on end, like a great Bible, with self-turning leaves—
although the historians did have the building of Babylon
going on later, according to plans held in the hands of boss
contractors, scroll fashion.

When the animals go into the ark in all the downpour of
tons of water, there are herds of zebras, and long cavalcades
of elephants and lions, instead of the two by two which we
are told in Genesis is correct. The ark was real cosily efficient

within. But Japeth was blinded, like Samson of a later date, and put to grind at the mill—which seems to be another Gaza.

Someone once said that the Paradise Lost is the dream of a Puritan who fell asleep over his Bible. Well, Noah's Ark must be the nightmare of a child who fell asleep over Dore's illustration of the Bible—without ever having read the text.

Well—it is something to have seen the world's best picture—*Joan of Arc*—and the world's worst—*Noah's Ark*—in the space of one month.

June 28, 1929

. . . . . .

There is a fascination about Claude McKay's *Banjo* after all. It is difficult to read, for there is no plot, no thread of narrative to hold it together; no raison d'etre. And yet, the quaint philosophizings of the stranded Negroes in the fascinating sewer of Marseilles are worth considering.

"For civilization had gone out among these native, earthy people, had despoiled them of their primitive soil, had uprooted, enchanted, transported and transformed them to labor under its làws, and yet lacked the spirit to tolerate them within its walls."

"As the rag is to the bull, so is the composite voice of the Negro—speech, song and laughter—to a bawdy world. More exasperating, indeed, than the Negro's being himself, is his primitive color in a world where everything is being reduced to a familiar formula, this remains strange and elusive."

* * *

And you cannot but chuckle, though you may be momentarily indignant, over Mr. McKay's gesture in the direction of the

Negro "intelligentsia." "Aframericàns, long-deracinated, still rootless among phantoms and pale shadows, enfeebled by self-effacement before condescending patronage, social negativism, and miscegenation." "The colored Intelligentsia lived its life 'to have the white neighbors think well of us,' so that it could move more peaceably into nice 'white' streets. . . . Hopeless, enervating talk of the chances of 'passing for white,' and the spectre of the Future that were the common topics of the colored intelligentsia."

* * *

You feel a common cause with Mr. McKay there. You feel like clasping his hand and saying with whole-hearted sympathy, "Brother, you know. I also have suffered from those conversations."

So Banjo and Ray and Taloufa and his ilk down in the bistro of Marseilles, according to Mr. McKay, "Possessed more potential power for racial salvation than the Negro literati, whose poverty of mind and purpose showed never any signs of enrichment, even though inflated above the common level and given an appearance of superiority."

. . . . . .

August 2, 1929

The worst of taking your vacation early is that when you come back to work, properly sun-tanned, healthy, blowsy and what not, after the congratulations and admiration have staled—everyone else goes on their vacation, and you are left, feeling defrauded somehow, and wondering why you have to work so hard in such hot weather. But this feeling of self-pity is momentary, when you remember those classic "last two weeks in August." If you went early you have escaped the hordes who try to crowd in two weeks what they have lost in the preceding fifty.

*   *   *

Mankind has much of the sheep in his makeup. And conservative withal. A generation ago someone discovered that the last two weeks in August were the logical time for the summer rest, as they came just before the cool weather, and just after the body was torn to pieces by the heat waves of the summer. So that became the classic time for the annual holiday. And for years men and women who have ample time during the entire twelve hot weeks of the summer to loaf, wait in patience until August fifteenth. Then the mad rush, the congested trains, overcrowded hotels, massed beaches, packed boats, inferior accommodations, wild-eyed amusement proprietors, motor roads where cars crawl at ten miles an hour, traffic jams, sunburn cures, wailing youngsters, dances and card games, the same as in winter, only now heat and haste are added to the usual irritation. And then the insane Labor Day crowds! A frenzied rush to "rest!" to pack into a fortnight what could never be done in twenty-five fortnights.

*   *   *

Therefore the wise ones of the earth, who have but four weeks out of the year, or even two, and who wish really to loaf and invite their souls, choose July as their time for holidaying. July, before the hordes descend upon the lovely spots of woods and sea and mountain, and spread sordidness in their train. July, before the mosquitoes, especially those with long names, speckled wings, and wicked tails, get in their fine work of injecting malaria into the system of the injudicious. July, before the sea-nettle, that innocent looking lump of colorless gelatine, with basting threads straying through its amorphous body, begins to operate in bays and

seas, to caress the body of the unwary swimmer with its
deadly sting. July, before the poison ivy has had time to reach
out evil and lusty leaves into every cluster of innocent looking
wild flowers. July, before the green corn has grown tough,
and the chef has lost his cunning with the little hot rolls. July
before the hotel keepers have grown harried and absent-
minded about extra service, and while the plate dinners are
still large and generous, and not depleted by an unexpected
forty carloads of trippers. July, before things have become
so formal and societyfied that you feel you must crawl into
evening clothes for dinner, and the bathing beach looks like
Peacock Alley. Oh, yes, commend me to July for a pure
unadulterated vacation—if that is what you wish, and not a
hectic, fevered social time.

* * *

Therefore July, and therefore Highland Beach. Washington
has known Highland Beach, and Arundel-on-the-Bay for
thirty-five years and loved it, when it was nothing much but
three cottages some sand dunes and a gorgeous bathing beach.
Then Baltimore looked upon it, and found it good. Then
Philadelphia realized its possibilities—and now, behold the
Mecca of those of us who would have a summer home in a
colony of congenial souls, or who would spend a few weeks
in a delightful spot, far enough from the madding crowd,
and yet near enough to some good companions, or who have
children whose heritage of freedom and happiness and unlimited play should not be denied. Hence Highland Beach, the
joy of the vacationist, whether in July or in August; the
delight of the "tripper" or motorist, who would come down
for a cooling dip in the Bay and a good dinner, and the
Paradise of children.

* * *

Yea, a veritable Eden for little folk. A safe beach, where one really would have to go to a lot of trouble to drown; two creeks full of crabs actually begging to be netted, oodles of sand, a lake full of fish, daring you not to catch them, tides that rise and fall not too high, waves that are never too rough to be troublesome, nights of moonlight and phosphorescent glow in the waves, just right for bonfires on the beach and weinie roasts; days of languorous softness, sunshine or gray glow; a Y.W.C.A. camp with plenty of jolly girls to enliven things by Friday night "stunts"—and plenty of children, big boys (like Douglass Lucas and Perry Howard with their immoral "Hesperus") and Fred, the Third, and Jimmy Henderson clear on down to the tiniest boy, McDougald Holmes, bravely bringing up the rear, not to be daunted by the deepest water or the heaviest crab net, mostly dripping Chesapeake Bay whether in his sun-tan bathing suit, or his best linen trouserettes.

And girls, plenty of them, girls from "Personality Plus" Carol Harris at the "Y" camp, and Betty Francis, the indomitable and fearless swimmer, down to tiny Peggy Lucas, the Queen of the Children's Playground, planned and constructed by her doting grandfather. Swimming matches, when the Wharton boys and others contended mightily with Benny Brown from Baltimore—who won the prize; swimming matches among the oldsters, at night, when the phosphorus in the heavy waves gleamed like miners lamps on the foreheads. Early morning dips, mornings of standing knee deep in the creeks, scooping up the unwary crabs. Wading excursions over to Arundel to the Curtis bungalow, where Buddy, the Life-Guard, aged two plus, tells you his name is Fleming Norris, the Second. Languorous afternoons on the Henderson pier in the lake, restful mornings in the hammock on Joe

Douglass' porch, waiting for the mail. Annozeans' the meeting place of everyone. Just standing still in her garden and everyone you know from everywhere, North, South, East or West, will come by Sunday afternoons. Dances in the evening, if you are frivolous, at Ware's—a dip in the bay, and wienies in Annapolis.

And your bridge maniacs—of course. Tournaments and games that move from the Howard porch, to the Freeman porch, to the Holmes porch, down to the Williams living room, come back and linger everywhere, and keep a standing game at Annozeans, with, on week ends, the champion of them all, Mrs. McCard presiding.

* * *

Oh, assuredly, July at Highland Beach. The wave of vacationists may gather and break where it will in August, but in the language of the prophet—I am content. It has been a lovely time, a perfect experience, a delightful and never-to-be-forgotten memory.

August 9, 1929

It would be interesting to take Oswald Harrison Villard's article in July *Harper's*, "The Crumbling Color Line" and compare it column by column with George Schuyler's "Keeping the Negro in His Place" in the August *Mercury*. Mr. Villard is almost all in a mood of optimism; Mr. Schuyler is plainly pessimistic. The one "points with pride," the other "views with alarm." Between the Scylla and Charybdis of their differing emotions, the mere outsider and looker-on, even though he be an "Aframerican" can steer a middle course of patient sailing to a goal nowhere visible on the horizon.

August 23, 1929

One of the joys which await me Monday mornings is the
Christian Review of Philadelphia. And that is mainly because
of Nannie Burroughs' column, "From a Woman's Point of
View." The week is only well started when I have had
Nannie's reactions to the homely problems with which she
deals—ministers' wives, clean babies, homemaking, manners
in public—all the things which we know so well, and practice
so ill.

This last week the caption is "Sidewalk Conventions." The
opening sentence, "Entirely too much of the business of our
conventions is attended to by sidewalk Solomons," gives an
idea of the sermon to be preached. And those of us who go
up and down in the land attending conventions know only
too well the spectacle of the convention overflowing on to the
sidewalks with the consequent loss of dignity and decorum of
the whole affair. Before the brothers and sisters go to another
convention—and there are legion yet to be held before August
and September have passed—they should read Nannie Burroughs' opinion of the "Sidewalk Solomons," and her slogan,
"Clear the sidewalk! The convention was called to meet IN
the church."

        . . . . . .

It is small wonder that "All Quiet on the Western Front" is
the world's best seller, and how significant that a world's best
seller should be an indictment of war—surely the most pitiful
yet written. Peace treaties and peace tracts fade into insignificance before this quiet and simple tale of the generation
which was destroyed by the war. Entering the war from the
public school, returning to—nothing. Millions with no per-

spective—wiped out as completely as if caught in a barrage of fire.

We say "Old men make wars"—and the rest. Herr Ehrich Remarque looks at the Russian prisoners and comments, "A word of command has made these silent figures our enemies; a word of command might transform them into our friends." Or, "Now just why would a French blacksmith or a French shoemaker want to attack us. No, it is merely the rulers." Or, "Why do they never tell us that you are just poor devils like us, that your mothers are just as anxious as ours, and that we have the same fear of death, and the same dying, and the same agony—Forgive me, comrade, how could you be our enemy?"

"I am young, I am twenty years old; yet I know nothing of life but despair, death, fear and fatuous superficiality cast over an abyss of sorrow. I see how peoples are set against one another, and in silence, unknowingly, foolishly, obediently, innocently slay one another. I see that the keenest brains of the world invent weapons and words to make it yet more refined and enduring."

The awfulness of it, the utter simplicity of this boy's "Why—why—why?" No one who has read this book can ever again think calmly of another war. If such books as this have come from the hideous debacle of 1914–1918, perhaps after all, it WAS the war to end war.

THE ULTIMATE INSULT *

The ultimate insult has been given to Presidential Candidate Hoover. He has been accused of calling upon and dancing with a colored woman!

Governor Theodore G. Bilbo, of Mississippi, is responsible for this latest horror of a bitter campaign. Gov. Bilbo says he was not the author of the story; that he merely repeated the statement that was made at a public rally in Jackson, Miss., some days ago. But whether the author of the story or not, he gave it wide publicity and drew upon his head the solemn and bitter wrath of one, George Akerson, assistant to the presidential candidate. Mr. Akerson's wrath was Jovean. He declared that the statement of the Governor was "unqualifiedly false," and characterized it further as "the most indecent and unworthy statement in the whole of a bitter campaign."

The Republican campaign managers in their attempts to dent the solid South have circulated a similar report about Presidential Candidate Smith, alleging that he dances with colored women in New York City—a statement which brought forth no such bitter denial from the Democratic National headquarters, as has come from the Republican headquarters. Denial there was, but nothing so scathing, so insulting, so vehement as this which has come for the defense of Mr. Hoover. But here we have Mr. Akerson solemnly alleging that he was with Mr. Hoover EVERY HOUR (manifestly

* Editorial, The Washington *Eagle*, October 26, 1928.

a physical impossibility) of the four months that he was in the flood area, and that the only contact he had with colored people was when they presented him with a memorial thanking him for his aid to them in the work of reconstruction. Mr. Akerson alternately weeps and gnashes his teeth in the face of this atrocity—that his master could be accused of such an unspeakable, such a dastardly crime against decency.

We do not believe that Mr. Hoover called on the colored lady, nor that he danced with her. He does not look like a dancing man; there is no particular reason for his socializing with the Mound Bayouites, and the thought is enough to provoke the risibles of anyone with a grain of humor. Left to itself it would have died the natural death of all jokes. But Mr. Akerson exalts it to a crime of lese majeste; to a breaking of the Decalogue, to the sin against the Holy Ghost.

And in so doing he hurls the vilest of insults in the face of every Negro in the United States. He wipes mud in their teeth, and he utterly destroys whatever lingering belief in the decency of the Republican party might have been left in the mind of the Negro. It is safe to assert that there is not a colored woman in the United States who would want to dance with Mr. Hoover, or would feel herself honored in so doing. But every woman of color feels her soul flame into a white heat of insulted rage at the characterization by Mr. Akerson, as "an indecent and unworthy statement."

The Republican party has fallen over itself repudiating the Negro in speaking to the South. It injected the race question into the campaign from the first, by spreading the propaganda in the South of Gov. Smith's affiliation with the Negro of New York; of Ferdinand Q. Morton's white stenographer, and considerable more such bitterness. It has out-Bourboned the Bourbons in flaunting the bloody shirt, and stirred up sectional hatred where sectional hatred had died down. It has grabbed frantically at every possible crevice to try to break into the solidity of the South. And now in a last wild stand against a possible loss of a doubtful gain, it shrieks insult and bilge at the Negro over the shoulders of the Governor of Mississippi.

"That any person in Mississippi should be led to vote for or against Mr. Hoover upon a representation of this kind would forever be a most infamous blot on the record of the State of Mississippi," continues Mr. Akerson.

And we paraphrase that statement by saying that any Negro who would vote for Mr. Hoover after his gratuitous insult to the womenkind of the race is unworthy of the trusting faith of a sister, the loyal love of a wife, or the tender self-sacrificing devotion of a mother.

ESSAYS

POLITICS IN DELAWARE*

An anomalous condition exists in the political situation in Delaware. The Republican Party in that State has been in power for twenty-five years and as the colored man has the balance of power and constitutes one-tenth of the voting population, it has been kept in power by his vote. Yet Delaware is the only State in the Union where the colored man may not practice law. In all that time, the colored people have not had one of their race serve on the jury. There are no colored policemen in Delaware. Some may be called but none are ever chosen. The courts practice a most humiliating segregation. It is definitely acknowledged that the Ku Klux Klan is controlled by and in turn controls the party in power.

Two years ago, the Negroes arose and turning against the Republican Party, defeated the candidate for re-election to Congress, Caleb S. Layton. He had voted against the Dyer Anti-Lynching Bill, a measure in which they, in common with all other Negroes in the country, were intensely interested. Dr. Layton boasted that he was proud of his record. He was left at home and his opponent, Judge William H. Boyce, who had a record for fair and impartial wielding of justice from his seat on the bench, was elected in his stead. At the same time, T. Coleman duPont, who had been appointed to the U.S. Senate through a manipulation facetiously known in Delaware as "the dirty deal," was also defeated.

T. Coleman duPont's record on the Dyer Bill was not

*Opportunity, November 1924.

good. While he did not have an opportunity to vote on it, he was one of the Senators who walked out when the question of bringing it to a vote was being debated in the Senate. The absence of a quorum prevented the vote being taken. T. C. duPont helped to make the absence of a quorum possible.

This subversal of tradition two years ago resulted in not only a Democratic Senator, Thomas F. Bayard, and a Democratic Congressman, Judge William H. Boyce, being elected, but a Democratic majority in the State General Assembly. When appropriations to State institutions were being cut and slashed in the interests of economy, one institution escaped, the Industrial School for Colored Girls, which received an appropriation of $53,000, more money than was ever given to any colored institution at one time in the history of Delaware.

The elections of 1924 present an amazing situation. The Democratic candidate for Governor, Joseph Bancroft, comes from a line of ancestry which has been a friend of the colored people for more than a hundred years. The Bancrofts are old line Abolitionists. They have educated more colored boys in higher institutions of learning than any other family in Delaware. The Joseph Bancroft & Sons Company, huge textile manufacturers, employs more colored men than any other corporation in Delaware. Mrs. Bancroft is the daughter of General O.O. Howard of Freedmen's Bureau and Howard University fame, herself a woman of large charities and earnest work among the colored people.

On the other hand, the Republican candidate for Congress against this same Judge Boyce, who was elected by the Negro two years ago, was a member of the Resolutions Committee in the Republican State Convention which killed a resolution presented to the body which read as follows: "The matter of segregation in the several courts of the State, the failure of colored men to be named as jurors in the several counties, and the debarring of colored men from the practice of law in Delaware, is unjust to a large group of our citizens. The same is hereby condemned as being subversive of the best traditions of the Republican Party, and the party in state convention assembled pledges itself to take immediate steps to correct the conditions herein complained of."

This resolution, though presented by a white member of the Republican State Convention, was not even allowed to be read.

Another peculiar situation which the colored people hold against this same duPont, the candidate for Senator, in addition to his walking out on the Dyer Bill, is the fact that he voted against the seating of Henry Lincoln Johnson's colored delegation from Georgia in the Republican National Convention, and that he was indiscreet enough, when a committee of prominent colored men waited on him, to refer to some of our most outstanding colored national leaders as "darkies."

Pierre duPont, who has given more to the education of the Negro than any other single individual in a specific State, is related to Coleman duPont, but is not to be confused with him. Pierre duPont has no political aspirations, and is reported to be a Democrat. There is frequent confusion in the minds of the Negroes of the rural sections as to the identity of these two men—the one a benefactor of the colored people, the other hardly a friend. And it is whispered that Coleman duPont is not averse to profiting by his cousin's contributions to the education of the Negro.

In the past several years three colored women and girls have been raped by white men. As the crime of rape is a capital one in Delaware, it is worthy of note that not one of the men charged with the heinous crime has been punished as the law provides. The charge is usually made a minor one, or a failure to indict remains. This has added to the political unrest of the colored people. Thus it can be truly said that the political situation in Delaware is an anomalous one, with party tradition on one side and the Abolitionists and Quakers heading the other. The colored people are facing this peculiar situation, and having decided that as the ballot is the most powerful political weapon that they have, it is in their power to use it effectively.

WOMAN'S MOST SERIOUS PROBLEM *

E. B. Reuter, in his latest book, *The American Race Problem,* makes this comment, "During the past decade there has been a somewhat marked improvement in the economic conditions of the Negroes. This is reflected in the decline of the number of women employed, and in the shift in numbers in different occupations." This statement is followed by a table showing the shift in occupational employment.

From one elevator operator in 1910, the number jumped to 3,073 in 1920. Those engaged in lumber and furniture industries in 1910 were 1,456. In 1920, 4,066. Textile industries jumped from 2,234 to 7,257. On the other hand, chambermaids in 1910 were numbered 14,071, but in 1920 they had declined to 10,443. Untrained nurses from 17,874 to 13,888; cooks from 205,584 to 168,710; laundresses, not in public laundries, from 361,551 to 283,557. On the other hand, cigar and tobacco workers jumped from 10,746 to 21,829, and the teaching profession showed a normal increase from 22,528 to 29,244.

Just what do these figures indicate? That the Negro woman is leaving the industries of home life, cooking, domestic service generally, child nursing, laundry work and going into mills, factories, operation of elevators, clerking, stenography (for in these latter occupations there is an almost 400 percent increase). She is doing a higher grade of work, getting better money, commanding better respect from the

* *The Messenger*, March 1927.

community because of her higher economic value, and less menial occupation. Domestic service claims her race no longer as its inalienable right. She is earning a salary, not wages.

This sounds fine. For sixty-three years the Negro woman has been a co-worker with the Negro man. Now that she is more than ever working by his side, she feels a thrill of pride in her new economic status.

But—"the ratio of children to women has declined from census to census for both races. The decline has in general been more rapid for the Negro than for the white elements in the population."* In 1850 the number of children under five years of age per 1,000 women from 15 to 44 years of age for Negro women was 741, for white women, 659. In 1920 the Negro birth rate had decreased to 439, the white to 471. While the percentage of children under five years of age had decreased in the case of Negro women from 13.8 in Negro families to 10.9, and in white families from 11.9 to 10.9!

"In spite of the considerable increase in the Negro population and in the increase of the marriage rate, the actual number of Negro children under five years of age was less in 1920 than at any of the previous enumerations."* In 1900 the number of Negro children under five years of age was 1,215,655; in 1910, the number was 1,263,288; in 1920 it was 1,143,699!

And this sharp decline in the face of increased knowledge of the care and feeding of infants; the work of the insurance companies in health, Negro Health Week, public health nurses, clinics, dispensaries, and all the active agencies for the conservation and preservation of health.

* E.B. Reuter.

One startling fact is apparent. Negro women are exercising birth control in order to preserve their new economic independence. Or, because of poverty of the family, they are compelled to limit their offspring.

The same author, Dr. Reuter, tells us that a recent study showed that fifty-five Negro professors at Howard University had come from families averaging 6.5 children, while the professors themselves had an average of 0.7 children. Some were unmarried, but for each family formed, the average number of children was 1.6. "The birth rate of the cultured classes is apparently only one-third of the masses."

The race is here faced with a startling fact. Our birth rate is declining; our infant mortality is increasing; our normal rate of increase must necessarily be slowing up; our educated and intelligent classes are refusing to have children; our women are going into the kind of work that taxes both physical and mental capacities, which of itself, limits fecundity. While white women are beginning to work more away from home, at present, even with the rush of all women into the wage earner's class, in New York City alone, seven times as many colored as white women work away from home.

The inevitable disruption of family life necessitated by the woman being a co-wage earner with the man has discouraged the Negro woman from child-bearing. Juvenile delinquents are recruited largely from the motherless home. That is the home that is without the constant care of the mother or head of the house. For a child to arise in the morning after both parents are gone, get itself an indifferent breakfast, go to school uncared for, lunch on a penny's worth of sweets, and return to a cold and cheerless house or apartment to await the return of a jaded and fatigued mother to get supper, is not conducive to sweetness and light in its behavior. Truancy, street walking, petty thievery and gang rowdyism are the natural results of this lack of family life. The Negro woman is awakening to the fact that the contribution she makes to the economic life of the race is too often made at the expense of the lives of the boys and girls of the race—so she is refusing to bring into the world any more potential delinquents.

This is the bald and ungarnished statement of a startling series of facts. The decline in the birth rate of the Negro. The rise in the economic life of the Negro woman. The sharpest peak of the decline—if a decline can be said to have a peak—is in the birth rate of the more cultured and more nearly leisure classes. The slow increase in the national family life, caused by the women workers not having time to make homes in the strictest sense of homemaking. The sharp rise in juvenile delinquency—in the cities, of course, and among the children of women workers. And worst of all because more subtle and insinuating in its flattering connotation of economic freedom, handsome salaries and social prestige—the growing use of married women of the child-bearing age as public school teachers, with the consequent temptation to refrain from child-bearing in order not to interfere with the independent life in the school room.

This is the situation. I would not suggest any remedy, make any criticism, raise any question, nor berate the men and women who are responsible for this crisis. For it is a serious crisis. I would only ask the young and intelligent women to give pause.

The new Negro is the topic most dwelt upon these days by the young folks, whom some call, frequently in derisive envy, the "Intelligentsia." In every race, in every nation and in every clime in every period of history there is always an

eager-eyed group of youthful patriots who seriously set themselves to right the wrongs done to their race, or nation or
sect or sometimes to art of self-expression. No race or nation
can advance without them. Thomas Jefferson was an ardent
leader of youthful patriots of his day, and Alexander Hamilton
would have been dubbed a leader of the intelligentsia were
he living now. They do big things, these young people.

Perhaps they may turn their attention, these race-loving
slips of girls and slim ardent youths who make hot-eyed
speeches about the freedom of the individual and the rights
of the Negro, to the fact that at the rate we are going the
Negro will become more and more negligible in the life of
the nation. For we must remember that while the Negro
constituted 19.3 percent of the population in 1790, and 18.9
in 1800, he constitutes only 9.9 percent today, and his
percentage of increase has steadily dropped from 37.5 in
1810 to 6.3 in 1920.

No race can rise higher than its women is an aphorism
that is so trite that it has ceased to be tiresome from its very
monotony. If it might be phrased otherwise to catch the
attention of the Negro woman, it would be worth while
making the effort. No race can be said to be a growing race,
whose birth rate is declining, and whose natural rate of
increase is dropping sharply. No race will amount to anything
economically, no matter how high the wages it collects nor
how many commercial enterprises it supports, whose owner-
ship of homes has not kept proportionate pace with its business
holdings. Churches, social agencies, schools and Sunday schools
cannot do the work of mothers and heads of families. Their
best efforts are as cheering and comforting to the soul of a
child in comparison with the welcoming smile of the mother
when it comes from school as the machine-like warmth of an

incubator is to the chick after the downy comfort of a clucking hen. Incubators are an essential for the mass production of chickens, but the training of human souls needs to begin at home in the old-fashioned family life, augmented later, if necessary, in the expensive schools and settlements of the great cities.

THE PROBLEM OF PERSONAL
SERVICE *

Most of us are familiar with the sight of the middle-class
white woman going from door to door in the frankly colored
neighborhood, ringing the bells and asking with honeyed
accents of condescension, "I wonder if you could tell me
where I can get a good cook (or laundress or housemaid)";
and the blunt reply of the stout colored dame, as she holds
the door against Nordic intrusion, " 'Deed, I couldn't tell
you ma'am, I need a girl myself."

That is one phase of the problem of personal service—
many of us dislike the term "domestic" service—it has collected such a variety of unpleasant connotations. But the
situation must have reached an acute condition if we are to
judge by the findings of the group of rich New York women,
headed by Mrs. Boardman, which has decided to place
servants in the professional class. Service is to be on a par
with other operations in the business world, and the supposed
stigma which is attached to domestic employment is to be
removed. The maid and cook and laundress will be graduates
of schools for their training. They will have regular hours.
They will be addressed by the title "Miss" or "Mrs." and all
the rest of it. But as the Philadelphia *Record* whimsically
objects, what about the price paid to these super-servants?

Our race knows that this solution will not touch us. When
super-servants are to be employed, with all the frills and
appurtenances, including the gracious form of address, we

* *The Messenger*, June 1927.

293

well know the Caucasian female of the species will not have to pay a dark-skinned girl the price, nor be willing to accord her the position of business employee rather than personal maid. And after all, there will be comparatively few even of the wealthiest class who will be able or willing to pay the price for this superior class of domestics.

So that leaves the problem exactly where it was at the beginning.

We have noticed before that the number of ladies maids has dropped from 10,239 in 1910 to 5,488 in 1920. Of chambermaids from 14,071 in 1910 to 10,443 in 1920. Of child nurses from 17,874 in 1910 to 13,888 in 1920. Of dressmakers and seamstresses from 38,277 in 1910 to 26,961 in 1920. Of cooks from 205,584 in 1910, to 168,443 in 1920. Of laundresses, not in laundries, from 361,551 in 1910 to 283,557 in 1920. We have noted, too, that women are leaving the ranks of personal service for the easier (so far as hours go) and better paid work in mills, industries, factories.

But there are phases of personal service that are attractive. Board and lodging being often included, the wages are "clear," and the work is often so planned that there is not the strain, the constant being on tiptoe that is necessary in the industrial and professional world. Often, too, contacts, that are afterwards remunerative, are made. If there were an adequate protection afforded the girl or woman who goes into personal service, either as a career, a stop-gap, a summer avocation, or a means to an end, there is hardly any phase of the work-a-day world that would offer better opportunities for the girl forced to leave school before she has gained her high school diploma, or for one who has done so.

And that adequate protection of the woman in personal

service can come only from intelligent organization into a union that will safeguard her interests, protect her morals, assure her of a home when temporarily out of employment, and give her accurate card catalogue information of prospective employers.

This is an idea neither new nor original. During the war, Miss Eartha M. White, of Jacksonville, Florida, had under her direction a most excellent union of women in war work, whether elevator runners, drivers of trucks, special domestic servants or what not. It had possibilities, that union did. It may still exist, but if so, its activities are of the soundless variety. Perhaps the closing of the war, releasing the women from their unusual duties caused a cessation of interest.

Four or five years ago, Miss Nannie Burroughs, of Washington, D.C., conceived the idea of a Domestic Servants Organization, with rules, regulations and projects similar to the unions among men laborers or skilled workmen. It was a magnificent idea, and with her customary smashing skill, Miss Burroughs put it across in quite a bit of the territory of the United States. A building was bought and operated for the girls in the heart of northwest Washington. It is a sort of Social Center, with classes, lodging rooms, recreation rooms, dining rooms, where excellent meals can be obtained at small cost, and all the rest of it.

But the appeal was never national. For one thing, to put such an idea across, trained organizers and speakers must be on the go all the time, reaching the women in small towns, as well as in large ones, and hammering, hammering away at the idea. And that takes money. And Miss Burroughs had no money. And not much time to do the work herself, since the life of her own school, the National Training School, depends upon her own efforts.

And that still leaves the problem in the air.

Only those who have had dealings with the middle-class employer of colored girls know that those girls sometimes have to endure to get a fair living wage. We know by heart the tales of the miserable sleeping quarters, the long and uncertain hours, the lonely evenings, which ofttimes end in surreptitious visits to any place where company and pleasure may be had. Small wonder then, that girls drift into factories—and they are pretty poor factories in the Middle Atlantic and Southern states which employ colored girls. Small wonder that domestic service is shunned. There is too much uncertainty about its operations.

Girls under the charge of institutions who are paroled to service, fare much better. The parole officer, or visiting officer, sees to it that the girl's room is adequately furnished, is warm and attractive. She insists upon recreation and hours off. She places a valuation upon the girl's services, and sees that she is so recompensed. And the paroled girl is correspondingly respected because there is law behind her. She is apt to be free from the unwelcome attentions of the men of the house—for no man relishes being hauled into court on the charge of "contributing to the delinquency of a minor" or "interfering with the safety of a ward of the state."

FACING LIFE SQUARELY*

The Girl Reserves in their beautiful ritual promise to "face life squarely." Surely a most essential thing for all young girls to know; to learn to look with honest, clear-eyed vision at life, stripping away shams and non-essentials, facing facts and not being lured from the truth by silly reticences and repressions.

I wish that every girl of our race could learn the code of the Girl Reserves—at least that one part of it. And I wish that every Aframerican woman in this country could take as the essential basic element of her life this one thing—to face life squarely. We have come a long way from the Victorian days of repressions and hidings of the truth, and silences about what everyone knew was true, and pretences and shams, when the mention of any portion of anatomy but the face was silenced with blushes, and no respectable woman wore silk stockings. But we still love to deceive ourselves, and while we are less prudish than our Victorian mothers, we are still afraid of the truth as it touches the fabric of society. And we love to make high-sounding phrases which mean nothing, and to talk glibly about progress and changes in the social order and the superiority of the age, and how mankind is marching on, and kindred banal stuff. And the mere mention of a question which might puncture the gossamer veil of pretense cloaking the meaningless words causes consternation.

Let me illustrate: We are fond of talking nowadays about

*The Messenger, July 1927, p. 219.

"Progress in Race Relations." It is a phrase that is on the tongues of white and black—those interested in sociology and economics. We are deluged with releases giving statistics of the increased good will between the races. Headlines of startling height in some of our papers record touching instances of affection and love between Nordics and Aframericans.

Much is doubtless true. Southern colleges and universities are studying the Negro as never before. Men and women of our race appear before their student bodies, and in the classrooms, getting respectful and interested hearings. A thing unthinkable in any term twenty-five years ago. The Negro just now is the pet subject of litterateurs and sociologists. He is in the hey-dey of an unprecedented era of popularity. And so his emissaries are given eager attention; his books are read avidly, and best of all, bought and circulated. Gatherings and meetings and conferences between the races in the South are common occurrences, and there is no longer fear and wonder on the part of the Southern white women lest fire from Heaven descend upon them in wrath at meeting black men on a quasi equality.

But—let us face the situation squarely. We are apt to be lulled to sleep by the beautiful and touching instances of Christian amity between our people and those of the Nordic race. And yet we ought to know that behind the web of honeyed words, under the skin of every Southern white man and woman there lies the venom of race hatred. As in older days it was said that if you scratch any Russian, you would find a Tartar. We may amend the proverb to say scratch every Nordic and you find a cracker.

The Mississippi Flood is a case in point. While Nature has unloosed the torrent of her wrath upon a hapless land and wrought devastation untold and horror inescapable, similar demons have been unleashed in the souls of the white men in the path of destruction. If there ever were truth in the statement that "one touch of nature makes the whole world kin," it has lost its applicability in this instance. If the progress in race relations had kept pace with its advertisements, we should not hear the pitiful tales which filter through from the Southland. The thin veneer of civilization has sloughed off the white men and the old slave-driving, whip-cracking, black-women-raping, antebellum, plantation overseer herds the helpless blacks to his own liking, and a virtual slavery exists in the vast flood area.

Let us face this fact squarely. True the plantation owners of Mississippi, Louisiana and Arkansas are not the highest type of Nordics. They are not the ones who go to colleges or universities, or are interested in lectures or literature. The only race relations they ever heard of are the relations of black man and white master, or black woman and white ravisher. But until the Negroes of the backwoods are safe in the knowledge of their own freedom; until peonage ceases to be winked at by the law; until the chain gang is abolished and simple, elemental justice is dealt the ignorant blacks, we are hiding our heads in the sand. And the women of our race must realize that there is no progress in sobbing with joy over the spectacle of two or three ordinary Southern white women sitting down to talk with several very high class black women over the race problem. We are deluding ourselves if we feel we are getting anywhere by having conferences, when hundreds of black women are wringing their hands because their men have been driven over the crumbling levee to certain death, while the white men stand out of the danger zone.

We have learned to face the issue of lynching squarely. We are no longer hoodwinked by unsupported statements. We know that there have been more lynchings in the present year thus far than in the past. But this phase of the question is a good one for the women to look firmly in the face. Lynchings only occur where Negroes are afraid. When they cease to fear, the white man turns tail and skulks away.

We talk much about the army of graduates who step forth proudly this month ready for their conquering march through life. And we quote statistics to show our remarkable progress and expansion educationally. But if we would face this educational question squarely, we would see that the problem is to keep the standard where it belongs. For as long as we have segregated schools, as long as our educational system in this country is a biracial one, unless every nerve of every one of us is strained to the uttermost, we will have a biracial standard, and the Negro one will inevitably be lower. We cannot afford to deceive ourselves; for the sake of the children we should fight segregation in schools as if it were a poisonous viper attacking the very heart of our race. To face this problem squarely we must admit that the schools are primarily for the children and not for teachers, and that it were far better that our youngsters be thrown into competition with all races in schools, where no quarter is given, and the rate must be kept high, and from whence if they get through, they can emerge strong from the battle, and with respect for their own ability to stand up in a contest of wits, than that they be swathed in the inevitable paternalism of a strictly "colored" school. The job for the women of the race is to abolish the double standard of measurement and achievement of the child. And we do not need to deceive ourselves by averring that such a double standard does not exist.

Perhaps the place at which we are apt to deceive ourselves most blatantly is at the point of political independence. The political independence of any American citizen is a joke. And not only the political independence, but the political participation of the Negro in the affairs of the body politic is something to make high Olympus howl with mirth. Even in New York where the Aframerican is largely Tammanyized, he is no free agent. For being wise, he is an opportunist and slips into the well-worn groove of the perfectly obvious.

But now and then we hear of groups among us having conferences, the women as well as the men. And we talk wisely about what will be done to candidates when they dare to rear their heads. And if we were honest enough with ourselves to face the issue squarely, we'd all go home and admit that we will all file in line, march to the ballot box and vote as we are told at the crack of the boss' whip.

I might go on and multiply instances in our racial and national life where endless confusion of thought and action are caused by our refusing to look situations in the face; by self- and racial deception, by weak acceptance of the obvious explanation—by "going along" in other words.

Oh, that the girls may teach the women and the boys teach the men the wisdom of "facing life squarely."

BIG QUARTERLY IN
WILMINGTON *

A throbbing, pulsing mass of dusky folk, a kaleidoscope of brilliant gowns, hats and hosiery and shoes; many-hued faces, variously clad in silks, cottons, velvets, chiffons, milling around aimlessly; frank blending of rainbow hues; massing of flesh and color; tall, dark men, short light ones; buxom women of all shades of brown, and yellow; slim, multi-garbed maidens of Oriental seductiveness. An Oriental bazaar in an American city in 1932; a piece of a Georgia camp-meeting transplanted in the Middle Atlantic States; an anachronism of the days of slavery in the middle of the twentieth century.

This, to a casual observer, is the famous Big Quarterly in Wilmington, Delaware, held annually on the last Sunday in August. Each year prophets gravely shake their heads and predict that this will be the last of the Big Quarterly celebrations: that the Negro has outgrown that sort of thing, that the crowds will cease to gather for so antiquated an event. And each year sees a huge crowd, ever-changing in its characteristics and methods of enjoyment, but still the same restless, laughing, pleasure-seeking mass of dark humanity.

No amount of disgust and frowning upon the quaint custom by the high-brows of the race can change the mental attitude of the hoi-polloi. The immemorial usage of meeting together on Big Quarterly is too deeply rooted in the minds and hearts

*The Wilmington *Every Evening*, August 27, 1932.

of the Negroes of the Eastern Shore of Maryland and Virginia, of Delaware and Southeastern Pennsylvania, to be broken up or rooted out by the mere disgust of a few intelligentsia.

Big Quarterly originated when Delaware was a slave state. In days gone by, when the harvest was in and the work of the summer done, it was the custom of the masters to allow the slaves to foregather on one glorious Sunday holiday. What better than to go to Wilmington, the center of life on the Peninsula, and there meet with old friends not seen for a year? And the church, always the center of social life among Negroes was the hub, around which revolved the festive occasion of Big Quarterly.

On French St., in early days one of the main arteries of the city, was located in a small grove, the little Union Church of Africans, organized by Peter Spencer in 1908. Here in the rude building, overflowing into the grove, the slaves congregated for the great foregathering of the year. Song and praise, allelulias and shoutings without restraint; glad greetings and happy intercourse, a chance to show off the garments acquired during a thrifty year, gustatory delights innumerable—all this was a rare holiday for Negroes, slave and free, and since the first great meeting of rejoicing in 1812, the custom has persisted. It died down for a brief while during the Civil War, only to be reestablished with more fervor and brilliancy immediately after Emancipation.

The great feature, however, then as now, for the one hundred and twenty years that "Big Quarterly" has been an institution of the metropolis of the Delmarva Peninsula, is eating. That is the business of the day. From the moment that the visitors begin to arrive in the dews of early morn,

until the last one straggles home through the midnight damp-
ness of the sea-laden air, to eat is the constant duty of each
and every one without any dissent.

Eating stands, closely phalanxed together, line French St.
on both sides, from Sixth St., to Tenth, overflow into the
side streets, east and west, up and down, and run around into
contiguous Walnut St. Weeks before the event, concessionaires begin to bargain and haggle for places, French St.,
between Eighth and Ninth, being the most profitable, and
bringing the biggest prices.

The occupants of busses along the favored way set out
stands and many use their living rooms for rest rooms and
impromptu restaurants. Side by side white draped tables set
out upon the sidewalk, piled high with ham and cabbage,
greens and side-meat, fried chicken, deviled crabs, chicken
potpie, hot corn, frankfurters, soft drinks, sandwiches, ice
cream, candies, home-made cakes and pies, cigars, watermelon, sliced in economic slivers, varicolored lemonade,
coffee, pigs' feet, everything that can tempt the palate of
man, the appetite of woman, the gormandizing of children.

Thrifty concessionaires set up gasoline stoves on the sidewalks, where the food may be kept hot, and the sight of
innumerable pots and kettles boiling in the August sunshine
in a city street is an unforgettable spectacle. The strident
voices of barkers, calling attention to the superior daintiness
and palatability of their cookery, rise above the din of greetings, the jubilation of the "Singing Bands."

On the west side of French St., where the church is situated,
is the "grove," a hollow block of land, formerly entered by
a stable yard, now by a service station. This is the heart of
the eating business. Here are long tables set up on trestles,

with white cloths and plates and knives and forks, and here the crowd surges and sways and sings and eats and enjoys life under the trees, safe from the humid, piercing rays of the sun.

It must not be forgotten, however, that this assemblage is primarily a religious one. Within the church, rebuilt since the early days and fairly commodious now, is jammed with worshippers. Without, in the more secluded part of the grove, is a continuous service, presided over by first one and then another of the pastors of the African Union Methodist Protestant Church. They have come from many nearby towns, to carry on the services, which begin at 6 o'clock in the morning, and end after 11 at night. Prayer and praise meetings, love feasts and communion services, sermons and class revivals, shoutings and singings and hallelujahs, in the most fervid camp-meeting style, go on uninterruptedly despite the throngs in the streets, the automobiles and other attractions, services at Zion M.E. Church, at Ninth Street, the religious services are thronged all day and far into the night [*sic*].

It is the "Singing Bands" who are the most picturesque of the revivalists. A "Singing Band" is a group of men and women who have joined themselves together as a sort of itinerant choir and revivalist band combined. They usually travel from camp-meeting to camp-meeting all Summer, making a grand finale at the Wilmington Big Quarterly. Their voices are a perfect blend. Soprano, alto, baritone, bass are there, with usually a good falsetto to carry the minor wail, so integral a part of Negro spirituals. They sing the latter excellently, but their best is done in improvisations.

The student of the folk song, of the epic lay would do well to follow one of these singing bands of Eastern Shore colored folk. The falsetto member will begin a wail or a song of praise in a weird minor, the soprano and alto swing in alternately, the tenor echoes the wail, the baritone carries the basic tune in a lower third, and the bass lays a fine background or support in a harmonic growl or repetition.

Never mind the words. They may be modern, or religious or what not. They may be praise or distress; they are always filled with vivid tropes and metaphor of Oriental imagery, but they fit the tune perfectly.

In a short time the rhythm of the song has communicated itself to the bodies of the singers, and they sway in harmony, patting their hands and shuffling their feet.

The women singers are always garbed in severe tight-fitting black, with little close black bonnets, tied with crisp white bows under the chins and the anomaly of the swayings and posturings with their Shaker bonnets is startling. The crowd which gathers around the Singing Band gets the infection of the music, and sways and sings with them. Then, when the religious fervor is at fever heat, and there have been one or two hysterical shoutings on the edge of the crowd, the music ceases abruptly, and one of the band, or it may be an itinerant preacher, who has drifted by, begins an impromptu sermon, to which a few listen, the hat is passed, a few pennies or dimes drop into its depths, and the band moves on to another part of the street or deeper into the grove.

There are to be found in the throngs many ballad singers. These are men and women, singing evangelists, who lustily and tunefully chant ballads from printed sheets, small, cheap affairs, which they have had printed, after singing, sell for five cents each. Much profit is derived thereby. The words of the ballad are generally free verse, which somehow fits the equally free chant, but their crudity of composition is atoned for by the wealth of imagery and trickiness of expression.

Big Quarterly is still picturesque, but with the commonplaceness of pageantry of a crowd on Lenox Ave. or Seventh St. in Harlem. That is, until you study through its multihued thronging. Vari-colored garments there still are, but cut in the latest style. Only now and then does "Uncle Tom" of day before yesterday totter through the swarming host. Only here and there is one of the severely upholstered purple satins or glittering beaded georgettes of yesterday, strutting pompously through the throng. Slim and modish gowns are in evidence, and crisp organdies and good looking rayons.

Old residents can tell of former days of grandeur, when there were crowds, indeed—often as many as fifteen thousand visitors congregating on French St. alone. From Sixth St. to Ninth, in three short squares, the major portion of the pilgrims crowded. From Saturday morning they begin to trickle in. Ox-cart and springless wagons, spavined mules and high-stepping horses.

All Saturday night could be heard the rumble and lumber of wagons and drays, buggies and sulkies and surreys, and whatever kind of vehicle could be mustered into service. And from these various equipages would alight occupants befitting their conveyances.

"Uncle Tom" in real life, white beard, square-rimmed spectacles, rheumatic back, cane, long linen duster. Children in crisp frocks, brilliant calicoes, or flowered lawns, holding firmly to chicken legs or cakes as they looked around wide-eyed and solemn. Girls and women in satins and homespuns, velvets and calicoes.

Cast-off finery of their white mistresses, or more gorgeous

apparel of their own choosing. Purple satin used to be a prime favorite, and reds of all materials. Picture hats, laden with feathers and flowers, like the hats worn by Cockney maidens on a London bank holiday. In later days, chiffon had a vogue of its own, and beaded frocks were the quintessence of elegance. The more sophisticated of the race would look on in disgust at the hordes of gaudily invested proletarians and leave the city, or at least French St., in disgust. But others, more social and less sensitive, would join merrily in the celebration and become themselves a part of the spectacle.

Time was when furniture dealers would reap a fat harvest in dimes and quarters. For trucks would be decorated in flags and bunting and flowers and leaves, even as the ox-carts came into town with tree "bush" drooping aesthetically over them. The younger folk, filled with the love of adventure and romance would go faring forth on a ride through the city or in Brandywine Park at a quarter the round trip. A very short round trip. A truck would fill and empty itself—rubber-neck wagons—thirty times in an afternoon. Those were harvest days! Many a tired truck horse testified to the thrift of his master on the Monday morning after that last Sunday in August.

In later days, the auto truck and tin "flivver" supplanted the dray. Fifteen or twenty years ago when the automobile was still a devil wagon or a wonder chariot, according to the viewpoint, it was a great adventure to take a ride in the horseless vehicle. Much pelf was gathered by the knowing ones, who with dilapidated cars, hastily acquired, made them pay for themselves on this one harvest day, or by drivers of trucks, renting them for a nominal sum, and pocketing the profit ten times over.

Laughter ripples now and then when some down-state or Eastern Shore Beau Brummel bedecked in a light blue suit, yellow toothpick shoes, and straw hat with rainbow band flashes his manly pulchritude upon the eyes of brown maidens.

No longer do drays and trucks and ancient flivvers of thrifty Wilmingtonians reap shekels by taking the wide-eyed yokel on a bit of sightseeing through the city. Said yokel comes with his family in his own gear-shift car, loaded down with his own fried chicken and ham and cake and pie, and spends his money only for soft drinks and ice cream. He parks his car in a spot chosen early as near the roped-off area of Eighth to Ninth St. as possible and picnics openly with visible enjoyment. From Chester, Philadelphia, West Chester, and other nearby Southern Pennsylvania towns, from New Jersey, just across the river, Penn Grove and Salem, from Maryland and Virginia, from all Delaware, the dusty country cars and overloaded busses toil in all day with throngs.

But there is growing sophistication or cynicism about the visitors now that was missing a few short years ago. It is as if they were saying, "Well, we're expected to do this sort of thing, so we won't disappoint the curiosity seekers."

Throughout it all there is a peculiar orderliness that is interesting. Arrests are practically nil. A decent regard for the Sabbath and a deeprooted respect for the occasion, primarily a religious one, makes for discipline. Vague rumors now and then about some feeble attempts at evasion of the Volstead Law float in the air, but are usually discredited. It is a church crowd, and it wants to sing and eat and greet its friends without interruption. Other things are unimportant.

Each year some of the intelligentsia of the Negroes in the city protest against this relic of slavery days. This frank enjoyment of public eating, this loud-voiced greeting of old friends, this street-singing, this crude evangelism, this stress of racial differences. But the protest is regarded as a mere gesture, like the dislike of some colored people of Negro spirituals, like the protests against *Green Pastures*.

The hordes which invade the streets enjoy the novelty of unrestraint; the merchants of the city reap a harvest in the sale of foodstuffs to concessionaires; the railways and bus and steamship lines revel in the all-day throng of excursionists from all points; the taxi companies are delightfully frantic in their endeavors to get autos enough for the demands made upon them; the street cars register an upward slant in the day's receipts and dollars, even in these years of depression, stream into the city all day long, for days in advance, in fact. The protests of the few avail nothing against the economic and gregarious delights of the many.

It is an anachronism, a flare-back, atavism, what you will, this Big Quarterly, but it holds within it incredible possibilities of suggestion for those who might wish to investigate a rich mine of folk-lore, custom, tradition among this growing Negro people.

Editor's comment:

We commend to our readers the article on "Big Quarterly" in Wilmington on this page. It is by Alice Dunbar-Nelson, who has caught the spirit and the color of the kaleodiscopic gathering and compares it with the Big Quarterlies of former times. Her word picture well reflects the activities of great fete day for the colored folks of all this section and recalls that these gatherings have been continued, with but brief interruption during the Civil War period for 120 years, to long remain, perhaps as the annual August fixture in the religious calendar of the colored people of Wilmington.

BRASS ANKLES SPEAKS*

The "Race" question is paramount. A cloud of books, articles and pronunciamentos on the subject of the white man or girl who "passes" over to the other side of the racial fence, and either entirely forsakes his or her own race, to live in terror or misery all their days, or else come crawling back to do uplift work among their own people, hovers on the literary horizon. On the other hand, there is an increasing interest and sentimentality concerning the poor, pitiful black girl, whose life is a torment among her own people, because of their "blue vein" proclivities. It seems but fair and just now for some of the neglected light-skinned colored people, who have not "passed" to rise and speak a word in self-defense.

I am of the latter class, what E. C. Adams in "Nigger to Nigger" immortalizes in the poem, "Brass Ankles." White enough to pass for white, but with a darker family background, a real love for the mother race, and no desire to be numbered among the white race.

My earliest recollections are miserable ones. I was born in a far Southern city, where complexion did, in a manner of speaking, determine one's social status. However, the family being poor, I was sent to the public school. It was a heterogeneous mass of children which greeted my frightened eyes on that fateful morning in September, when I timidly took my place in the first grade. There were not enough seats for

*Typescript, authored by "Adele Morris" (a proven pseudonym) at "20 South Twelfth Street/Philadelphia, Pa.," the headquarters of the American Friends Service Committee, where Dunbar-Nelson worked between 1928 and 1931.

all the squirming mass of little ones, so the harassed young teacher—I have reason to believe now that this was her first school—put me on the platform at her feet. I was so little and scared and homesick that it made no impression on me at the time. But at the luncheon hour I was assailed with shouts of derision—"Yah! Teacher's pet! Yah! Just cause she's yaller!" Thus at once was I initiated into the class of the disgraced, which has haunted and tormented my whole life— "Light nigger, with straight hair!"

This was the beginning of what was for nearly six years a life of terror, horror and torment. For in this monster public school, which daily disgorged about 2500 children, there were all shades and tints and degrees of complexions from velvet black to blonde white. And the line of demarcation was rigidly drawn—not by the fairer children, but by the darker ones. I had no color sense. In my family we never spoke of it. Indian browns and cafe au laits, were mingled with pale bronze and blonde yellows all in one group of cousins and uncles and aunts and brothers and sisters. For so peculiarly does the Mendelian law work in mixed bloods, that four children of two parents may show four different degrees of mixture, brown, yellow, tan, blonde.

In the school, therefore, I felt at first the same freedom concerning color. So I essayed friendship with Esther. Esther was velvet dark, with great liquid eyes. She could sing, knew lots of forbidden lore, and brought lovely cakes for luncheon. Therefore I loved Esther, and would have been an intimate friend of hers. But she repulsed me with ribald laughter— "Half white nigger! Go on wid ya kind!", and drew up a solid phalanx of little dark girls, who thumbed noses at me and chased me away from their ring game on the school playground.

Bitter recollections of hair ribbons jerked off and trampled in the mud. Painful memories of curls yanked back into the ink bottle of the desk behind me, and dripping ink down my carefully washed print frocks. That alone was a tragedy, for clothes came hard, and a dress ruined by ink-dripping curls meant privation for the mother at home. How I hated those curls! Charlie, the neighbor-boy and I were of an age, a complexion and the same taffy-colored curls. So bitter were his experiences that his mother had his curls cut off. But I was a girl and must wear curls. I wept in envy of Charles, the shorn one. However, long before it was the natural time for curls to be discarded, my mother, for sheer pity, braided my hair in a long heavy plait down my back. Alas! It, too, was ink-soaked, pulled, yanked and twisted.

I was a timid, scared, rabbit sort of a child, but out of desperation I learned to fight. My sister, a few years older, was in an upper grade, through those six, fearsome years. She had learned early to defend herself with well-aimed rocks, ink bottles and a scientific use of sharp finger-nails. She taught me some valuable lessons, and came to my rescue when my nerve had given out. She had something of the spirit of an organizer, too, and had a gang of "yellow niggers" that could do valiant service in the organized warfare between the dark ones and the light ones.

I used to watch the principal of the school, and her fellow teachers with considerable interest as I grew older and the situation unfolded itself to me. As far as I can remember now, they were all mulattoes or very light brown. If their sympathies were with the little fair children, who were so bitterly persecuted, they never gave any evidence. The principal punished the belligerents with an impartiality that was heart-breaking. Years afterward, I learned that she had told my mother and the mothers of other girls of our class and complexion that she understood and appreciated our sorrows and troubles, but if she gave any evidence of sympathy, or in any way placed the punishment where she knew it rightfully belonged, the parents of the darker children would march in a body to the Board of Education, and protest against her as being unfit for the job.

Time went on, and a long spell of illness took me out of the school. That too, was due to color prejudice. There was a small-pox scare, and the Board of Health ordered one of those wholesale vaccinations that are sometimes worse than the disease. My mother sent a note to the principal asking her not to have me vaccinated on the day selected, but that she would take me to the family physician that night, and send the certificate to school in the morning. The principal read the note, shook her head, looked at me sorrowfully, "You should have stayed at home today," was her terse comment. So I was dragged, screaming and protesting to have my arm scratched with a scalpel instead of a vaccine point. Terror and rage helped the infection which followed, and for a long while my life was despaired of. It seemed certain that I would lose my arm. Somehow, I did not, and when I was well enough, about eighteen months later, to think of education, my mother sent me to a private school.

The bitterness that had been ingrained in me through those six fateful years, from six to twelve years of age, stayed. The new school was one of those American Missionary Schools founded shortly after the war, as an experiment in Negro education. Later, these same schools became the aristocratic educational institutions of the race. Though the fee was only a nominal one, it was successful in keeping out many a proletariat. Thus gradually, all over the South these very schools which were founded in a missionary spirit by the descendents of abolitionists for the hordes of knowledge-seeking freedmen, became in the second and third generations, the exclusive stamping grounds of the descendents of those who were never slaves, or of the aristocrats among freedmen.

And because here I found boys and girls like myself, fair, light brown, with educated parents, descendents of office holders under the reconstruction regime or of free antebellum Negroes, with traditions—therefore was I happy until the end of my high and normal school career.

Except for Eddie. I loved Eddie. He represented to me the unattainable, for he was in the college department, and he won prizes in oratory and debate and one day smiled at me understandingly when I was only a high school freshman. I walked on air for days. But Eddie was of a deep darkness, and refused to allow me to love him. With stern dignity he checked my fluttering advances. He would not demean himself by walking with a mere golden butterfly; far rather would he walk alone, he told me. It broke my heart for nearly a month.

Out in life, I found myself confronted, as did most of my friends and associates, with the same problems which had confronted the principal of that public school. I became a public school teacher. There were little dark children in my school. I had to watch them tormenting the little fair children, and not lift my hand to protect them, at the risk of a severe reprimand from my principal or supervisor, induced by complaints from parents. I had to endure in hot, shamed silence the innuendos constantly printed in the weekly colored newspaper—a sort of local *Smart Set*—against the fair teachers, every time one was seen with a new coat or hat. How could they afford to dress so well? was the constant query. Light colored girls, it was well known, were the legitimate prey of white men. Were not the members of the Board of Education helping out the meagre salaries of the better looking teachers? What price shame? Protest? The editor was a black man and owed allegiance to no proprietary. His daughter had failed to pass the teachers' examination; she had failed in the normal school; she had failed in the high school. She was really stupid. But her father would not believe it. There were some darker girls who had made brilliant records in school; were brilliant teachers. He shut his eyes to their prowess, and vented his spleen upon the light ones who had succeeded.

After teaching a year or two, I had saved enough to embark upon my cherished ambition—to go to college, and so I came North. Here I found a condition just as bitter, but more subtle. You come up against a dead wall of hate and prejudice and misunderstanding, and you cannot tell what causes it.

During the summer session I had lived with a colored family in the town. The room was uncomfortable, the food not good, and the prices as high as in the school dormitories. Therefore, when I decided to return for the winter, I applied for and secured a place in one of the college cottages. This branded me at once among the colored students. I was said to be "passing," though nothing was further from my mind— especially as there were no race restrictions in the dormitories. I tried to make friends among the colored girl students—all of whom that year were brown. Success came only after the hardest kind of hard work, and it was only a truce. I had to batter down a wall, which had doubtless been erected by my erstwhile dark-skinned landlady.

I had registered from my own religious creed. The rector of the white church in town called at once, made me welcome, and asked me to connect myself with his church. I waited three weeks for the colored minister to make a like overture. I would have preferred the colored church, for I had always taken an active part in our little church at home among my own people. But no gesture was made, so I went to the white church. Then an entertainment was given at the colored church. I saw a flier for the first time on the day of the affair, with my name down for a recitation. Naturally, I did not go on such slight notice, and forever afterwards was branded among the colored townspeople as a "half white strainer, with no love for the Race."

And yet, in spite of all the tragedy of my childhood and young womanhood, I had not been able to develop that color sense. When I say this to my darker friends, they simply laugh at me. They may like me personally; they may even become my very good friends; but there is always a barrier, a veil—nay, rather a vitrified glass wall, which I can neither break down, batter down, nor pierce. I have to see dear friends turn from a talk with me, to exchange a glance of comprehension and understanding one with another which I, nor anyone of my complexion, can ever hope to share.

In the course of my peregrinations, after college days, I came to teach in a small city on the Middle Atlantic Seaboard. A little city where hate is a refined art, where bitterness is rife, and where prejudice is a thing so vital and potent that it makes all other emotions seem pale and insignificant. I shall never forget the day that I was introduced by the principal to the faculty of the high school where I was to teach. There were two other faces like mine in the group of thirty. The two who looked like me, exchanged glances of pity—the others measured me with cold contempt and grim derision. A sweat broke out on me. I knew what I was up against and an icy hand clutched my heart. I felt I could never break this down; this unreasoning prejudice against my mere personal appearance.

With the children it was the same. The day I walked into my classroom, I head a whisper run through the aisles, "Half white nigger!" For a moment I was transplanted to that first day at school twenty odd years ago.

The agony of that first semester! The nerve-racking terror of never knowing where there would be an outbreak of unreasoning prejudice among those dark children, venting itself in a spiteful remark, and undoing in a moment what I had spent weeks to create. The heart-breaking rebuffs when I tried to be cordial with my fellow-teachers; the curt refusals to walk home with me, or to go to church or places of amusement. The scathing denunciations of irate parents when their children did not get the undeserved marks they wanted. I was accused of everything except infanticide. Mine had been the experiences of the other two teachers, I was told. The principal protected as far as he could, but what can a busy man do against a whole community? If I had a dollar for every bitter, scalding, hopeless tear that I shed that first school year, I should be independently wealthy. It was only sheer grit and determination not to be beaten that kept me from throwing up the job and going back home.

Small wonder, then, that the few lighter persons in the community drew together; we were literally thrown upon each other, whether we liked or not. But when we began going about together and spending our time in each other's society, a howl went up. We were organizing a "blue vein" society. We were mistresses of white men. We were Lesbians. We hated black folk and plotted against them. As a matter of fact, we had no other recourse but to cling together.

Much water has passed under the bridge since those days, and I have lived in many other communities. Save for size, virulence, and local conditions, the situation duplicates itself. Once I planned a pageant in one community. "You'll never put it over," my friends adjured me; "You haven't enough pull with the darker people." But I planned my committees always to be headed up by black or brown men or women, who in turn selected their aides, thus relieving me of all responsibility. It went over big, in spite of misfits on committees. But had I actually placed thereon men and women of real ability, who could have handled the situation more efficiently, the whole thing would have fallen to the ground if they were light in color.

I have served on boards and committees of schools, institutions, projects. I have seen the chairmen, or those with appointing power, look at me apologetically, and name someone whom they knew and I knew was unfit for a place, where I could have best helped and worked. But they did not dare be accused of partiality on account of color. I have had my offers of help in charity affairs refused, or if accepted grudgingly, credit withheld or services forgotten. I have been turned down by my own race far more often than many a brown-skinned person has been similarly treated by the white race. I have been snubbed and ostracized with subtle cruelties that I am safe to assert have hardly been duplicated by the experiences of dark people in their dealings with Caucasians. I say more cruel, for I have been foolishly optimistic enough to expect sympathy, understanding and help from my own people—and that I receive rarely outside of individuals of my own or allied complexion.

As if there is not enough stupid cruelty among my own, I have had to suffer at the hands of white people because of my likeness to them. On two occasions when I was seeking a position, I was rejected because I was "too white," and not typically racial enough for the particular job. Once when I was employed in a traveling position during the war, I came into headquarters from a particularly exhausting trip through the South. There I had twice been put off Jim Crow cars, because the conductor insisted that I was a white woman, and three times refused food in the dining-car, because the colored waiters, "tipped off" the white stewards. When I reached headquarters I found three of my best so-called brown skinned friends protesting against sending me out to work among my own people because I looked too much like white.

Once I "passed" and got a job in a department store in a large city. But one of the colored employees "spotted" me, for we always know each other, and reported that I was colored, and I was fired in the middle of the day. The joke was that I had applied for a job in the stock room where all the employees are colored, and the head of the placing bureau told me that was no place for me—"Only colored girls work there," so he placed me in the book department, and then fired me because I had "deceived" him.

I have had my friends meet me downtown in city streets and turn their heads away, so positive that I do not want to speak to them. Sometimes I have to go out of my way and pluck at their sleeves to force them to speak. If I do not, then it is reported around that I "pass" when I am downtown—and sad is my case among my own kind then.

There are a thousand subtleties of refined cruelty which every fair colored person must suffer at the hands of his or her own people. And every fair colored woman or man, girl or boy who reads this knows that I have not exaggerated. If it be true that thousands of us pass over into the white group each year, it is due not only to the wish for economic ease and convenience, but often to the bitterness of one's own kind. It is not to be wondered at that lighter skinned Negroes cling together in their respective communities. It is not so much that they dislike the darker brethren, but the darker brethren DO NOT LIKE THEM.

So I raise my tiny voice in all this hub-bub of "Race" clamor; all this wishy-washy sentimentalism about the persecuted black ones of the race, and their inability to get on with their own kind. As in Haiti, as in Africa, the bitterness and prejudice have always come from the blacks to the yellows. They have been the greatest sufferers, because they have had, perforce, to suffer in silence. To complain would be only to bring upon themselves another storm of abuse and fury.

The "yaller niggers," the "Brass Ankles" must bear the hatred of their own and the prejudice of the white race. If they do not choose to go over to the other side—and tens of thousands feel, like myself, that there is no gain socially in so doing, though there may be some economic convenience— then they are forced to draw together in a common cause against their blood brothers who visit upon them hatred and persecution.